Wakefield Press

The Boys from St Francis

A born storyteller, Ashley Mallett was asked to write the story of *The Boys from St Francis* by Ngadjuri elder and former resident of the home, Vince Copley, AM. Ashley's 30-odd books include the definitive history of the 1868 Aboriginal Australian Cricket Tour of England, *The Black Lords of Summer* (UQP 2002).

Ashley Mallett, who lives in Adelaide, regards *The Boys from St Francis* as his most important work.

By the same author

Autobiography
Rowdy
Spin Out

Biography
Clarrie Grimmett: The Bradman of spin
Trumper: The illustrated biography
Chappelli Speaks Out
One of a Kind: The Doug Walters story
Thommo Speaks Out
Nugget: Man of the century
Scarlet: Clarrie Grimmett, test cricketer
No Beating about the Bush

Historical
The Black Lords of Summer: The story of the 1968 Aboriginal tour of England and beyond
The Catch that Broke a Bank

General non-fiction
Bradman's Band
100 Cricket Tips
Eleven: The greatest eleven of the 20th century
The Diggers' Doctor:
The fortunate life of Col. Donald Beard, AM, RFD, ED (Retd)
Great Australian Test Cricket Stories

For children

Master Sportsman series
CRICKET: *Doug Walters, Dennis Lillee, Rodney Marsh, The Chappell Brothers, Allan Border, Geoff Lawson, Kim Hughes* and *Don Bradman*.
FOOTBALL: *Mark Williams, Tim Watson* and *Robert Wayne Johnston*.
SOCCER: *John Kosmina*.
TENNIS: *Evonne Cawley*.

The Boys from St Francis

Ashley Mallett

Wakefield Press

Wakefield Press
16 Rose Street
Mile End
South Australia 5031
www.wakefieldpress.com.au

First published 2018

Copyright © Ashley Mallett, 2018

All rights reserved. This book is copyright. Apart from
any fair dealing for the purposes of private study, research,
criticism or review, as permitted under the Copyright Act,
no part may be reproduced without written permission.
Enquiries should be addressed to the publisher.

Aboriginal and Torres Strait Islander people are advised
that this book contains names and images of deceased
Aboriginal and Torres Strait Islander persons.

Cover design by Liz Nicholson, Wakefield Press
Edited by Margot Lloyd, Wakefield Press
Typeset by Michael Deves, Wakefield Press

ISBN 978 1 74305 580 9

A catalogue record for this
book is available from the
National Library of Australia

Wakefield Press thanks
Coriole Vineyards for
continued support

This book is dedicated to all Indigenous Australians who have suffered discrimination and racial barbs through the ignorance of their white brothers since the day the First Fleet arrived in 1788.

The Boys from St Francis was a highly emotional literary journey for me. My eternal thanks to my wife, Patsy, the love of my life, who provided me with never-ending support, encouragement and sage advice throughout the writing of this important work.

Going to school, 1950. From left: Lawrie Bray, Des Price, Ken Hampton, Richie Bray, Malcolm Cooper, Gordon Briscoe, Ronnie McCoy, Vince Copley, Gerry Hill and Wilfred Huddleston. Photo courtesy John Smith.

Contents

Foreword ix
Preface xiii

Stolen 1
The first six 17
A 'better place' 32
The house that 'Jack' built 45
The boys from St Francis 51
Our own 'William Tell' 67
By a hand so cruel 81
Sunshine and shadow 89
High achievers 101
The Colebrook girls 118
Faith 130
The flag 142
Their hero 153
Charlie 162
Home 171
A year to remember 180

Kidnapped	194
The power of education	209
A black white man? Never!	223
Joy and sorrow	235
Two brilliant careers	245
Rising from the ashes	257
Author's note	269
Acknowledgements	273
Index	275

Foreword

Vince Copley, AM
Ngadjuri Elder
St Francis House old boy

When I was about nine years old I got to know some of the St Francis House boys when they spent Christmas at Alice Springs. So a few months later I thought my arrival at the home wouldn't be so daunting. We'd flown to Adelaide from the Alice and Father Smith greeted Mum and I. Because she considered it such an important occasion Mum dressed me up in a neatly pressed grey suit, highly polished shoes and a little blue cap. You can imagine how I felt when Father Smith, Mum and I entered the dining room at the home. There the boys were tucking into their food. Their clothes were clean enough but threadbare, and they hardly turned a hair when I was introduced, stopping briefly to throw me a cursory glance, then with a collective sigh they carried on eating. Embarrassed by my toffy outfit, I wondered what sort of flak I might cop later on from the older boys. I didn't have to wait too long. My roommates were Peter Tilmouth and Lawrie Bray.

There was a pecking order at the home and the new kid on the block was the lackey. He made the bed, scrubbed the floor, washed the dishes, chopped the wood, milked the cow, stoked the boiler and never questioned an order from the older ones. It took me a year before I summoned the courage to stand up for myself. For months Gordon Briscoe (who would become the first Indigenous man to gain a PhD in history) and I were always fighting. The older boys made a decision, 'If they want to fight, they'll fight.'

A bout was set up in the gymnasium. We wore gloves and fought in the ring before a noisy crowd. Although Gordon and I both had seconds, there was no referee. After a few rounds of the most frantic flurry of fists, as luck had it I won the fight. At the ripe old age of 11 I had earned my wings. Nothing was said, but I knew I was welcomed into the fold.

Soon it was my turn to show a new kid who was boss: everyone had to earn their stripes.

There were two distinct groups of boys at St Francis House. In the first instance there were six lads – David Woodford, Malcolm Cooper, Peter Tilmouth, Bill Espie, John Palmer and Charlie Perkins – who came to the home with the blessing of their mothers. Father Percy Smith, the Anglican priest who ran the home, had encouraged these boys' mothers to have their sons move to St Francis House because of the perceived greater educational and lifestyle opportunities on offer.

Others, such as Wally McArthur, John Moriarty, Jim Foster and Gordon Briscoe, were boys of the Stolen Generations, who came to the home via a Church-run institution in Mulgoa, NSW.

We attended Ethelton Primary School and later Le Fevre Boys Technical School. Initially the white kids taunted and teased us, but we got our own back on the sports field where we were faster, more agile and smarter. At Le Fevre we learnt to use our fists and the headmaster Fred Vickery gave us the thumbs up to fight our own battles in the schoolyard. Perhaps it was our having to stick together that created the extraordinary bond we enjoy today.

Father Smith was a kind man and a mentor to us, however, he left after just two years at St Francis House. We never discovered the actual reason for his abandoning us. Was it for the good of his health? Was it for the new job he was offered, and a title within the church? The men who replaced Father Smith were largely incompetent, uncaring; some downright cruel, brutal cowards who wielded a baton or bashed us with a rubber hose for the most minor indiscretion. Our battles at school and in the street and at the home steeled us for the years ahead.

The bonds the boys formed were and are unshakeable to this very day. *The Boys from St Francis* is a story which exposes all the emotions – sadness and joy; achievement and failure; love and hatred; humour and hope; bigotry and strength. The book may inspire others who are in or were in institutions to come forward and tell their stories. Why did St Francis House succeed in producing a number of inspirational people – successful in commerce, politics, history and sport – where other Church-run institutions failed? You may find the answer in the following pages.

As a lasting tribute to the boys and their story it would be something if the City of Port Adelaide Enfield allocated a small room at St Francis House (Glanville Hall) so that not only memorabilia could be housed but we old boys could tell our story. Such knowledge would prove invaluable for students as part of the local schools' curriculum; another positive for the Closing the Gap initiative.

All Australians should read *The Boys from St Francis*.

Preface

The prone figure stirred.

Muhammad Ali slowly lifted his head from the massage table and like a big cat eyeing his prey he focused on the two Australians who dared to enter his domain.

Trainer Angelo Dundee, a towel slung over his shoulder, stood beside the champion boxer being massaged and all eyes zoned in on the two Australians who stood transfixed in the centre of the room.

Aboriginal activist Charlie Perkins and Ngadjuri elder Vince Copley had just flown in from Australia to meet with Ali at Kuala Lumpur's plush Hilton Hotel.

They were on a mission to persuade Ali to visit Australia to help inspire their people, especially young Aboriginal boys, to seek a proper education so they could build a successful future for themselves.

Ali sat bolt upright and yelled: 'Get my cheque book. Get my cheque book!'

Vince Copley will never forget the moment.

'Charlie railed against any inference that we were there pleading for money. He grabbed me and started pushing toward the door, all the while shouting in the direction of the naked champion, "We don't want your money. We are not here for a handout."

'Charlie continued pushing me toward the door and I blurted, "Charlie, what the hell are you doing? This bloke can fight a bit."

'But Charlie was a very determined man and Ali's inference that we were there "on the take" cut deeply. He was still pushing me toward the door, but Ali's minders formed an impenetrable human wall and we were stuck fast.

'Suddenly Ali's mood changed. He put on a dressing gown and approached us; the human wall vanished.

'"What can I do for you gentlemen?" he said warmly.

'We put our case.

'"Hey, flying is not my thing," Ali confessed. "I hate flying. It took all manner of persuasion to get me to fly here from the States. I am not keen on flying to Australia."'

Understandably, nerves were on edge. It was 6 am, Sunday 29 June 1975, eve of the world heavyweight boxing championship title fight.

Ali had already completed an early morning run and was looking forward to rest, a hearty breakfast and rest again. The champion knew that his opponent, Britisher Joe Bugner, would be a worthy adversary. Ali's minders wore worried frowns.

As Ali continued chatting with Charlie and Vince there was a resounding bang, a sound eerily like a gun shot. The dozen minders, who had been standing tall, legs astride, like statues, suddenly came alive. They all drew their guns and everyone in the room froze.

A clumsy young cameraman helping the main photographer had been stumbling about for some time and had eventually knocked a chair and upset a tall upright, which, in turn, had fallen against a large light above their heads. The light had fallen with a loud bang.

When everyone realised the source of the noise momentary terror turned to uproarious laughter.

Before Charlie and Vince left the room, the champion boxer nodded in the direction of his trainer: 'Hey Angelo, see to it that these two Australian gentlemen come to the fight tomorrow night and are treated to ringside seats.'

Ironically, when Charlie and Vince arrived at the Kuala Lumpur airport earlier that day they had bumped into Keith Butler, sports journalist with Adelaide's morning newspaper, the *Advertiser*. When Charlie and Vince explained their reason for seeking an audience with Muhammad Ali, Butler offered to help secure them a couple of tickets for the fight. He would never have dreamt that the two men would obtain ringside seats.

But it came to pass.

As the two great heavyweights slugged it out, there sat Charlie Perkins and Vince Copley in $1000 ringside seats, and there was Keith Butler, watching the fight through binoculars from a spot high in the back row of the crowded Merdeka Stadium.

Perkins and Copley were no ordinary Australians. They had left their families in the Northern Territory as youngsters and were taken to St Francis House, an Anglican home in Port Adelaide, where kindly Father Percy Smith had created an environment of trust and belonging for dozens of Aboriginal boys.

Some of the boys were taken from their families, while others were sent to the care of Father Smith in their mothers' hope that they would gain a decent education.

While Charlie and Vince experienced discrimination at the home, at school and on the street, they also found solace in Father Smith's care and determination to help them make something of their lives.

St Francis House in Semaphore ran from 1946 to 1959, catering for dozens of young Aboriginal boys.

Like Muhammad Ali the boys endured racism and bigotry throughout their life journeys. They didn't experience great wealth and status on the world stage, but St Francis House taught them well. They developed a great work ethic; they bonded like brothers and they discovered the greatest power of them all – education.

Stolen

As the truck roared away in the heat, Alice Foster felt a shiver engulf her body: the chill wind of oblivion.

In a cloud of choking dust the big green army truck suddenly appeared. With the engine still roaring, two khaki-clad figures jumped from the vehicle and hit the ground running. They rushed toward the veranda where Alice Foster had gathered her two children to her side. Hearing wails of anguish emanating from behind the canvas canopy at the back of the truck, Alice feared the worst. She knew that this was the latest attempt by government officials to steal her children away from her. The two men approached. They said nothing as they separated the children – Rose, 10, and Jim, nine – from their mother's grasp.

As Rose and Jim Foster were taken to the vehicle, little hands carefully parted the canvas canopy at the front of the truck. From her position on the veranda, Alice could see a row of children of varying ages sitting on a wooden bench seat on one side of the truck.

Her heart skipped a beat when she noticed that one of the older girls held a tiny baby in her arms. Jim Foster later learned that this infant was eight-month-old Phyllis Hamilton. Apart from Phyllis, there were other babies aboard, including Robert Huddleston and Fay Hall (both 11 months), a 12-month-old and three two-year-olds. The 30 children rounded up in the Roper River district that day ranged in age from eight months to 14 years, the age of Wilton Huddleston. Among the mix was four-year-old John Moriarty, who would later become a leading academic, a well-known businessman and the first Aboriginal soccer player to be picked for an Australian team. The round-up was completed with four army trucks and after officials were satisfied that they had collected all the children they rendezvoused at a prearranged spot in Roper River. Officials timed the round-up for the middle of the day. They were confident that no adult males would be about at that time of day to challenge them, and had only to contend with a number of distraught mothers.

The children rounded up that day in July 1942 came from a wide sweep of settlements and camps across the Roper River district, Groote Eylandt, and Borroloola.

As the truck roared away in the heat, Alice Foster felt a shiver engulf her body: the chill wind of oblivion.

Jim Foster has an enduring image of his bewildered mother weeping uncontrollably as she slumped to her knees on the veranda. Would she ever see her beloved children again? Alice Foster's maiden name was Bajamalanya, of the Yanyuwa People. She had a long, loving relationship with Horace Mole Foster, a self-made man who loved the outdoors.

In 1918 Horace had built himself a home of wood and paperbark, using a blanket made from the hide of a bullock as his mattress. Horace's hut was near a bubbling hot spring on Lorella Station, north-west of Borroloola. The spring would prove a godsend for his vegetable garden.

In 1923 Horace and two other men, Bill Haerney and Jack Keighran, were hauled before the Borroloola Police Court charged with 'poddy dodging,' the illegal activity of stealing unbranded young cattle. Bill Haerney would say that Horace 'could quote from the classics while wearing a sarong and eating bush tucker', and Horace no doubt used his skilful oratory to sway the magistrate. The men walked free.

Horace, born at Jamestown in 1887, was 22 years older than his wife. Alice Bajamalanya was born in January 1909 and she married Horace in Darwin in 1930. Their firstborn, Rose, was brought into this world at Manangoora Station in November 1930. Their only son, James, arrived on 16 January 1933. Unlike the majority of white men who fathered children with an Aboriginal woman, Horace Foster did not scuttle off into the night. He stayed true to Alice and he was fiercely protective of his family.

'My dad was a knockabout sort of bloke,' Jim says. 'He wasn't keen on studying law and following in his father's footsteps.'

Back in 1928 Horace Foster and his pal Bill Haerney had bought a lease for part of Manangoora Station on the Wearyan River for obtaining and removing salt.

'Dad eked out a living by working the salt pans,' Jim explains. 'During the wet season the plains would be flooded and when the water subsided and the sun shone huge deposits of salt were left.

'A bit of casual work here and there suited him and he did well from droving, however, his main source of income was the money he earned from bagging salt. Horace's joy came when he was paid cash for his bags of salt, which were collected by steamer at the Foster landing at Borroloola.

'Although Dad was intelligent and well read he didn't have a lot of formal education. But he did teach us well; the three Rs and much more during the early days. We didn't attend a formal school. Dad was our teacher and because there were no luxuries such as electricity, we studied under the light of a kerosene lamp and we turned out okay.'

While Horace loved manual labour he also had an enquiring mind. He loved the English language and constructing clever, succinct sentences. Round the time he was tutoring his children, Horace took a correspondence course in journalism. Perhaps he had in mind to one day pen his life story.

Two years before Rose and Jim Foster became victims of the Stolen Generation, Horace Foster had confronted two government officials who arrived unannounced at their home to take the children away. Word was the government men were close by, so Horace had hidden his children in a shed half an hour before they turned up. When they approached he stood his ground, brandishing a loaded double-barrelled shotgun. When the government men got within 10 metres of the shed, Horace levelled his shotgun at them and shouted, 'Clear off! Now!' Those two agents of darkness made a hasty retreat, but they were back again in that army truck two years later, knowing that Horace Foster would never again threaten them.

Some 18 months before the July 1942 round-up, Horace had an incident while cleaning his shotgun. There was a cartridge jammed in the breach and he had attempted to dislodge it with a knife, but his efforts failed. In frustration he grabbed hold of the gun by the barrel and slammed the butt on a huge tree slab which doubled as a tabletop for cutting meat. The instant the butt struck the wooden slab the gun discharged.

In anger and pain, Horace realised he had accidentally shot himself in the groin. He bled profusely and with Alice's help he tore a bed-sheet into strips and managed to fashion a crude tourniquet.

Stolen

The tourniquet stopped the bleeding, but in that harsh bush environment, devoid of any sort of antiseptic, Horace's chances of surviving diminished with every passing hour. He was in terrible pain, there was blood everywhere, and he knew that he had done serious damage to the bone in his right leg.

He asked for paper and pen and wrote a note:

> *Have shot myself accidentally. Think I am settled. Can you come out? Shot the bone in two above the knee. May bleed to death.*

It was 24 February 1941, at the height of the monsoon season in the Gulf of Carpentaria. The Wearyan River was running fast and all the creeks and swamps in the area were overflowing. Deadly snakes found refuge on fallen logs protruding from the floodwaters and the river was infested with saltwater crocodiles. Access to the outside world was severely restricted. There was no electricity, no telephone and certainly no wireless.

Any communication would have to be delivered personally to the policeman stationed at Borroloola, some 100 km away from the Foster family campsite. Horace carefully wrapped his written SOS in an oilskin. A brave Aboriginal boy carried the precious note for Constable Ted Heathcock through miles of swamp and flooded plain, infested with snakes and crocodiles. The boy completed the journey in less than two days.

Was there still time?

Unfortunately when the boy arrived with the note, Constable Heathcock was away, attending a murder trial in Darwin. However, immediately the policeman's wife, Sister Ruth Heathcock, a qualified nurse, read Horace's SOS she sprang into action. She radioed the Royal Flying Doctor Service, which was stationed at Cloncurry, 1440 km away. Next day an aircraft went out, but torrential rain, zero visibility and boggy conditions prevented all possibility of a plane making a successful landing near Horace Foster's camp. The pilot flew on to Borroloola and informed Sister Ruth of his frustration.

Five days had passed since the accident and Sister Ruth held out little hope of Horace surviving the gunshot wound and subsequent infection. Still she decided to mount a rescue mission of her own.

She gathered together a team of people – two men, and a Mrs Bessie Marshall (nee a-Kithibula) and her husband – and, armed with medical supplies, the rescue party set out on their mission in an Aboriginal-made dugout canoe. Hollowed out from the trunk of a tree, the dugout canoe needed expert handling as it had no keel and was in constant danger of capsizing. They paddled down the flooded McArthur River for 90 km and traversed the turbulent mouth of the river before negotiating 30 km on the open sea of the Gulf of Carpentaria, which at that time of the year is one of the roughest, most treacherous stretches of water in Australia. They reached the Wearyan River three days after leaving Borroloola.

To her dismay Sister Ruth found Horace in a bad way: he was suffering from blood poisoning and tetanus. She dressed his wounds and made him as comfortable as possible, but the tetanus infection had already progressed to the point of no return. Horace had to be fed through a gap in his teeth as his jaws had clamped shut: lockjaw, the greatly feared condition associated with tetanus, had the poor man in its deadly grip. Horace was barely alive when Sister Ruth arranged for her helpers to clear ground near the homestead to make it possible for the Flying Doctor plane to land.

Stolen

'We washed him [Horace] where he had shot himself,' Mrs Bessie Marshall said afterwards. 'The bone was completely broken. She [Sister Ruth] waited with him and made things better for him. His thigh was in pieces. It was a mess.

'After we cleared the area for the plane to land we heard it flying overhead, so we carried him [Horace] toward the place where the plane would land. As the pilot came in for the final approach, Horace Foster died.'

It had been eight days after Foster had accidentally shot himself.

Sister Ruth Heathcock's courage won widespread praise. Mr C.A.L. Abbott, Administrator of the Northern Territory, described her rescue attempt as 'one of the bravest acts I have known in the Territory.'

Alice Foster had lost her beloved Horace, husband and father of Rose and Jim. With Horace gone, the family was now at the mercy of government officials. Soon came what Alice had long dreaded: the round-up.

Jim Foster recalled it with a faraway look of sadness in his eyes: 'Barely 18 months before the trucks came to steal us away, we watched our father die an agonising death from a gunshot wound. As we were shoved onto the back of the truck there was our darling mother slumped to her knees on the front veranda. Her sobs were clearly audible from where we sat on a crowded bench seat on the truck. That final glimpse of my mother was the last time we saw her.'

A number of properties were visited in the region and more children were torn from their mothers' arms. More than once that traumatic day Jim and the others witnessed a distraught mother wailing and hitting herself on the head with a rock.

The Boys from St Francis

The official list of 30 'half-caste' children forcibly taken from their families and transported to Mulgoa, near the town of Penrith at the foot of the Blue Mountains in New South Wales, is:

Surname, first name	Birthplace	Age
Hamilton, Phyllis	Groote Eylandt	8 months
Hall, Fay	Roper River	11 months
Huddleston, Robert	Roper River	11 months
Wesley, Billy	Katherine	1 year
Burke, Wendy	Roper River	1 year
Hamilton, Joan	Darwin	1 year
Roberts, Glen	Roper River	2 years
Burke, Laurel	Roper River	2 years
Wesley, Kenneth	Roper River	2 years
Hall, Trevor	Roper River	3 years
Hamilton, Betty	Groote Eylandt	3 years
Huddleston, Wilfred	Roper River	3 years
Moriarty, John	Borroloola	4 years
Wesley, Heather	Roper River	5 years
Hamilton, Hubert	Groote Eylandt	6 years
Campbell, Tim	Borroloola	6 years
Hall, Carey	Roper River	6 years
Huddleston, Cecily	Roper River	6 years
Herbert, Joyce	Roper River	7 years
Hamilton, Eileen	Groote Eylandt	8 years
Foster, Jim	Borroloola	9 years
Herbert, Alfred	Roper River	9 years
Hamilton, Melva	Groote Eylandt	10 years

Stolen

Wesley, Helen	Roper River	10 years
Foster, Rose	Borroloola	10 years
Hamilton, Arnold	Groote Eylandt	11 years
Huddleston, Ida	Roper River	11 years
Pearce, Nettie	Alice Springs	12 years
McCaw, Frederick	Roper River	14 years
Huddleston, Wilton	Roper River	14 years

A few months before the Roper River district round-up, war came to Australia's doorstep. In the wake of the 19 February 1942 Japanese bombing of Darwin, there was a very real threat that the Japanese Imperial Army would invade Australia. After the first bombing run there were another 62 raids on the city; more bombs were dropped on Darwin than at Pearl Harbor. The Darwin bombings killed 243, mostly civilians, and injured a further 300. They destroyed half the city. The military moved in and the Australian government decided to close all Aboriginal institutions including the native hospital, isolated refuges for people suffering leprosy, government ration depots and many of the religious missions. Incredibly the Australian government feared that Aboriginals would collude with the invading Japanese forces as they advanced from a possible beachhead established in the far north. Just as German and Japanese citizens were rounded up and placed in detention centres to sit out the war, so too were Aboriginals. Now, not only were Indigenous people discriminated against for their colour, they had become veritable aliens in their own land.

The children were loaded into four army trucks and the convoy took the long, dusty road to Alice Springs. After four or

The Boys from St Francis

five days in Alice Springs, they were taken to the railway station and placed aboard the Ghan, bound for Adelaide.

Those from the Roper River region were followed by others in the Northern Territory. Among the children taken from their mothers in Alice Springs was Wally McArthur, a boy who developed amazing athletic prowess. Like so many others, Wally was born of a liaison between a white man (in his case a white policeman called Langdon) and his Aboriginal mother.

Wally came into this world under a giant gumtree on the banks of the McArthur River. He was given the surname McArthur and, like the turbulent fury of a swollen creek at the height of a flash flood, Wally's explosive athletic power left all the others in his wake. According to his peers no one grew up to be stronger or run faster than Wally McArthur. He became the hero of the boys at St Francis House; their ideal role model. Wally possessed the perfect build: long muscled legs and a torso to make even the most gifted and toned Olympic champion sit up and take notice. In fact, Wally was considered by a range of good judges to have been fast enough as a sprinter to win an Olympic gold medal, but racism and bigotry proved a hurdle too hard for him to negotiate.

In 1947 Wally ran the world's fastest 440-yard event for 14-year-olds. He had the form, and then some, to win a place on the 1952 Australian Olympic athletics squad bound for Helsinki. He yearned for the chance to compete in trials in Hobart, however, he could not afford the fare to travel to Tasmania. As it turned out, a benevolent gentleman came to the rescue and paid his fare. Now aged 18, Wally wiped the field, defeating a young Western Australian, Kevin Gosper, who four years later won the silver medal for the 440-yard event in Melbourne in 1956.

Stolen

Wally's brilliance in both the 100-yard dash and the 440 didn't resonate with the officials. Perhaps they were simply following the apartheid-like guidelines of the horrendous White Australia Policy, for Wally was not even shortlisted for the Helsinki Olympic Games. Officials would go to their graves denying anything untoward ever happened over Wally McArthur's non-selection for Helsinki.

In 1953 Wally turned professional and in 1958 he recorded far better times for the 100-yard race and the 440 than the gold medallists at the Cardiff Commonwealth Games on the very day of the finals.

Undoubtedly Wally McArthur was the Usain Bolt of his day. But in the 1950s another sport captured his attention: rugby league.

In 1953 Wally was 'man of the match' in an interstate clash for South Australia against Western Australia. He signed for Rochdale Hornets and flew out of Sydney bound for England on 19 November 1953.

Under the banner headline, A NEW BLACK FLASH IS ON HIS WAY TO ENGLAND, the *Daily Express* announced details of Wally McArthur's imminent arrival. Over seven years in England he played 165 games for Rochdale, Blackpool Borough, Salford, Wigan and Worthington Town. During that time he played alongside fellow former St Francis House boy, Jim Foster, who was like a terrier in his desperate forays into the heart of any scrum. More often than not Jim would burrow in and get the ball, only to hand it to Wally – 'the fastest winger in football boots' – whose incredible speed enabled him to scythe through the opposition defensive cordon like a hot knife in butter. When the Rochdale Hornets players first set eyes on Wally they couldn't believe his strength and speed. Soon all of England heard of the 'black flash.'

But all of that was ahead of Wally. Even all those years later, the pain of being dragged from his home and taken to a foreign place stayed with him.

The method of his being stolen from his family was different to Jim Foster and the others from Roper River, but the motive was entirely consistent with the government's racist policy. A government car arrived at Wally's home and he was placed in a seat alongside the driver. He waved to his mother and members of his family, all seated round a camp fire. It would be 55 years before he would set eyes on any family member again.

Seven-year-old Wally McArthur was bound for a refugee camp in Mulgoa, New South Wales. Unbeknown to Wally his four-year-old cousin John Moriarty had also been stolen, taken straight from school and put onto a truck. All this happened without John's family's knowledge. John's mother only learned what had happened when she arrived at the school to collect her son.

Gordon Briscoe and his mother were among hundreds of Aboriginals ordered out of the Northern Territory in 1942. They were also transported to Mulgoa.

'I felt the dark green canvas rubbing across my face as I was lifted into the army truck,' Gordon says. 'I recall being with my mother and her two young sisters. We left Alice Springs mid-morning and travelled south by military convoy to Oodnadatta. From there we were transported on cattle trucks to Quorn, where we caught a train. The smell of steam engines has never left me.'

Gordon, his mother and her two sisters stayed briefly at the

Balaklava Railway Station before travelling onward to Adelaide, where they were met by Father Percy Smith, the Anglican priest who had run St John's Hostel in Alice Springs.

'Wearing an army uniform, Father Smith was there to meet us and from there we were taken to a church mission society tearoom opposite Adelaide Railway Station,' Gordon says.

There they met up with the 30 children who had been rounded up in the Roper River district. Among those who were transported from Alice Springs was Millie Glen. Millie, whose white father (Fred Raggatt) worked Glen Helen Station, was given the surname Glen. She was taken from her mother when she was two years old and placed with carers at the Bungalow, the Old Telegraph Station in Alice Springs.

'I'm unsure what year I was born in, but I know my birthday was 1 December because all Aboriginal girls at that time were given that,' she smiles.

'The boys' birthdate was 1 April ... I can only suppose that giving the boys April Fool's Day as their birthdate amused the government officials.'

Interestingly, Wally McArthur gives his birthdate as 1 December 1933, so perhaps the official at the time was none too coherent or aware (or both) when he made the notation in the birth register.

After a couple of weeks, which must have seemed a lifetime for those poor little souls, the 30 children from the Roper River district plus those from Alice Springs arrived in Ashfield, where they were given a quick-fire physical check-up so the matron could apply to government agencies for child endowment. From Ashfield, 13 km south-west of the Sydney CBD, the children were taken to Mulgoa.

The Boys from St Francis

These boys in a Mulgoa class photograph all came later to St Francis House. Back row, far left: Ken Hampton. Second row, starting second from left: John Hampton, Harry Russell, Wally McArthur, Cyril Hampton, Jim Foster. Front row, starting second from left: Gerry Hill, John Moriarty, Wilfred 'Boofa' Huddleston and, far right, Tim Campbell. Photo courtesy John Moriarty.

Mulgoa means 'black swan' and in the old days two groups – the Dharug and the Gandangara people – shared the Mulgoa valley. The Roper River contingent arrived at an imposing 15-room mansion, solidly built of stone by the best convict labour available in the 1830s; a stately building befitting the glory days of the pastoral 'king,' Governor Lachlan Macquarie. A gift to the Anglican Church by a wealthy colonial pastoralist, the mansion was complemented by a majestic 20-acre sweep of lush pasture next door. Wide verandas encircled each of the three floors of the building. The girls slept next door. Jim Foster was free to visit with his sister, Rose, and the boys and girls were encouraged to mix during the daylight hours.

Stolen

One of the church missionaries at Mulgoa was a short, stout woman with a kindly disposition. Sister Dove 'owned' Saturday mornings, although this didn't always sit well with the children: this was the day their hair was shorn and they were deloused with a white powder, said to be a magical formula for killing nits.

It was also the day when each child was given a compulsory dose of Epsom salts, malt molasses and, on occasion, milk emulsion. As the boys filed into the door leading to the dining room on Saturday mornings before football, an attendant would wait with a spoonful of the dreaded Epsom salts.

Later at St Francis House there was a like process with the nurse holding the dreaded medicine. She stood tall like a grenadier guardsman at the dining room door.

'You'd hold the liquid in your mouth,' Vince Copley says, 'after enduring the time it took to hear the reading of morning prayer. You'd sit down, cast a bit more sugar on your porridge, then swallow the Epsom salts and gulp down the sugar-soaked cereal. It was the only way to kill the bitter taste. But by the time you got out onto the ground to play football, you'd be cursing the Epsom salts because they tended to make an impact on your body by the end of the first quarter.'

At Mulgoa the indomitable Sister Dove also introduced the children to three Christian hymns: 'Bring in the Sheaves', 'Rolling Over, Rolling Over' and 'Jesus Wants me for a Sunbeam'.

Sometimes when a relative visited and they took their child to the Blue Mountains there was the opportunity to supplement their diet by fishing, or catching *perentie* (a black tree goanna), rabbits and witchetty grubs, which could be roasted over an open fire.

The children were well treated and far better off at Mulgoa

than living in a detention camp, as many Aboriginal people did during the war years,.

The children taken to Mulgoa were there three years before Father Percy Smith started his 'assimilation experiment' by picking six boys in Alice Springs and taking them to Adelaide to realise his dream of providing them with a better education and generally a better chance in life.

The first six

The tribal people thought they were too white for their own good and the whites ostracised them because of their black blood.

The train belched steam as six little boys clambered aboard. Under a relentless late January sun their mothers linked arms as they stood on the platform watching their boys disappear through the door of the carriage. Millie Woodford, Dido Cooper, Tilly Miller, Hetti Perkins, Edie Espie and Melva Palmer were confident their boys were in safe hands. Father Smith had long been a calm and trusted friend of the women and their children. He had convinced the women that by taking their children to Adelaide he could lead them on a journey to a better future. The mothers also had great faith in Father Smith's wife, Isabel, who they believed would assume the role of foster mother to their boys during their time in Adelaide. Soon the boys were back in view, competing for the best vantage point, hanging their heads out of the window above the carriage door and craning their necks for one last lingering look at the familiar faces gathered on the platform. The women felt a raw mix of emotion: joy that their sons were to receive a quality education, but also great sadness that the boys had to be taken all the way to Adelaide.

For the six boys – David Woodford, Malcolm Cooper, Peter Tilmouth, Charlie Perkins, Bill Espie and John Palmer – the journey was one of excitement; an adventure.

In no time the stationmaster raised his right arm holding his

The Boys from St Francis

flag aloft. There was a nod from the guard, the shrill sound of a whistle and the Ghan slowly chugged away, slowly but surely working up a good head of steam. The smiling mothers were still standing on the platform, their faces glistening with tears, as the steam train sped into the distance.

As the Ghan pulled through the famous gap in the majestic MacDonnell Ranges, nine-year-old Charlie Perkins had a fleeting glimpse of Rainbow Town, the place so named because of the varying skin colours of the groups living there in the heart of Alice Springs. Even the high vantage point of Anzac Hill soon became a distant speck on the landscape.

The word was well and truly out for at intermittent points along the railway line family members stood and waved. They couldn't see the boys' faces as the train steamed past them, but they knew the boys could see them.

While the other boys chatted excitedly, Charlie kept his thoughts to himself. As with many other Aboriginal children in those days, Charlie never really knew the date of his birth. According to the official register the date was 16 June 1936, but often in those days an official would not record birthdates until he had a long list of names, so a baby born in July might not be officially recorded until December. To his family Charlie was born 'around 1936 to 37'.

Even the exact place of his birth was a mystery. Some maintained that Charlie was born on a dry river bed near the Old Telegraph Station, but others were adamant that Hetti Perkins gave birth to Charlie on a table at the old station itself.

Hetti Perkins was an Arrernte woman. Charlie's father's name was Connelly, but Charlie saw him only once. However, he learnt that his father came from Mt Isa. He was an Aboriginal man of

The first six

the war-like Kalkadoon group, whose mother was Kalkadoon and father Irish.

Charlie's mother kept her maiden name. She didn't marry Connelly, who fathered a number of Charlie's brothers and sisters. One of Hetti's children was the result of her liaison with a man named Lake, and Charlie never discovered how many other siblings were fathered by a man named Jim Turner.

According to Hetti the family was 'split up', but nevertheless Charlie had a happy childhood and he loved hearing the stories of his father and his feats of strength. Connelly took on all and sundry in bare-knuckle fist fights; he drank little and had a good sense of humour.

His father had six brothers and four sisters, one of whom gave birth to 17 children. Charlie was to say years later than 'I hope my children love me as much as I love my father.'

Charlie peered out of the carriage window and wondered what was in store. He was excited at the prospect of gaining a good education. It was his mother's dream that Charlie be given a decent opportunity in life, but he had already developed a strong sense of right and wrong. He couldn't understand why there was such a determination on the part of the European people to take all part-Aboriginal children away from their people and keep them separate, often forcibly so.

It was this injustice and other acts of discrimination against his people which defined Charlie Perkins and eventually drove him to make a difference in public life. As the other boys chatted excitedly, Charlie closed his eyes and dreamt of happy times.

Charlie was always happiest running about the bush near the Old Telegraph Station, joyfully playing in the nearby waterhole with the other children. He always loved the hills, valleys and rivers of the MacDonnell Ranges, which almost encircle Alice Springs like nature's Colosseum. In the late afternoon to nightfall the ranges shimmer in a kaleidoscope of colours that capture the imagination. The country, the animals and birds meant everything to Charlie. He was proud to have a skin grouping of the Arrernte group called Purula and to have the caterpillar as his totem, for this was his ancestry.

Charlie also discovered a good way to find money in and about the town theatre in Bath Street. Hetti was employed as a cook in a café near the theatre. She worked late into the night and often there was no one to care for her children, so they were left to their own devices. Charlie found money dropped by soldiers while they were buying their cinema tickets.

If he found a £1 note he quickly thrust it into his pocket. Any coin, be it a two shilling or a threepenny piece, he hid in the dust in front of the pay box. He would rise at the crack of dawn, grab a rake and scratch at the dusty ground in search of more booty.

Sometimes in those happy times playing with mates about the area, they would venture into what was then known as the 'new' Alice Springs.

The boys would climb up to the top of part of the ranges which surround the town like ancient stone sentinels. Forbidden to enter the town after dark, the boys always looked down on Alice Springs with a tinge of sadness. They were staring at another world, the white man's world. On more than one occasion, Charlie and his mates stayed longer than authorities would tolerate and they were picked up by the police and driven back to the reserve.

To put one over the troopers was a thrilling challenge for Charlie. From the time he was a toddler he sensed something

The first six

was amiss in his life. Because the white man decreed that part-Aboriginal people could not fraternise with the tribal people, his grandmother Nellie Errerreke Perkins could never get close enough to hold her grandson. When Charlie was five, his grandmother pressed her face to the cyclone wire fence that segregated the tribal people from the 'half-caste home' in Alice Springs. He stared at her, longing to be held. Why was she barred from coming to him and his mother, Nellie's beloved daughter?

Charlie's grandmother was among a handful of Eastern Arrernte Aboriginals who, along with two white men, had by 1905 extracted 500 tonnes of gold-bearing ore from the Great Western Mine at White Range. Nellie's father was murdered near the site of the mine, a place where the late summer heat sweeps across the Simpson Desert, shimmering above the treeless ridges of the world's oldest mountain range, the MacDonnells. Nellie Perkins knew the tree at which her father was shot in cold blood. She forever had nightmares after witnessing men chained together and force-marched to Alice Springs jail. Nellie yearned to be with Hetti and her grandsons, but all she could do was find a vantage point on the rise above Wollatjthere and call out for her daughter.

'Hetti? Hetti Perkins!'

It was forced separation; no less than Australia's own form of apartheid.

Charlie didn't understand his grandmother's anguish until years later, and Nellie Perkins died in 1947 without ever comprehending why the whites prevented her from living with her family.

At that very time Gordon Briscoe was rubbing shoulders with Wally McArthur and Jim Foster at Mulgoa. Gordon was interested in history and he sought to learn all he could about the subject, especially the real story of his people.

Gordon learnt about the itinerant workers – European, Afghan and Chinese men working as cameleers, rail workers, pastoral labourers and telegraph station staff – who came to the Northern Territory during the mid to late 1800s. These intruders brought alcohol with them and often left the women pregnant and their children destitute.

Gordon wrote in his highly acclaimed book, *Racial Folly*:

> Some Mardu women were very young and left their children in the camps. Others were either already burdened with too many children or had left to meet ceremonial obligations in distant communities. In many instances Aboriginal women were raped thus exacerbating the population explosion of unwanted children of mixed descent, most of whom were abandoned by their white fathers. Many Mardu people were killed by pastoralists and brutal marauding police. Some Aboriginals were killed at will and others for spearing for food cattle and sheep which had crossed their traditional hunting lands. Cultural practices that had continued for 1000 or more years were lost. Animal game, so much a staple diet of hunter-gatherers, was soon changed as sheep and cattle meat entered the Mardo diet. What began as a strange phenomenon ended up as everlasting death or perdition. From our grandmothers, who lived through this brutal past, we learned that most of the white men, who ventured into the Tywerentye, Western MacDonnell Ranges and the river regions of the Leratupa and Umbarntuwa, came along with wives. They came to build and operate telegraph stations, the pastoral leases, the small

stores and railway stations. Slowly, between 1890 and 1914, a few white women began migrating from South Australia and other colonies, and many learned that their white husbands had black children whom they abandoned in Aboriginal camps.

As the half-caste population grew, the small number of white women residing in the service towns dotted along the arterial route from Oodnadatta to what is now Darwin began to panic. They panicked not only because they saw the presence of half-caste children in the same classrooms as disadvantaging their white children, but also because their white husbands had sired those same children.

The increasing presence of half-caste children aroused deep-seated fears and anxieties in the settler women. Their men were equally intent on denying the existence of these offspring. Each morning when these men washed their faces and looked out across the creeks in service towns, they would see their abandoned children in the Aboriginal fringe camps running around before their very eyes, barely existing.

The stark realisation that these part-Aboriginals would forever be disowned by the tribal people and ostracised by the whites has taken its toll on generations of men, women and children. To recent times they were outcasts in their own land, but the six youngsters sitting on the train bound for Adelaide that January day in 1945 were largely oblivious to this history.

Ten-year-old Charlie Perkins knew right from wrong alright, but the word *discrimination* was not then in his vocabulary. However, he would soon grow to learn of it and all its evil ramifications.

The Boys from St Francis

As Charlie sat by himself alone in his thoughts, Father Smith closed his eyes, satisfied with his decision to take the boys to Adelaide. In 1933 when Father Smith took up his post in Alice Springs he was told that he must do all in his power to help the mixed-blood children, especially those living in what was called the 'half-caste institution', the Bungalow, at the Old Telegraph Station. In Father Percy Smith's typed writings, *The Story of St Francis House* (now in the possession of his son John), he says:

> They were looked upon by the blacks as those who were born in an infringement of their tribal laws and were looked upon as the 'cheeky ones.' The white man ostracised them, except when they wanted cheap labour. Their normal pay was 5/- a week, even those employed by the government.

Father Smith found that the Aboriginal children living at the Bungalow were sad; they often cowered and hid their faces when he approached. Something was terribly amiss. He soon discovered the problem. The superintendent of the Bungalow was a drunkard and a bully. He was the 'Protector of Children' and he wore that title like a badge of dishonour. A month after Father Smith arrived, the superintendent was dismissed, convicted of raping a number of young Aboriginal girls and jailed.

Immediately the rogue superintendent was replaced the environment changed. Better conditions and humane treatment were, according to Father Smith, certain to work, although the children's ill-treatment had taken its toll. Father Smith knew that you can't paint a smile on a child's face. It took 18 months before he noticed the children were speaking out confidently and, like all happy, normal children, asking questions of their peers and elders. They no longer averted their eyes when Father

The first six

Smith approached, but for most of the children the psychological scars would remain forever.

The collective ill-treatment of 'half-caste' men, women and children by whites has sadly had a long and undistinguished history in Australia, and Father Smith was dismayed to learn the history of the Aboriginals' institutional life in the Territory. In 1914 a teacher, Ida Standley, established a school in a little tin shed behind the Stuart Arms Hotel. She taught white and Aboriginal children, but the white parents railed against her teaching 'mixed' classes. Her solution was to teach the white children in the morning and Aboriginal children in the afternoon. The sequence was reversed next day. While the prejudice of the white mothers was evident, Ida had found a strategy to provide an education in equal measure for black and white.

It may have escaped the attention of those in Canberra, but Ida Standley had established the first multi-racial school in the land. Some attest that the schooling went well, although the Aboriginal youngsters were getting under two hours tuition daily and the rest of their day was spent running about the streets. The boys coped best for the girls were vulnerable and targets. Ida was deeply concerned about the welfare of the young Aboriginal girls, many of whom were destitute.

Unhappily the humble schoolhouse was right next door to the hotel and often when an Aboriginal girl left the school house she would be accosted by a drunken lout emerging from the front bar. Ida tried locking the girls in at night, but they often broke out, many of them seeking company.

In 1927 the Ida Standley school was moved to a so-called refuge at Jay Creek, some 40 km from Alice Springs. Ida's concerns were increased at Jay Creek because the Aboriginal children from the school were added to a growing number of half-caste children who had been rounded up by police from the stations and outlying camps and dumped there.

In 1928 Territorians turned a blind eye to the illegal unions between white men and Aboriginal girls. These part-Aboriginal babies were often 'conveniently' allowed to fall into a fire or disposed of in some other horrendous manner. The babies were contemptuously called 'yeller fellas' and from the outset they were destined to become veritable outcasts in their own land.

Legendary anthropologist Professor Ted Strehlow estimated that no child born in the area in and around Alice Springs after 1875 was educated in the full traditions. He once famously said: 'We have to train ourselves to look upon the land of our birth with the eyes, not of conquerors overcoming an enemy, but of children looking at the face of their mother. Only then shall we truly be able to call Australia our home. Our native traditions can help us become finer and better Australians.'

When Father Smith caught sight of the way the Aboriginal children were being treated at Jay Creek he set about getting many of the children moved to the Bungalow at the Old Telegraph Station, which was no longer run by the superintendent.

In the late 1930s the Bungalow was at its lowest ebb. Racism was rife, with whites having a low opinion of the 'half-castes.' There were two teachers to school more than 100 Aboriginal children, 24 of whom were toddlers, most of them at the Bungalow because they had been forcibly removed from their mothers. The chief dormitory girl was Hetti Perkins, Charlie's mother. Because the rooms were overcrowded, there were periodic outbreaks of measles, conjunctivitis, colds, and even pneumonia, tuberculosis and influenza.

The first six

In 1940 the authorities decided to return all the Eastern Arrernte to Jay Creek. The Western Desert people were placed in a new depot at Haasts Bluff and the children of the Bungalow were to be evacuated to distant towns.

Father Smith wrote (in part) of his experiences with the Aboriginal people:

> In taking the boys to Adelaide, what we were aiming at was assimilation and we started to do it before it became government policy in 1954. There is a lot being said about the Aboriginals being allowed to keep their own culture and this is how it should be for the full-blood native people. As I see it, there are many of Aboriginal blood who never had anything to do with tribal life which is the basis of Aboriginal culture, laws and customs. I refer to those of mixed blood who have never been admitted by initiation to tribal life. In fact, the mixed bloods have no real culture of their own. They are people in between the black and white cultures and to a large extent belong to neither and in certain places, even now, are ostracised. Therefore, the best way to help these people is to assimilate them and give them equality of opportunity. It is up to our white society to receive them as equals. That many white Australians are not willing to do so is a disgrace, for they are part-white and it is our duty to accept them! This was my aim in bringing the six boys to live and be educated in Adelaide.

But had the white man missed the point? The part-Aboriginal person was no more ostracised by the white man than the full-initiated Aboriginal. General discrimination and racism did not separate them. It is worth noting that then Prime Minister Paul Keating said in 1992:

the starting point might be to recognise that the problem starts with us non-Aboriginal Australians. It begins, I think, with the act of recognition. Recognition that it was we who did the dispossessing. We took the traditional lands and smashed the traditional way of life. We brought the diseases. The alcohol. We committed the murders. We took the children from the mothers. We practised discrimination and exclusion...

Father Smith was determined to prove that Aboriginal children were just as good as any other. He was buoyed by the success of Joe Croft, a boy who gained a qualifying certificate at school. Father Smith convinced the Darwin-based Department of Native Affairs that Croft be sponsored for higher studies at All Souls School in Charters Towers, Queensland. Croft became a star pupil, getting his junior and senior certificate and being appointed captain of the school.

He later attended Queensland University studying engineering, and during his war service he gained invaluable training on his way to becoming a licensed surveyor. His outstanding qualities saw him recruited to the Department of Aboriginal Affairs in Canberra.

Joe Croft was perhaps the first high achiever among those boys who came under the influence of Father Smith. But however kind Father Smith happened to be, assimilation smacks very much of policy by stealth: 'breed the black out of them' and over time the individual merges into white society, gradually losing his culture and sense of belonging.

Governments throughout Australia were actively involved in taking 'half-caste' children from their mothers and placing

The first six

them into institutional care. It was long argued that they were ostracised by full-blood relatives and discriminated against by the whites. According to the European rulers of Australia, assimilation with whites was the only possible course to follow.

From 1910 until well into the 1970s this policy of forced removal of children from their Aboriginal mothers and placement in institutional 'care' was pursued relentlessly.

We know now that children of Australian Aboriginal and Torres Strait Islander descent were forcibly taken from their families by Australian federal and state government agencies as well as church missions. Newspaper articles and reports to various parliamentary committees consistently argued that such removals were a form of 'child protection': that the catastrophic decline in population of the Aboriginals after white contact would, unless an effective policy of assimilation was properly enacted, continue unabated. Typical of the official line between the wars was this statement by Dr Cecil Cook, the Protector of Aborigines in the Northern Territory, from 1930:

> Generally by the fifth and invariably by the sixth generation, all native characteristics of the Australian Aborigine are eradicated. The problem of our half-castes will quickly be eliminated by the complete disappearance of the black race, and the swift submergence of their progeny in the white.

Around the same time the Chief Protector of Aborigines in Western Australia, A.O. Neville, wrote in the morning broadsheet the *West Australian*: 'Eliminate in future the full-blood and the white and one common blend will remain.'

In 1982 I interviewed tennis player Evonne Goolagong about her childhood, with the view of including the story in a series of children's books about prominent Australian sportsmen and women. Evonne talked about her mother coming into the children's bedroom in the dead of night in their home at Barellan in country New South Wales, thumping an upturned mop on the floor and saying theatrically, 'Quick, children outside; hide in the car, the bogey men are coming.' As with the other Goolagong kids, Evonne thought that her mother was just playing a game.

Evonne didn't realise it then, nor did I, that her mother was hiding her children from the government agencies. Evonne and I 'caught on' at the time of the first Sorry Day in 1998. British-trained journalist, author and critic Phillip Knightley said of the Stolen Generations in 2000:

> This cannot be over-emphasised – the Australian government literally kidnapped these children from their parents as a matter of policy. White welfare officers, often supported by police, would descend on Aboriginal camps, round up all the children, separate the ones with light-coloured skin, bundle them into trucks and take them away. If their parents protested they were held at bay by police.

In February 2007 then Australian Prime Minister Kevin Rudd did what previous governments of all persuasions should have done years ago: he delivered a public apology to the Stolen Generations. The apology came very late, but it came. It was appropriate and it was greatly appreciated by all thinking Australians. In 1997 Sir Ronald Wilson, a former High Court judge and co-author of the *Bringing Them Home* report on the Stolen Generations said publicly that he believed the taking of the children from their mothers was a form of genocide.

The first six

But all of that was way down the track. As the Ghan steamed along toward Adelaide in 1945, Father Smith believed he was setting out on a blessed mission.

A 'better place'

He stared at the envelope addressed in a beautiful copperplate hand. To this dedicated man of the cloth, those two crisp £1 notes were pennies from heaven.

As the Ghan chugged along, the hours dragged and the boys became restless. Father Smith initially eased their boredom by reading to them, but even the good man's animated oratory began to wear thin. The boys wanted to get off the train and run about in their new world. They knew Adelaide would be different from Alice Springs, but they could never have envisioned how different.

Father Smith's wife Isabel wasn't aboard the train. As the time had approached for the party to leave Alice Springs, Isabel had received an urgent telegram. Her father was gravely ill. She cancelled her rail fare and flew from Alice Springs to Adelaide. Sadly, upon her arrival at Parafield Airport she learnt that her father had died minutes before her plane landed.

Father Smith's move to Adelaide from Alice Springs had to do with his own ill health, too. During the last years of the war, he had run St John's Hostel, in Bath Street, Alice Springs, which included providing spiritual sustenance for the troops based in the area. A legend in Alice Springs where he had been priest-in-charge since 1933 of the mission district, which embraced a parish covering a staggering 600,000 square miles, Father Smith was continually plagued by bouts of bronchitis and pleurisy. By 1945, his health was failing to the point where he felt the need to make a decision about his future.

A 'better place'

Isabel and Percy Smith on their wedding day, 8 June 1943.

Indeed, the army doctor suggested to him that for the good of his health he should seek to live in a 'less severe clime.' Adelaide, with its mild Mediterranean climate, seemed ideal.

The boys' mothers had long planned for their sons' journey to Adelaide. They bought clothes for them and paid their railway fares. In addition they made good their pledge to Father Smith to make available their child endowments for their sons' daily expenses.

Money was always going to be a problem in his mission, but Father Smith had been promised financial help from the Northern Territory branch of Native Affairs.

After an exhausting three-day journey, the party finally

arrived in Adelaide. They spent the night at the home of a relative of the Smith family in the seaside suburb of Semaphore. Charlie and the others were so excited to get to the seaside that they rushed headlong toward the sand hills. But to their dismay they found the water was salty and the beach strange for boys who had spent all their years in Alice Springs. Semaphore would come to play an important role in their development.

Before Father Smith and the six boys – David Woodford, Malcolm Cooper, Peter Tilmouth, Charlie Perkins, Bill Espie and John Palmer – set out from Alice Springs, arrangements for accommodation and schooling in Adelaide had been finalised.

Miss Murphy, a former nurse and charitable woman, offered rent-free hostel accommodation in an old nursing home building which stood next to her home in Pembroke Street, Kensington Gardens.

Father Smith's first task was to conduct the funeral service for his father-in-law at Cheltenham Cemetery. He was also keen to see the boys wearing good quality clothes and walking in proper shoes, so he took them all along to Myers department store in the city and bought them a suit of clothes, shoes and socks. Most of the boys had never worn shoes, but Father Smith knew if his boys were well dressed it would go a long way toward their being accepted by the other children. Despite promises of financial help from the church and well-wishers, little money was pushed his way. Still, the boys settled in nicely to Marryatville Primary School, where they mixed happily with their fellow students and the teachers.

The home in Kensington Gardens had an attached sleep-out, complete with six beds, perfect for Father Smith's purpose. However, Percy and Isabel Smith's sleeping arrangements were not ideal. They slept on the front veranda while Isabel's recently widowed mother, Mrs Almond, used the bedroom.

Not far from their hostel in Pembroke Street was Kensington Oval where the legendary Don Bradman played grade cricket, and often the boys would go to the oval to play cricket or football either after school or on Saturdays. On rare occasions Father Smith would take the boys for a stroll to nearby Holden Street where Sir Donald Bradman and Lady Jessie Bradman lived in an impressive two-storey house. On such occasions Father Smith would regale the boys with stories of Bradman's exploits in international cricket. A friend of Father Smith's happened to be a member of the South Australian Cricket Association and the friend often invited him to state or test matches at Adelaide Oval. Sometimes Father Smith would offer one of the boys a chance to join him at Adelaide Oval.

As the weeks passed the boys settled in well. They studied hard and the Smiths helped them daily with their homework. First among the initial batch of boys from Alice Springs to show genuine artistic talent was John Palmer. At his very first attempt to draw, John painted a copy of one of Albert Namatjira's ghost gum paintings. The painting was displayed at a school function where the state governor, Sir William Norrie, selected the work for special commendation. Father Smith was excited about John's artistic future and he enrolled him at the South Australian School of Art, where he studied for two years. Sadly, John did not continue to paint in later years when he returned to the Northern Territory.

All of the initial six boys Father Smith brought to Adelaide in 1945 studied and worked hard becoming productive workers and solid citizens, managing to forge successful careers. Charlie

The Boys from St Francis

Bill Espie as a young constable with the NSW Police Force. Photograph taken at his Greenacre (Sydney) home. Photo courtesy John Smith.

Perkins became a national figure, a strong advocate for Aboriginal affairs. He played international soccer and he became a fierce agitator against wrongdoing. Awarded an AO and an honorary PhD from the University of Western Sydney, Charlie became the first Aboriginal to head a federal government department. He was a champion for his people.

Bill Espie rose to a high rank in the New South Wales Police Force and was awarded the Queen's Medal for bravery after he risked his life dragging an injured man to safety from a car engulfed in fire.

Malcolm Cooper became an electrician in the public service and later was officer-in-charge of Aboriginal employment for the state government. Malcolm, a half-back flanker, was the first

A 'better place'

Aboriginal footballer to play for Port Adelaide in a grand final.

David Woodford gained an apprenticeship with South Australian Railways and worked his way up from cleaner to stoker to driver. He has retained his mischievous sense of humour.

Peter Tilmouth became an apprentice fitter and turner. He spent some time in the merchant navy, married and had two children. But tragedy struck when he was just 34 years old; Peter was killed when an opal mine he was working in Coober Pedy collapsed.

The boys later said that during their time at Pembroke Street they felt closer to Father Smith and his wife, Isabel, than at any other time. The Smiths created an environment which was High Church of England and the epitome of decorum and decency. Mrs Smith would always set the table with lace tablecloth, bone china and silverware. Part of the ritual during evening meals was the 'passing of the tea'. The teapot was passed from place to place and on more than one occasion one of the boys spilt a few drops or knocked over a cup. When a mistake occurred, Isabel Smith never scolded them harshly. She would utter softly, 'My dear, you are not supposed to ...'

Some of the boys found it difficult to immediately be comfortable with their clothes. They had to wear underpants, some for the first time; they were compelled to wear shoes; and they wore suits on special occasions, such us Sundays.

Sundays were special. The boys donned their suits and went to Holy Communion. Father Smith always ensured that each of the boys wrote a letter home of a Sunday afternoon. Writing to their mothers on a regular basis was a non-negotiable commitment for the boys and they all dutifully complied. Usually the Smiths would offer a starting point for the boys, such as 'I do hope you are well,' but other than that they wanted each boy to write from the heart to his mother and there was never any hint of censorship. Often he took the boys to fellowship tea and, as always, his message was clear: 'give these "half-caste" boys an equal chance with the others and they are just as equal in all ways'. The Smiths cherished the boys as their own and the boys loved them pretty much as surrogate parents. After supper most winter nights, the boys huddled together on the floor in front of a roaring fire of Father Smith's study and he would read passages from *Winnie the Pooh*, always ending with the gentle, 'Okay, boys, into bed.'

The Smiths were strong in their convictions, but gentle in the commonsense way they guided the boys. Church underpinned their daily lives and twice daily they attended chapel. On Sundays they worshipped at St Edward's Church, Kensington.

The boys enjoyed their schooling and were polite and respectful toward the Smiths and Mrs Almond. Despite this, by mid 1945 Father Smith was fast losing confidence in his mission. Money had become a huge issue. Because of delays by government agencies and church he had found that he was forking out money from his own pocket. And by August 1945 the money had run out. Father Smith was at his wits' end. How would he cope? How could he possibly pay any of the staff?

The heavy workload was also affecting Isabel, who did all the cooking and the housework. She also had to care for her bedridden mother, who had suffered a stroke. House help was desperately required and one woman in particular had been highly recommended for the job. Father Smith agonised over the decision, as he could only offer Mrs Blaiklock part-time

A 'better place'

employment at the rate of £2 a week, which he knew he would have to raise by the end of her first week. At that very point in time, £2 was £2 more than he could afford.

There had been an offer of £100 from the Australian Board of Missions, but that money was not immediately forthcoming, so his mission to feed, clothe and educate the boys was in jeopardy.

The very day that Father Smith was due to pay the part-time housekeeper her first week's wages, an anonymous letter arrived. He stared at the envelope: it was addressed in a flowing copperplate hand: *Fr Percy Smith, Pembroke Street, Kensington Gardens, South Australia.*

He opened the envelope and came upon two crisp £1 notes.

Father Smith raised his head and smiled. Those two notes were like pennies from heaven. He immediately took up his pen to write Mrs Blaiklock.

But the anonymous gift was nowhere near enough for him to continue his mission. He had been promised money from a variety of well-meaning organisations including the church, but nothing had been forthcoming. There had been a tentative offer by All Souls School in Charters Towers, Queensland (the school Joe Croft had attended), to provide for the boys, but Father Smith was unsure that it was a realistic option. He worried that his mission was destined to fail and the boys would have to return to Alice Springs.

Just as despair reigned, deliverance emerged in the form of the bishop of Adelaide, the Right Reverend B.P. Robin, who had enthusiastically taken up their cause with Canberra. Maintenance was paid and the Smiths received other allowances to ensure their dream was kept alive.

In addition to the bishop of Adelaide's interest, the Australian

The Boys from St Francis

Board of Missions, who had by then honoured their promised donation of £100, wished greater involvement and asked that Father Smith find larger, more suitable accommodation so they could help a greater number of boys. On 12 November 1946 at a meeting at Miss Murphy's Pembroke property, church stakeholders and Father Smith resolved to try and run a home for up to 50 boys. Father Smith had reservations because his dream was to help the boys acquire the best education within an environment which encouraged hard work and spiritual strength without losing the culture of their Aboriginality. He believed his cause to help the boys would work best if numbers were kept to a minimum. However, he eventually agreed.

The first task was to find a suitable home for up to 50 part-Aboriginal boys. Having looked far and wide, Father Smith decided to negotiate to buy Glanville Hall, a substantial stone building in South Semaphore, which he first set eyes on from his seat on a trolley bus on a trip with Isabel. He thought aloud, 'What's that place?'

'Glanville Hall, Percy. I used to play hockey on the grounds.'

Father Smith smiled. Perhaps it had been ordained. He vowed to see Glanville Hall and meet the owner.

Father Smith's belief in human nature was heightened by an agreement between the South Australian Education Department and the Australian Board of Missions to provide up to £5000 for the purchase of the hall.

The owner initially gave Father Smith a 'yes', then followed up in writing with a flat 'no' to any suggestion that the building be sold. But Father Smith wasn't taking no for an answer. He knew he had to find another way to secure a good deal, so he put the matter in the hands of a real estate company (Shepherds) in the city. Eventually the owner relented and the asking price was £5000. Father Smith countered with an offer of £4000 and a compromise was reached with a handshake. Glanville Hall was bought for £4500.

The Commonwealth government wanted the South Australian Education Department to pay an additional £800 in cash for repairs in return for a swap of land. A proposed road was closed which gave Glanville Hall more land and a total area of some 13 acres. Agreement among the Commonwealth government, local council and the other parties was cumbersome and the sale dragged on to 1953.

However, the renovation and occupation of the newly named St Francis House forged ahead. New bathrooms were built, along with a coke-fired boiler, which provided hot water throughout the building, and renovations to a small room for the cook.

St Francis House was close to Bower Road, a short walk to Semaphore Beach. The house comprised 28 rooms and a tower. In addition there was a coach house, laundry, stables and an impressive cobblestone courtyard.

The coach house was used as a gymnasium. Attic rooms were used as the boys' sleeping quarters and all the ground-floor rooms were in good order, except the kitchen, which was in disrepair. There was also a large room off the passage in the southern side of the building. This had been a billiard room, but the table was sold and the room converted into a chapel.

During the renovations, the usually reserved and conservative Father Smith had a brain wave. He discovered a splendid cedar toilet seat and thought it could be re-fashioned by a master craftsman into something quite special. And so it came to pass that the old cedar toilet seat that had served the lavatory at

The Boys from St Francis

Glanville Hall since 1856 was transformed into a missal stand in the chapel.

Isabel, then pregnant with their son John, moved into Glanville Hall in mid November 1946. About a week later Father Smith and the original six boys joined her, plus two others: Gordon Briscoe, whose mother brought him from Balaklava (South Australia) to Father Smith's care in Pembroke Street early in 1946, and Brian Butler.

While everyone had moved in to Glanville Hall at the end of 1946, the home was not officially opened until the following October.

On Saturday, 27 September 1947, a front-page story appeared in the Adelaide-edition of *Truth* under the heading: ABOS. FIND FAIRY GODFATHER.

> While the bedraggled procession of half-caste offenders grows week by week in the police courts of the Commonwealth, a silver-haired Adelaide clergyman is quietly going ahead with an experiment which seems like a beacon in the dreary story of Aboriginal welfare. He is the Rev P. McD Smith, former rector of Alice Springs and now superintendent of St Francis House, Semaphore, where since the beginning of the year 12 half-caste children, drawn from squalid humpies of the backblocks, have been living the happy, healthy life, which, he says, it is our duty as a Christian community to give them – and whence, Mr Smith hopes, they will return as doctors, lawyers and the like to minister among their own unhappy people.

Another part of the article quotes Dr Charles Duguid, the 'pioneer of Aboriginal welfare' and world-famed explorer:

A 'better place'

Comparing the achievements of Mr Smith, who is working with limited funds far from the spotlight of publicity, with that of the Aborigines' Friends Association, he told *Truth* that the natives were receiving a mere pittance of the vast sums subscribed by sympathetic white people.

The bulk of the money, he claims, is being spent in providing a retired minister with a comfortable job as secretary, on honorariums for various individuals, and in general office expenditure. In 1946, says Dr Duguid of the money collected through the years by the Aborigines' Friends Association in South Australia about £13,000 was invested in Government stock and £500 on War Loans.

Of the interest of £506, £175/17/- went to Aboriginal missions scattered through the Commonwealth and only £1/9/11 found its way to local Aborigines. Set alongside this paltry 30 bob – barely enough to buy a pair of boots – the figure of £329 for 'honorariums, printing and office,' seems on the face of it to be disproportionate, Dr Duguid said.

On 4 October 1947 (St Francis Day), Bishop Robin officially opened and blessed St Francis House. Father Smith thought it appropriate to so name the home, in honour of Saint Francis, 'the little friend of the poor and loved by all of God's creatures'. Non-stop rain that October day failed to dampen Bishop Robin's enthusiasm as he dashed from room to room, blessing every open space, nook and cranny.

A number of the St Francis House boys were confirmed earlier in the day at a ceremony performed by the bishop at St Paul's Church in Port Adelaide. But best of all to Father Smith and the boys was the warm welcome and blessing to their new home. Father Smith lived until 1982 and he may well have seen

The Boys from St Francis

Choir of St Paul's Anglican Church, Port Adelaide, c. 1950.
Second from left: David Woodford. Sixth from left: Vince Copley.
Seventh from left: Bill Espie. Far right: Charlie Perkins.

Margaret Thatcher's interview on 4 May 1979, at the beginning of her long-running tenure as prime minister. As the press swarmed about her outside No. 10 Downing Street her opening salvo paraphrased part of the prayer of St Francis of Assisi, saying it was 'particularly apt at this time':

> *Where there is discord may we bring harmony*
> *Where there is error may we bring truth*
> *Where there is doubt may we bring faith*
> *Where there is despair may we bring hope.*

While Margaret Thatcher's take on part of St Francis's prayer was more than 30 years on from the opening of St Francis House, the words rang as true then as they do today.

By 4 October 1947 the spirit of the boys from St Francis had already been established.

The house that 'Jack' built

Glanville Hall was Captain John ('Jack') Hart's residential pièce de résistance, built on land that had been the exclusive territory of the Kaurna people for more than 8000 years.

St Francis House resembled an English castle. Solid stones walls embraced a handsome coach house, impressive tower and a labyrinth of rooms, stairwells and little nooks, perfect for children to hide in and dream up mischief to impress their peers. The boys' new home was close to Semaphore Beach and from the lookout on the St Francis House tower, added in 1865, one could see for miles, across the sand hills and well across the water.

Built in the Victorian Tudor style, St Francis House was designed by a famous pioneer of the colony, George Strickland Kingston. But it was built by a man even more famous: the adventurer Captain John ('Jack') Hart – seafarer, whaler, drover, trader and thrice premier of South Australia.

The well-to-do Captain Hart owned 80 acres of lush pasture known as Buck's Flat in Semaphore South and he built Glanville Hall there in 1856. The name didn't change until 4 October 1947. After the last St Francis House boy left in 1959, St Francis House was purchased by the Port Adelaide Enfield Council and the name reverted to Glanville Hall.

The stone used in the construction of St Francis House was quarried in Port Vincent and transported by a fleet of flat-bottomed barges across the gulf to be offloaded at spot near where the Ethelton Railway Station now stands. At the ebb of the tide the barges would run aground and when the water level was low enough carts were run onto the sand whereupon the stone was loaded and carted to the building site.

Captain Hart had retired from the sea in 1846. He became a prominent merchant in Port Adelaide, where he built, at a cost of £3750, the first flour mill in the colony. It began operating in 1855, a year before he constructed his new home, which he named Glanville Hall after his mother, 'the beautiful Mary Glanville'. When he added the distinctive tower almost ten years later, the locals took to calling the captain's home 'Hart's Castle'. From the tower Captain Hart was often first to set eyes on the billowing sails of a visiting merchant ship heading for port.

He knew a thing or two about seamanship and the colony

Glanville Hall *(known as St Francis House 1947–1959)*, *by Port Adelaide artist, John Ford.*

of South Australia, having provided critical topographical information to Colonel William Light before his departure from England in HMS *Rapid* to survey the new colony. Apart from his long experience as a whaler in Tasmania and Encounter Bay, he was also a sealer in Victoria and he amassed vast knowledge of and contact with a range of Aboriginal people during his many voyages.

After his seafaring days were over Captain Hart took what many thought to be an 'armchair ride' for the old adventurer: he became a politician. Elected to parliament in 1851 he was treasurer six times, premier and chief secretary three times and a member of nine ministries.

Captain Hart entertained lavishly at St Francis House and due to his standing in the community he hosted many dignitaries, including two South Australian governors, Sir Dominick Daly and Sir James Ferguson. But the most distinguished guest of them all was the Duke of Edinburgh, Prince Alfred, who enjoyed a lavish dinner in his honour at St Francis House in October 1867. In fact, Captain Hart was among a distinguished committee that received the Duke when his ship, HMS *Galatea*, berthed at Glenelg jetty. There was a slight hiccup when the leading horse of the Duke's carriage fell and the postilion (a person who rides the leading near horse of a team drawing a coach) was injured.

The Duke of Edinburgh was also to forge a strong relationship with the Australian Aboriginal Cricket Team which in early 1868 was preparing for a seven-month tour of England.

Over two days (4 and 5 February 1868) the Aboriginal cricketers played a match in Sydney against the army and navy team, drawn from those who sailed the Duke's sloop plus two famous cricketers, Australian Ned Gregory and Englishman Billy

Caffyn. The Duke watched the match closely and he especially enjoyed the Aboriginals' skilful demonstration of spear and boomerang throwing after each day's play. Two days after the match against the Duke's combined eleven, the Aboriginal team sailed for England on the *Parramatta*, a fully rigged wool clipper of 1521 tons.

On 24 May 1870 the newly formed Port Adelaide Football Club played its first match against a team touted as 'The Young Australians'. Significantly, the match was played on part of Buck's Flat, specifically the stretch of land right in front of St Francis House.

Given that Port Adelaide's first match was played so close to St Francis House and that Captain Hart was the club's patron, it is almost impossible to dismiss the notion that the players and officials were feted by a reception in St Francis House on the evening of the match. There has long been a strong bond between St Francis House and the Port Adelaide Football Club. Four of the St Francis boys – Vince Copley, Richie Bray, Malcolm Cooper and Wilfred 'Boofa' Huddleston – played football for the Port Adelaide Magpies. Chad Wingard, a Port Adelaide champion in the AFL, is a cousin of Vince Copley.

During his long service with the South Australian parliament, Captain Hart was head of the ministry that co-ordinated construction of the Overland Telegraph Line. He had a hand in building the Old Telegraph Station in Alice Springs, the place that became known as the Bungalow, birthplace of many of the boys who later found themselves living at St Francis House. Captain Hart became a Companion of the Order of St Michael and St George and he was Grand Master of Freemasons. Among his many and varied pursuits, he invested heavily in the copper mines at Paringa, Kapunda, Moonta and Burra.

According to his personal diary, by the year 1865, Captain John Hart was worth £35,000, a staggering fortune in Colonial times. He died suddenly on 28 January 1873, while attending a meeting in Adelaide.

Captain Hart did many fine things for South Australian generally, but it was in the Port Adelaide region that his reputation became legend. Glanville Hall was his residential pièce de résistance, built on land that had been the exclusive territory of the Kaurna people for more than 8000 years. The Kaurna name for Port Adelaide is Yerta (land) Bulti (sleep). What is now called Le Fevre Peninsula used to be a hard, flat stretch of land which, at low water, resembled the a nose, so the Kaurna people called it Mudlanga, meaning 'shape of the nose'.

On Buck's Flat, including where Captain Hart built Glanville Hall, was an important Kaurna meeting place where for centuries the ancient ceremony of the corroboree was held.

Take a train from Outer Harbor to Adelaide and you are travelling through the heart of Kaurna country. Two of the train stations along the way are Midlunga and Taperoo. The Kaurna interpretation of Midlunga means 'place of the *midla*'. The *midla* was a vital piece of hunting equipment, a spear thrower, used in league with a *kaya* spear to kill large game, such as kangaroo or emu. Taperoo is the European word for *tapurio*, a drum made by stretching the skin of possum over a round basket, which women and girls played during a Corroboree.

Before European occupation, the entire area was thick with trees, in part an extensive she-oak forest with paperbark, tea tree and gum; and the creeks and river teemed with blue crabs, water fowl, kangaroo and emu. It was a summer playground for the Kaurna who camped there during the hot weather. When the autumn arrived the Kaurna took to the foothills where they spent the winter months. And thousands of years before Port Adelaide's first football match on an oval right in front of St Francis House, young men of the Kaurna people played an early form of football. It was a kick-and-catch game played with a possum-skin ball called a *pando*.

Those St Francis boys who went on to play top-flight football, rugby and Australian Rules are linked back to the genesis of these games, played by their forefathers with a ball fashioned from possum skins.

The boys from St Francis

For a minute I froze, then I turned, looked him in the eye and said, 'Father, I'm just following the teaching of the Bible where it is written that God helps those who help themselves.' – David Woodford

Isabel and her infirm mother had already settled into St Francis House before Father Smith and the boys from Pembroke Street arrived in late 1946. Long before the boys left Pembroke Street, Kensington Park, they were joined by Gordon Briscoe, whose mother brought him there to give him better opportunities.

In his book *Racial Folly*, he recalls:

> Because these boys knew me as a baby at the Bungalow they immediately called me 'Nicky' the name my mother had always called me. As soon as Father Smith heard the boys calling me this name he scolded them and ordered that I was to be called Gordon, the name on my birth certificate. . . .
>
> Most of the boys were much older than me; their ages ranged from about ten and 11 to 14. I was seven going on eight and the only relief I got from the taunts of the older boys was when Brian Butler came or when I went to stay next door with Miss Murphy.

Brian Butler was the oldest son of a white contractor in Alice Springs and when his Aboriginal mother became sick he was sent to Pembroke Street. Gordon goes on:

The Boys from St Francis

> The older boys rigged up a punching bag in the backyard where they taught me how to punch, evade a blow and learn to skip. All this came in handy when Brian was added to our numbers because we were made to fight each other.

Gordon found solace in drawing.

> I would draw gum trees, desert and acacia trees (*Kalka* in my mother's language). Other boys from the home such as John Palmer could reproduce Albert Namatjira-style paintings and he would tell me about the *Kalka*. He would tell me about the *Kalka* nuts that his mother would make into necklaces for her many sisters. John's mother was a sister to my mother and we were very close to each other in the half-caste institution. John drew me to him in two ways. First he and Malcolm Cooper were good boxers and, second, both were really good footballers. Soon after settling down they taught me how to box and kick the footy.

Gordon cannot recall ever being threatened, bullied or discriminated against by white people during his time at kindergarten. However, during those formative years he had reason to question his carers when he realised that he could never depend on receiving protection from either Father or Isabel Smith from the relentless ongoing threats, taunts and bashings from the older boys.

The older boys dominated the young ones. Gordon got the most menial tasks, such as collecting hens' eggs or washing the bath tub. He also developed a habit of discarding his shoes: throwing them into the stream on the way to or from school, a painful habit as it turned out for whenever he threw his shoes away one of the older boys gave him a belting.

The boys from St Francis

It was an anxious time for young Gordon and he occasionally wet the bed, and that always attracted a thrashing from one of the older boys. Eventually the promising artist, John Palmer, bigger and stronger than the older boys, befriended Gordon and protected him from the others.

Gordon also recalls his first Christmas with the Smiths.

> At Christmas time I listened to stories about how Santa Claus would come down the chimney and fill my pillowcase full of toys, fruit and presents. I imagined I saw him in the dark as he moved across the room to attend to my stocking. Christmas Day turned out to be an exciting day and I received a big toy top, the first one I had ever had. True to the Father and Isabel Smith's stories Santa left quite a lot of presents and other nice things.

Every Christmas most of the boys went home to Alice Springs to see their families, but Gordon's mother lived in Victor Harbor, so he once accepted an invitation to stay at the home of Isabel's brother, Jim Almond, on Semaphore Road. This was in the Pembroke Street days, before the boys moved to Semaphore.

> This was only the second time I remember going to the beach. The first time was at Collaroy, a northern Sydney beach in about 1943. There I recall the large expanse of water and being swamped by a big wave, nearly getting drowned in the process. Later I learned to swim at Mulgoa and because Semaphore was a very calm beach, I took to the water with gusto....
>
> We swam most days from early morning until dusk and later returned after our evening meal to attend the sideshow and revolving swings in the funfair on the foreshore.

The Boys from St Francis

The district became significant in Gordon's growing years because St Francis House in Semaphore was destined to become his home for more than 10 years. One day Father Smith called at the house on Semaphore Road and collected Gordon and the whole Almond family and drove them to an impressive building some five kilometres south along Military Road.

That building was Glanville Hall.

While still at Pembroke Street, Gordon remembers distinctly how conversation round the dinner table focused almost entirely over many days on British testing on the rocket range, the test sites cutting a swathe through Pitcha Pitcha Lands.

> Early in 1947 Dr Charles Duguid, a friend of Father Smith's, spoke to him about the Australian Board of Missions getting involved in protests that were soon to take place in Melbourne, Adelaide and other places. Dr Duguid asked Father Smith if he would help to organise the Adelaide protest at Willard Hall in the city on March 31, 1947, and at a later date co-ordinate another protest at the Adelaide Town Hall. The day of the first protest sticks in my mind because Father Smith rounded up all the boys to attend the protest meeting. I heard Father Smith talking about the tests when Prime Minister Chifley announced the British-Australian compact in 1946. The project angered Father Smith and Dr Duguid and I overheard other prominent persons' names mentioned, such as Elkin, Thomson and Strehlow.
>
> The newspapers were full of how Elkin [Professor of Anthropology at the University of Sydney] had betrayed Aborigines by helping government to steal Aboriginal lands. I wrote to my mother in Victor Harbor and asked if her mother

was affected and I asked Father Smith if my grandmother could stay with us.

Later it came to me that following Chifley's statement, an Aboriginal man called Bill Ferguson could be heard on the wireless protesting about the infringement by the British and Australian governments in taking Aboriginal land for rocket testing. Again I thought of my grandmother but Father Smith talked not about poor Aborigines but the poor Church and nothing more happened as the purchase of Glanville Hall at Semaphore took over the table-talk.

But the talk about rocket testing and protests resonated with Gordon.

The move to St Francis House proved a revelation for the boys. They loved the wide open spaces. Just 500 metres from Semaphore Beach, the sand and the surf became their summer playground. There also were ample playing fields next to St Francis House where they kicked a football.

Early in 1948 Jim Almond, his wife, Judith (always known as Jingle), and their 12-year-old daughter Judy moved in to St Francis House. Jim was to have been employed as a handyman but, while the Almonds' flat was being renovated, but he took on a job as a machinist at General Motor's Holden in Croydon While there he lost all the fingers on his right hand in a machine accident.

Judy attracted the attention of some of the older boys, although they also sought the company of the girls next door, among the migrant 'village', where refugees from war-torn Europe lived in temporary houses scattered across the expanse of parkland in front of St Francis House. Gordon Briscoe felt an affinity with

The Boys from St Francis

these 'new Australians' who had mostly emigrated from Latvia and Estonia, 'because they suffered much the same indignities as we experienced'. Indeed some of the migrant women found employment at St Francis House as cleaners. They were often referred to by the general population as 'balts' and 'wogs', and many of the boys became close friends with their children. The older boys from St Francis were constantly planning how they might meet one of the migrant girls away from the glare and perceived hostility of their parents.

To find your way to the older boys' quarters, you had to walk past the pantry, which was in the main thoroughfare of the house, through the servery and up the rickety wooden flight of stairs. The pantry always seemed to lead the boys into temptation and the boys invariably raided the biscuits and cake tins there, after which they made a hasty retreat finding refuge in their top-floor room via the fire escape or by scampering over the roof.

The staff cake tin was just inside the door and to the boys' delight the door was rarely closed. However, they had to time their run because during the day there was a hive of activity in and about the kitchen and at night the boys were supposed to be safely tucked up in bed. Father Smith was often at his desk in his study and would randomly get up and go for a stroll. One evening when they thought the coast was clear David Woodford and Peter Tilmouth stole into the staffroom. They found a huge lump of fruit cake, but they had no knife. Improvising, they broke off chunks with their hands and wolfed them down. David Woodford remembers the time as if it was yesterday.

'As I gulped a piece of cake, I got a tap on the shoulder. The voice behind me said gently, "Can I have a piece, please?"

The boys from St Francis

The first boys at St Francis House. Back row: Charlie Kunoth, Bill Espie, Peter Tilmouth and John Palmer. Seated: Lawrie Bray, Charlie Perkins, Ernie Perkins, Malcolm Cooper and David Woodford. Front row: Brian Butler, Gordon Briscoe and Alice the dog.

'For a minute I froze, then I turned, looked him in the eye and said, "Father, I'm just following the teaching of the Bible where it is stated that God helps those who help themselves."

'"Yes, David so it does ... and God help those boys I catch stealing!"'

Despite creaking and rotten floorboards, the attic rooms on the top floor were popular with the boys, for they were away from the prying eyes of Father Smith and staff. However, the poor condition of the floorboards became evident to all when one morning a boy's foot fell through a rotting floorboard and his leg, up to the knee, crashed through the ceiling below.

Despite the obvious need for renovation in some areas of the

The Boys from St Francis

Mucking about at St Francis House. Boys in striped t-shirts: Richie Bray (left) and Robert Walker. Behind them: James Bray (left) and Trevor Reid.

building, the boys settled in quickly. The ground floor rooms were in good order, yet the kitchen was a disgrace. Even mild-mannered Father Smith was moved to use his most colourful language, describing the kitchen as 'substandard'.

By the end of 1948 St Francis House was brimming with boys of varying ages. There were the original six from Alice Springs – Malcolm Cooper, David Woodford, Charlie Perkins, Bill Espie, Peter Tilmouth and John Palmer – plus Gordon Briscoe and Brian Butler and a contingent of lads from Mulgoa, among them Jim Foster, Wally McArthur and John Moriarty.

Soon others would arrive including Vince Copley from Point Pearce and three boys from Alice Springs – Ernie Perkins (Charlie's brother), Richie Bray and Max Wilson. They soon learned that there was a pecking order among the boys at

The boys from St Francis

Jim Foster, David Woodford, Peter Tilmouth and Malcolm Cooper at St Francis House.

St Francis House where the older boys who had 'paid their dues' ruled the roost.

'We younger boys copped all the menial tasks,' Vince recalls, 'Chopping wood, milking the cow – yes, we had a cow – cleaning and sweeping the courtyard and generally going about our tasks without upsetting the older lads.'

The young ones idolised Wally McArthur. At the age of 14 Wally, who had arrived at St Francis House from Mulgoa, was already a champion athlete and dubbed 'the fastest 14-year-old runner in the world' with the potential to become an Olympic champion. Wally often dragged the younger boys from their beds at the crack of dawn to run with him on Semaphore beach.

'Sometimes we'd sneak a look at Wally shaving. There he would be standing naked from the waist up, and there we would be admiring his incredible physique and rippling muscles,' Vince recalls.

Semaphore Beach was their playground.

For thousands of years the beach and surrounding area had been a popular summer camping spot for the Kaurna people. When the Europeans arrived in 1836, Ityamaiitpinna, or King Rodney, was the first Aboriginal man they encountered. King Rodney and his family camped every summer at what is now the Adelaide Botanic Gardens in winter. The river's water was blue when the first settlers came, but they soon wrecked a beautifully maintained ecosystem by using the river and its tributaries as sewers.

A little-known fact is that the original Port Adelaide Council coat of arms depicted an Aboriginal man and a sailor holding a crest with the motto *'Haud pluribus impar'* ('Second to none.'). In its entirety the complete quote is *'Deo favente haud pluribus impar'* or 'By the grace of God to no one equal.'

That an Aboriginal person was shown on the coat of arms tells us that the Kaurna people were held in high esteem back in the mid 1850s. How attitudes changed.

In the early summer of 1948 it was time for the boys from St Francis to go to school.

A few days beforehand Father Smith took the boys to Semaphore where he bought shirts, trousers and shoes for everyone. Some of the boys' mothers provided socks for their sons. Gordon Briscoe was amazed to get two pairs of socks, the only present he ever received from his mother. Those socks ran the gauntlet of time and wear, but repairs had them last almost as long as his shoes.

The boys from St Francis awoke early, made their beds,

The boys from St Francis

Father Smith with Malcolm Cooper and Charlie Perkins in the St Francis House common room, c. 1948.

showered, dressed in their new clothes and shoes and had a good breakfast, all in a state of nervous excitement. There had been much publicity about the new school attendees. Local bigots and parents were alerted to what Father Smith was planning. It was common at the time for newspapers to carry stories about the government's assimilation policies and its ideas about altruism and 'race'. Father Smith believed strongly that equality would eventually emerge through social interaction between white and non-white and in his boys demonstrating a hard-working, God-fearing character of such magnitude that they would earn the trust of all. However, not everyone in the community shared Father Smith's vision.

As the group neared the school they were confronted by a throng of angry white mothers and fathers and adolescent boys and girls; 60-plus people barred their passage through the school front gate. There were plenty of catcalls and ugly racist taunts, but Father Smith was determined to make things right. He left the boys some 50 yards from the front gate and brushed his way through the madding crowd and headed straight for the headmaster's office.

Father Smith found an ally in the school headmaster, who, upon learning of the commotion, angrily stormed out of his office and rushed to the front gate whereupon he gave the protestors a dressing down, telling them that if they continued to bar passage to the new students he would call the police.

Father Smith rejoined his group of Aboriginal boys and they walked unimpeded through the front gate to be registered. Gordon Briscoe believes Father Smith 'had no illusions about forcing order, but he always sided with the boys' view when we had a couple of fights to settle our differences in the schoolyard.'

Back at St Francis House there were squabbles as there are in any group of young people. Some were over and done with in a few minutes; others were long-lasting.

The first group to come from Pembroke Street had the wood on the younger boys because they could fight. Charlie Perkins and Lawrie Bray, who were first cousins, made up one tight group and depending on the issue and conflict would support each other. Then Vince Copley became a close friend of Lawrie Bray and would get caught up in any fights, too.

Most of the boys got nicknames. Jim Foster gave Peter Tilmouth the tag 'Truck' because Peter worked Saturday mornings on a vegetable truck. Foster's nickname was 'Frog' and he was the main man when it came to dreaming up names for the others.

The boys from St Francis

The boys from Mulgoa brought their biases with them to St Francis House. The younger boys became very street smart early, for the older Mulgoa mob dominated and would pick on Vince and Lawrie and Ernie Perkins for the most trivial of 'misdemeanours'.

Vince Copley and Ernie Perkins shared a room upstairs in the southern wing, while Lawrie Bray and David Woodford had the last room on the same side. When in later years Gordon Briscoe made it his business to learn more about his family he found that David Woodford's mother, Millie, married Lawrie Bray's brother Norman Bray. Millie was a full sister both to Peter Tilmouth's mother Tilly Tilmouth and to the deceased May Hill, Gerry Hill's mother.

> We were kept in the dark and discouraged from knowing more about our Alice Springs relatives. The inference was that our future was with the white world.
>
> By the time I was 10, in November 1948, I was acutely aware of the 'rigid controls' others in society had over me. News items about Aborigines made me and the boys I grew up with, sensitive to new ways the government would or could impose conditions on us. The news bulletins often contained information about how far governments would allow Aborigines to be educated, to receive full legal rights, how to behave, to enter licensed premises or even shops – where often we would be asked to leave for no other reason than the colour of our skin.
>
> These events had an impact on us and we would often hear about other Aboriginal boys who were the victims of discrimination.

The Boys from St Francis

News items gave white people ammunition as "know-alls" to tell us what to do. As we came to know people more intimately they would reveal to us either our lack of civil liberties or our human rights, sometimes in advance of us knowing them. Fear of breaking these customary barriers, or even laws, was a constant threat. When we played football we would be required to leave the training sheds immediately, similarly at swimming pools and picture theatres. On one of my mother's rare visits to Adelaide, I recall being asked to leave the Balfour's Cake and Coffee shop in King William Street in Adelaide. When we sat down there were still seats spare but we were nevertheless asked to leave. Although Father Smith encouraged us to be proud of our past, the contradictions of religion and state policy played against their education theory and the relentless prejudices of white society.

This was counterbalanced to some extent in that the boys were encouraged to write home on a regular basis. Writing letters meant that we did have some contact with relatives and we always hoped that this would improve our chances of school holiday breaks.

But as the years passed the dream sold to our mothers came crashing down around our ears with a bang not a whimper. The image in everyone's mind was of an education of excellence. Father Smith's dream in 1945 was crystal clear in the minds of everyone who read about it in the Adelaide *Advertiser* or heard it from Father Smith's lips.

Pembroke Street was in a bourgeois suburb of Adelaide that gave everyone involved a warm glow that success had arrived. By 1947 and 1948 stresses began to show that assimilation was an ideology void of confidence. As the population of the House increased with new faces from Alice Springs and Mulgoa the image and the original idea was soon lost. There was a feeling that the House was being gradually transformed from a home for better education and care to an orphanage for motherless half-castes, a reform school for wayward half-caste children who were classified as 'welfare'.

It had taken more than a decade for Father Smith to fashion his ideas on solving the 'half-caste problem' through education. The wartime chaos in central Australia provided him with the opportunity to apply his belief that whatever he did would resolve itself in the end by faith alone. In spite of what the effects might have on us young children, he went ahead. His vision was grounded in a lot of hope. He hoped that the boys would cope away from their families; he hoped that the Church would find the money to feed the boys and his own family; he hoped that his own family would cope with the pressure; and his final hope was to find the money to pay the staff that came to work for him.

Father Smith left St Francis House in 1949, the year I felt, rightly or wrongly, that he abandoned us for a new job and title: Canon the Reverend P MacD. Smith.

At the outset Father Smith moved to Adelaide for two reasons. First, he wanted to improve the lot of six Aboriginal boys by providing them with what he envisaged to be a better chance at life than their mothers could give their children in Alice Springs. Second, he had been advised by an army doctor to live in a cooler clime because of his failing health. The heat and dust of Alice Springs was thought to have been the major factor in his deteriorating health. So why did Father Smith go back to the Northern Territory? Certainly he had a running battle to get sufficient money to maintain standards at St Francis House. Maintenance of the old building was an ongoing expense, so too food and clothing for the boys.

From the outset Father Smith wanted to create an environment of love, care and a high standard of education for a limited number of Aboriginal boys. But his dream was slowly eroded by a lack of funds and a lack of vision by the Anglican Church. Initially the boys turned out immaculately in their new clothes and shoes, but as time passed and funds dwindled the boys' clothes became threadbare, their trousers and socks patched. Only a lot of Kiwi black and elbow grease gave their shoes a thinly veiled appearance of quality footwear.

The boys helped fundraising efforts by holding fetes and giving gymnastic displays. They even staged a play, *William Tell*, but were highly embarrassed when asked to stand in front of an audience and sing 'God Save the King' and 'Land of Hope and Glory'.

They also worked about St Francis House. Every morning before school two boys made sandwiches for their mates. Vince Copley said everyone loved this particular 'chore' because they found themselves in the privileged position of having access to all the food – be it bread, sliced fritz, tomatoes, cucumber, peanut butter or Vegemite – and close proximity to the cake tin.

Father Percy Smith, Isabel and baby John left St Francis House bound for Alice Springs in 1949. All the boys felt sad over their decision to leave. David Woodford and Jim Foster were further saddened for they would no longer be able to dip baby John Smith's dummy in salt and delight in the infant's reaction after they handed it back to him.

Our own 'William Tell'

Before he took aim, Peter tied a piece of string to the feathered end of an arrow. With unerring skill he shot the apple through the hole in the floor. Bullseye!

Every weekend for six months the boys toiled to make a road on the western side of St Francis House. Vince Copley was among a dozen workers who cracked rocks, carted sand and spread gravel. In rain and sweltering heat the boys worked diligently to ensure that their special visitor would be delighted by their efforts to fashion a professionally fashioned road surface from meagre materials and crude implements.

The road was being lovingly prepared for a visit by none other than the bishop of Adelaide, Bryan Robin. On Saturdays, the boys worked on the road from the instant they finished their breakfast until sundown, with only a brief break at morning and afternoon tea and a good lunch to interrupt the rhythm of their toil. Sundays were different for it was compulsory for the boys to attend church. But when they had walked back from the Sunday service and had lunch the rocks, sledgehammers and shovels awaited them.

An Englishman, Bryan Percival Robin had spent some time in Australia between the wars, then returned to England. There he was appointed rector of Woodchurch, Cheshire, in 1931. Incredibly, patronage of the incumbency at Woodchurch had been held by his family since 1612. Robin then became rural dean of Wirral North (1936 to 1941), honorary canon of Chester

The Boys from St Francis

Cathedral (1940 to 1941) and an air-raid precautions warden during World War II. Robin was consecrated bishop of Adelaide by the archbishop of Canterbury on 25 July 1941 in Westminster Abbey. He was enthroned at St Peter's Cathedral, Adelaide, on 2 December 1941. He would go on to serve as the Anglican bishop of Adelaide from 1941 until 1956. He replaced the long-term bishop Nutter Thomas who presided over his Adelaide flock from 1906 to 1940.

Bishop Robin was on the same page of the Bible as Father Smith in that he was High Church in his leanings, but he was also comfortable with the wide range of Anglican 'churchmanship' in the Adelaide diocese. An enthusiastic and energetic man, Bishop Robin was ever 'spiritual', and was said to have enjoyed life within the embrace of his faith and his people. He was said to have been a stately fellow, yet his sense of humour sometimes challenged people for he had the habit of raising one eyebrow, a feature beautifully drawn by Ivor Hele in his portrait of the bishop in 1956. Given his sense of humour Bishop Robin must have had a giggle about his first official visit to St Francis House in 1950.

Vince Copley recalls well the day the bishop arrived in his chauffeur-driven Bentley: 'We worked for months to make the road and there we were in our Sunday best lined up along the side of the road – our road – when the car loomed into sight. But to our great disappointment the bishop's vehicle slipped past the entrance to our road and disappeared round the back of the building. The bishop's driver had taken him to a spot on the courtyard, under the Moreton Bay fig tree between the back of St Francis House and the stables.'

At St Francis House there was a work roster for the boys.

Our own 'William Tell'

Everyone had to do their share, whether it was cleaning toilets and showers, helping staff clean floors or milking the cow.

None of the boys ever knew how the cow got to St Francis House, but it proved rich in milk and every week a different boy was allocated the job of milking her early in the morning and immediately after he returned from school.

One morning Vince Copley was walking from his room to the stairway when he noticed his roommate Ernie Perkins sitting on a stool milking the cow in the paddock beyond the southern wall of the main building. Vince would not have thought much about it had it not been for him spotting Ernie accidentally placing his right foot in the bucket of fresh milk as he got up from the milking stool and clumsily stumbling backwards. As he witnessed the entire scene from an upstairs window, Vince roared laughing. And from his vantage point Vince saw Ernie lift his boot out of the bucket and look about him hoping his clumsiness went unnoticed. Confident his little accident would remain his secret, Ernie stood tall and proceeded to carry the milk into the kitchen. When Vince entered the building for breakfast, he confidently announced to the kitchen staff, 'No milk for me today, thank you very much.'

Just down the corridor on the first floor from the room occupied by Vince Copley and Peter Tilmouth was a sizeable hole in the old wooden floor. And the gaping hole, wide enough for two apples or a medium-sized rockmelon to pass through, just happened to be directly above the pantry, where a large bowl laden with fresh fruit rested on a cupboard directly below the boys' gaze.

Peter Tilmouth was a good spear thrower and could also use a bow and arrow. As the boys loved fruit and that of the forbidden kind always tasted sweeter, Peter devised a cunning plan to steal from the bowl. Before he took aim, Peter tied a piece of string to the feathered end of an arrow. With unerring skill he shot the apple through the hole in the floor. Bullseye!

One by one his arrow pierced a choice piece of fruit and he carefully lifted his prize up from the bowl, through the hole and straight into the safe hands of Vince Copley. Peter proved to be a splendid archer, although inevitably the boys' craftiness was exposed and the hole in the floor patched up.

Tilmouth's expertise and ingenuity has forever lived in the boys' hearts. He was perfect for the role of William Tell in the play the boys performed in front of a hall full of Port Adelaide citizens in 1951. When the crucial moment came the crowd fell silent. Gordon Briscoe, playing the part of William Tell's son, stood stock still, eyes tightly shut, an apple perched precariously on his head. The famous archer took aim and the crowd held its breath. He shot the arrow and after initial screams of anguish the crowd roared – our modern William Tell's arrow fell after a couple of yards. Peter Tilmouth's attached string again worked brilliantly. A quivering Gordon Briscoe wasn't convinced about the string attached to Peter's arrow. Would the string break? When the arrow fell short of its target and clattered to the wooden floor a great feeling of relief coursed through Gordon's body.

The boys were fascinated with the story of William Tell, which seems to be as close to fiction as it is historical fact. Peter Tilmouth, while not armed with a crossbow so expertly used by William Tell, won fame among his peers for making good use of his bow and arrow.

David Woodford was as mischievous as any of the boys.

Our own 'William Tell'

David Woodford proudly astride his motorbike at St Francis House, c. 1957.

'One boy, Brian Butler, used to put his shoes on the wrong feet,' he laughs.

'Mrs Smith was always pointing this out to him and she asked us to help him. Then, one day, Brian actually got it right, but we just couldn't resist telling him he'd got it wrong again. So he changed them over and went on the usual inspection with Mrs Smith before church of a Sunday. When she laid eyes on Brian and looked at his shoes, she said with a sigh, "Oh Brian, you've done it again."'

Did Woody and the others feel guilty? Not on your nelly.

Every Sunday the boys walked from St Francis House to St Paul's Church in Jervois Street, Port Adelaide, a good 2 km away. Church became a favourite haunt for the boys, not because any of them showed much interest in religion, but for the very reason that after the service was over they each received a hearty meal. Charlie Perkins loved the egg and bacon rolls and he was among the majority of the boys who secreted food away from church to eat later back at St Francis House. Hunger was never too far away for these growing boys. To and from school the boys supplemented their diet by stealing fruit from numerous backyards along the way.

Father Smith had negotiated a deal with the cinema manager so that every Saturday afternoon the boys were could watch the latest film as a treat. Often the main feature was complemented by a short serial and the boys didn't want to miss an episode. Charlie Perkins was greatly aggrieved when he was accused of damaging the back of a pew at church. He felt discriminated against, and when he discovered that he had, along with two others, been given the task of filling all the offending holes with putty – at the very time the second week of a four-episode serial was been screened – he could hardly contain his anger.

White girls often met one or more of the boys at the cinema and they sat together throughout. However, as Vince Copley and Charlie Perkins would attest later, a white girl never walked the street with an Aboriginal boy in the light of day.

'It was fine for a white girl to sit in the dark with us,' Vince Copley says. 'And they would have been happy to walk down the street with us after the show were it not for them being afraid their parents might get to hear of it.'

Vince Copley, David Woodford and others had an overall positive experience at St Francis House. Max Wilson, however, hated his time there.

Born in Darwin Hospital on 30 April 1941, Max was the son of Phillis Gallagher and Steve Wilson. As with hundreds of mixed-race families, they were evacuated by the military in the wake of the Darwin bombing in 1942. They were taken to a migrant hostel in Balaklava, spending most of the war living among people of German and Japanese descent; people interned for the duration of the world conflict.

Before Max was sent to St Francis House he spent time in the shadow of Anzac Hill at the Catholic school in Bath Street, Alice Springs.

'I believe this was all linked with government's assimilation policy, which was nothing short of genocide,' Max says.

After World War II, to be able to gain some sort of equality with the white population, Indigenous Australians could apply for what was known as an 'exemption certificate'; they had to deny their heritage and their families. Understandably the exemption certificate was treated with contempt by Aboriginal people, most of whom regarded them as 'dog licences'. Only 1500 licences were ever issued, however, the stigma cut deep. It was similar to black South Africans having to carry a pass which depicted them as 'second-class citizens' throughout the apartheid period. When Max Wilson discovered the truth about assimilation it only confirmed what he thought of the system in its treatment of First Australians. Aboriginal people were always being told they had to be more 'white' but they were never given the freedom to change. They were told they had to take responsibility for assimilating into society, but they had never been given the opportunity to assume responsibility for anything – many of them had spent their entire lives being controlled by a reserve manager or a church-run missionary.

Even though they were expected to act like 'whites', assimilation never gave Aboriginals the same rights as other

The Boys from St Francis

Australians. Assimilation was an abject failure, but it did leave its mark, an ugly scar on the collective Indigenous psyche.

Max Wilson's two brothers – Harry Quartermaine and Henry Baker – were with him at the school on Bath Street, but after a while 'they just disappeared'.

'Next thing I remember is being on a train and waking up at the Adelaide Railway Station,' Max says. 'When I boarded the train in the Alice I was wearing shorts and T-shirt and thongs. When I got off the train it was freezing. I looked about at the group of boys, all of whom stood and shivered. Just the realisation that my mum wasn't there, Dad wasn't there ... my two brothers, I was so very cold and lonely and sad. I was on another planet and no one gave a shit.'

The boys were taken to St Francis House in a bus. There they were given tea and sent to bed. Max's room was on the top floor of the building.

'As I tossed in my bed all I could hear was children sobbing. Imagine waking up as we did that morning, shivering in summer clothes on a freezing railway platform, then being taken to a strange place and going to bed without your mum kissing you and saying "I love you."

'We were rudely awakened to the fact that we were in a very strange place where white people ran the organisation. There were Aboriginal people around us, but we didn't know them. I don't think we stopped crying for two weeks.'

Many of the St Francis boys developed very strong bonds with the others, but Max Wilson found it difficult.

'I don't bond with anyone,' he blurts.

Max did develop a good friendship with Des Price, however,

Our own 'William Tell'

whose mother took him under her wing when Max's mother was dying.

'Des's mother Annie promised my terminally ill mother that she would become my tribal mother after Mum passed,' Max says with a faraway look.

At the beginning of my interview with Max he shifts uneasily in his seat. We're sitting in the garden of Vince and Brenda Copley's home in Hillcrest. It's warm. There's a slight breeze and the occasional bird flutters overhead. Because of the seeming built-up anger, I don't expect to extract a lot from the interview.

I'm wrong.

'The regimented way of life at St Francis House was something I resented very much,' Max says. 'If I was threatened I hit out with my fists. I was a rebel and I didn't want to be there. I hated everyone.' Max didn't like Ethelton Primary or Le Fevre Boys Technical School, either.

> One day we were walking toward Ethelton Primary and we passed a little white kid sitting on the fence. We looked at him and he yelled, 'Nigger, nigger on the block.' We'd never heard the word 'nigger' before and didn't know that it was a derogatory term. But we soon found out about that word and two days later we again passed by where the kid was sitting on the fence. He had only just opened his mouth when we set upon him.

It is a sad fact that a child of a racist mimics their mother or father. Metaphorically the white kid wasn't sitting on the fence at all, he was reflecting the redneck attitude he most assuredly would have heard in the family home.

The Boys from St Francis

Max Wilson then hits on something that resonates: 'We had a rotten time at St Francis House until they [the white children and school teachers] found we had something they wanted – or if they didn't want it they admired us – because of our sporting ability.'

This appears to be a common thread in the boys' stories about their time at the home.

'Sport made us better than equal,' Max says. 'It made us better than the rest. I played junior soccer for the state and, of course, we had some great players such as John Moriarty and Gordon Briscoe who played internationally.'

In fact, John Moriarty became the first man of Aboriginal descent to play soccer for Australia.

Years earlier a group of St Francis boys, among them Wally McArthur, John Moriarty, Gordon Briscoe, Charlie Perkins, Gerry Hill and Max Wilson, were sitting on a fence watching the South Australian under-18 soccer team training on the oval near St Francis House.

'Hey, look at that round ball that bloke's kickin' about. Gee, that's a funny-looking ball,'

Charlie Perkins laughed. He reckoned it was a basketball, but Max said, 'That's soccer. That's soccer them blokes are playin'.'

The state players then invited the boys to form a team and have a game against them.

They knew about the Aboriginal kids' brilliance in ball games. The boys from St Francis played Australian Rules, rugby union, rugby league and cricket. In fact St Francis House provided the best sportsmen in the district. At Ethelton Primary through to Le Fevre Boys Technical School the boys from St Francis ran faster, jumped higher and hit harder than anyone else.

Our own 'William Tell'

A gathering of the St Francis children, c. 1953. Left to right: Wilfred 'Boofa' Huddleston, Tim Campbell, Richard Wilson, John Moriarty, Vince Copley, Susan Wilson and Gerry Hill. The Wilsons (Richard and Susan) were children of warden 'Whickey' Wilson.

They were the best fighters, so no one took them on because they knew they'd come off second best. Excelling at sport elicited immediate and long-lasting respect from their peers of a different hue.

As the boys jumped down from the fence, Charlie yelled, 'Just tell us the rules.'

One of the state boys said, 'Okay, don't touch the ball with your hands, that's important. You can hit it with your head.'

'Okay,' Charlie said. 'Where do we stand?'

For the next 90 minutes the boys from St Francis, barefoot and clad in shorts and singlets, thrashed the South Australian under-18 soccer team, all of whom wore their official state tops and highly polished football boots.

The Boys from St Francis

Ethelton Primary School football team, 1948. Back row: sixth from left, Peter Tilmouth. Middle row: third from left, Lawrie Bray. Front row: fifth from left, David Woodford; far right, Vince Copley.

Max and Gordon kept asking, 'Is this how you play?' and one of the red-faced opponents answered, 'Yeah, but take it easy a bit, will ya?'

They beat the state team 10 goals to nil!

A couple of the victors called, 'We'll come and play you again next week.'

'Oh, no. Don't bother,' one of the under-18s yelled.

Charlie Perkins realised why the Aboriginal boys were so effective that day.

'Our opponents were all skilled players. They attacked properly, but we were so lightning fast that by the time they got round to attack we were gone.'

While the boys had a good belly laugh about the extraordinary result against bigger, older opponents from an under-age state team, they also discovered they liked the game.

For Charlie Perkins the experience proved life-changing.

'That year I played for the Scottish club (Port Thistle) in Adelaide. I got on well with the club crowd. They treated me like a human being. That was where I first felt free, when I began to play soccer. The soccer club became my home and I found a new security in my ability to play well.

'I found some friends in soccer. Most of all I found a place where I could be *somebody*, because I could play soccer better than most and I was improving all the time.'

Charlie played one year as a junior before entering senior ranks at the age of 15. From his first senior game Charlie was destined to enjoy a grand career in first-division soccer.

In 1949 Port Thistle Soccer Club approached Father Smith asking for permission to rent a large field in front of St Francis House. It was the same stretch of turf where Port Adelaide Football Club had played its first official match in the winter of 1870. In 1949 the ground was owned by the Anglican Church and Father Smith agreed to rent it to the club.

The boys from St Francis filled the club's junior team that year, while Charlie Perkins, Peter Tilmouth and Harry Russell played for the colts eleven. At school, both primary and secondary, all the boys, including Charlie Perkins, played Australian Rules football in addition to soccer. While brilliant at both football codes, Charlie chose to pursue soccer.

Around 1955 Max Wilson went to the South Parklands to play the game.

'There were spotters [talent scouts] about and I excelled at inside left or left wing. Then one day I booted a goal from centre of the ground – gee, I was brilliant, ha! – and I not only became the team's centre-forward but I was selected in the state under-17 football squad,' Max recalls.

The boys of St Francis were generally a close-knit group, and Father Smith's departure from the house in 1949 impacted on all of them. Despite pangs of hunger, threadbare clothes and worn shoes, the boys had found comfort in the generosity and love of Percy Smith and his wife Isabel. But they were soon to discover that they had already lived through the halcyon years of St Francis House.

A new order was about to start.

It was a harsh new order; this new regime brought beatings and an atmosphere foreign to a once loving and caring environment.

By a hand so cruel

Most mornings when the older boys were in the shower, the short, plump Mrs Taylor wore a lewd smile as she casually strolled into the wet area.

In the wake of Father Smith's departure from St Francis House came a new superintendent: a thick-set, ill-tempered man named Taylor. He was immediately dubbed 'Squizzy', the tag given a notorious Melbourne-based gangster at that time. Squizzy Taylor was known for his bad temper and how he would lash out at anyone within range with his thick metre-long rubber hose. He used the rubber hose like a policeman's truncheon and he wielded it with impunity, like a burly Nazi prison guard.

Charlie Perkins was often flogged by Squizzy Taylor because Charlie did not hold back if he thought the superintendent was racist or just plain unjust or wrong. He infuriated Taylor. Some of the beatings with that infernal hose left Charlie with a mass of bruising and weals, and he often found it difficult to walk the next day.

Gordon Briscoe well remembers Squizzy Taylor, the man he calls a 'sadist'.

'The boys will never forget Taylor's time at the house. It was a period of brutal repression. Taylor, I suspect, was a sadist who revelled in the power he exerted over a bunch of hapless half-caste kids. I have not been able to find one boy from the home who could say a good thing about Squizzy and his family. The period from 1949 to mid 1952 was the most authoritarian regime

The Boys from St Francis

at St Francis House. First inkling that things were changing was that Squizzy used to control us with a one-metre long rubber hose. Squizzy would wake us up in the morning and give us 10 seconds to be downstairs from breakfast. If his orders were not obeyed he would wait at the bottom of the stairs and flog boys indiscriminately and with force. If you were hit by this hose it caused great swelling and this was not the only time he used it. He would hit boys when they were in the shower for taking too long; this overstay may have been by seconds.'

Vince Copley, Peter Tilmouth and a couple of the other boys were late for breakfast one morning and knew Squizzy, holding his hose, would be waiting for them at the foot of the stairs. So, just as they reached the bottom few steps, they leapt over the balustrade, thus avoiding Squizzy's lashing, and scrambled into the breakfast room. The boys were fit, strong and agile and Squizzy could never have matched them for speed or hand-eye coordination. All four boys made good their 'escape' and they were relatively safe sitting with their peers eating their cereal in the common room, for even Squizzy baulked at flogging a boy under the gaze of the kitchen staff.

There was a general feeling of fear among the boys at the prospect of being trapped by Taylor in the showers, though. Due to the narrow passage there was no escape and any boy flogged by Squizzy in the shower room was left with great red stripes on his legs and back. This was nothing, however, compared to the punishment for stealing fruit from the pantry.

After his mostly successful forays into shooting fruit through the hole in the floor directly over the pantry, our would-be William Tell, Peter Tilmouth, was often singled out as the likely fruit-stealing suspect, but until someone owned up Squizzy held the floor. The superintendent would demand all of the boys assemble in the common room and made them sit down at the school desks spread around the outside of the room. In that little room crammed full of fearful St Francis House boys stood Taylor, holding his rubber hose in his clenched right hand. Squizzy held court like a holier-than-thou accuser of heretics, knowing one or more had disobeyed the commandment 'Thou shalt not steal.'

It seemed a never-ending tale of woe, for hungry teenagers will do anything to sate their appetite and the pantry often proved too great a temptation.

One winter's day there were more than 40 boys in the common room. They stood shivering before their accuser. Squizzy Taylor loved to intimidate the boys. He made them place their hands on the desks and suddenly he lurched forward, slamming the rubber hose between their fingers.

'Who stole the fruit?' bellowed Squizzy. 'I know the culprit is here in this room and you will all suffer if someone does not own up.'

There was a long silence.

Then Bill Espie, who years later became a decorated and highly ranked police officer in New South Wales, stepped forward and said, 'I didn't do it sir, but I will own up.'

Squizzy should have had the title Commandant Taylor because he ran the house like a concentration camp. He ruled with an iron fist and always managed to create an atmosphere of fear and intimidation. He even had an elaborate intercom system installed by the Scouts for his convenience. He used it to summon children to his study for a dressing down and, more than likely, a flogging.

The Boys from St Francis

Taylor's wife was not violent like her husband, but she was nonetheless an unsavoury type. Most mornings when the older boys were in the shower, the short, plump Mrs Taylor wore a lewd smile as she casually strolled into the wet area. The boys never felt comfortable or game enough to protest as they knew such protestations would not only fall on deaf ears but that they would fall foul of Taylor's Law of the One-Metre Long Rubber Hose.

Frequently, Superintendent Taylor would hold a hearing: a kangaroo court. All in one package this church-appointed dictator and sadist was accuser, prosecutor and the modern equivalent of a hanging judge.

Floggings of boys by Superintendent Taylor after a hearing was always carried out in front of the others. It was a ploy to strike fear into the hearts of the boys. These floggings took place regularly.

The Taylors' cruel and sordid behaviour was so openly discussed within the St Francis House community that it inevitably came to the notice of the bishop of Adelaide. He intervened and Superintendent Taylor was sacked in 1952.

The next superintendent was the Reverend Goff Sherwin. Reverend Sherwin was an Australian Army veteran, a former commando who specialised in hand-to-hand fighting. By every account he was as bad as his predecessor, perhaps worse.

Reverend Sherwin had fought the Japanese in the jungles of New Guinea and, when not wearing his holy cassock, wore army-style khaki shorts. He was big and strong with powerful legs and soon, probably encouraged by the nickname-creator Jim Foster, the boys were calling him 'General Goff'.

General Goff introduced early morning rises and mid-week

chapel. Much to the annoyance of the boys, especially the older lads, he also took confessions every Friday night. In addition he ordered lights out at an earlier time for all junior and apprenticed boys. In Port Adelaide and Semaphore Friday nights were reserved for a night out with a girlfriend at the pictures. The older boys found a way to go to General Goff's confessional early of a Friday and they would bribe the younger boys with money to help fool the General when he made his regular nightly rounds. The younger boys became especially creative in arranging bed clothes and pillows to hoodwink the General into thinking that everyone was tucked up in bed for the night.

Those Friday nights were not the only time the older boys wanted to get away from the house. There was also the thought of an arm round your girl in the darkened Odeon Picture Theatre of a Saturday afternoon.

David Woodford expanded on the free Saturday afternoon pictures.

'Thanks to Father Smith's arrangement with the Odeon Theatre manager we got in free of charge. We were given a small amount of pocket money with the requirement that we saved one penny for the church collection plate the following day. The St Francis boys' queue at the pictures always grew considerably as we could get our mates in free of charge in exchange for lollies or ice cream at interval. No one complained.'

Just as inmates in prison find a commodity to trade with their fellows, the boys from St Francis became adept in procuring, buying, selling and trading. A fire escape was attached to each upstairs dormitory and the boys would stealthily slip down the ladder, sometimes in the dead of night, to meet their girl in the outer grounds. Earlier 'escapes' often became a night at the local dance or pictures at the Odeon Theatre on Semaphore Road.

One day General Goff was holding court in his study, regaling the boys with stories of his wartime adventures fighting the Japanese in New Guinea and how he would approach an enemy soldier from behind and quickly despatch him. Suddenly he grabbed Jim Foster and threw him to the floor and applied a choke hold. The gasping youngster was quickly released and no harm was done, however, the boys saw first hand the immense physical power the General possessed.

General Goff would have been the first to encourage the boys to learn to defend themselves. Just before Father Smith left the house, he organised a gymnasium class each week. The former coach house at the rear of St Francis House was quickly transformed into a makeshift gymnasium complete with punching bag, a variety of weights, climbing net and skipping ropes. Classes were held by Tommy Murphy, a former boxing champion. For any Aboriginal boy living in Port Adelaide in those years just after the war, learning the art of self-defence was essential. The boys learnt to defend themselves and their territory.

Semaphore Beach was firmly in their territory, and it was a favourite haunt all through the summer months. As the boys grew older and reached puberty the beach became a vastly different proposition. It was not all running, swimming and throwing spears into the heaped seaweed. Suddenly the boys noticed girls. Vince Copley still refers to their favourite summer haunt as 'Ticklebelly Beach'. But for teenage boys their newfound insight into a world with women was offset by fierce competition. The white guys were also keen on the girls.

The boys from St Francis were fiercely protective of 'their

patch', beach that stretched from Glanville Fort to Estcourt House in Grange. It was here that Wally McArthur ran like the wind; where Charlie Perkins and Peter Tilmouth threw their spears, mostly during the winter months; and the place where all the boys ran to try and emulate the great speed of Wally and to chat up members of the opposite sex. Inevitably they would come face to face with the Port Adelaide 'push', led by Jimmy and Freddy Wright. The brothers Wright attacked the boys with sticks and bottles, but the boys from St Francis were street-fighters from way back. They could use their fists, evade a thrown bottle or stick, and they could use their dingers (shanghais) with unerring skill.

Most of the St Francis House boys carried a shanghai on the beach. They were made by cutting the fork from a branch of a young gum tree. The boys then attached heavy-duty rubber from a truck inner tube to each side of the fork. The result could shoot quite a large pebble a great distance and they soon discovered that the shanghai was a formidable and potentially deadly weapon. When a day of battle against the 'push' arrived, all the boys from the house were gathered and marched off to war in defence of 'their patch'. The boys from St Francis gave their opponents a belting in the sand hills on Semaphore Beach. The Wright brothers took flight along with their defeated cohorts and were not seen in the vicinity of the beach for two years.

After a year of too much church and army-type 'early to bed and early to rise' demands, the General left St Francis House.

A few years ago Gordon Briscoe was gathering material for his book, *Racial Folly*, and to his dismay he was unable to find any reports or records about Superintendent Taylor or his replacement, Reverend Sherwin. A cover up? Or were the

The Boys from St Francis

documents mislaid? Certainly revelations about the unsavoury activities of Anglican Church appointees to St Francis House would have cast widespread disgust about these so-called 'trustworthy' citizens.

Sunshine and shadow

Max, you can't do anything to help. They will lower her into the ground and cover her in dirt ... now, go to school.

After Reverend Sherwin left St Francis House in 1953, laypersons Mr and Mrs Morris Wilson ran the home for the next three years. Morrie, as his wife called him, tried hard to make the experience for the boys as enjoyable as possible. 'Whickey', as the boys dubbed him, was a personable man, but he caused a lot of amusement among the boys because he walked like a duck. He was a big, strong man, with rusty brown hair, a freckled face and the sort of bow legs you associate with a cowboy who'd been in the saddle for more years than the locusts have eaten. Whickey wanted a better life for the boys, but still they wore the same cheap shirts and the same shoes, which they mended themselves or with help from one of the helpers at the home. They became used to wearing the same patched pants and darned socks.

Mothers' clubs sometimes came to the boys' rescue to mend their clothes, sheets and pillow cases. This weighed heavily on some of the boys. Having to accept handouts and charity was demeaning, but living conditions at St Francis House continued to deteriorate with the passing of the years. There also seemed to be an ongoing procession of newcomers, but the rooms were not changed. It simply meant more boys being crammed in to each room.

The Boys from St Francis

During the boys' time at St Francis House the cobbled brick courtyard between the main building and the coach house was quite flat. There the boys practised their soccer and played cricket with stolen tennis balls. Today the stumps painted on the brick wall between the two arched coach house walls are a little faded, but still clearly visible to the naked eye. However, the cobbled brick surface is now riddled with lumps and bumps due to the roots of an enormous Moreton Bay fig tree. The tree was there in the 1950s, but it was then a mere sapling.

Mr and Mrs Wilson tried their best, but they never quite worked out the best and fairest way to treat those older boys who had left school and were in paid employment and still staying in the house. Some of the older boys, especially those who came to St Francis House from Mulgoa, were successful apprentices. They were no longer boys but strapping young men and commonsense dictated that they be given a certain amount of leeway, given that they were working for a living and paying board. These older boys included Wally McArthur, Harry Russell and four of the originals from Alice Springs: Charlie Perkins, Malcolm Cooper, Peter Tilmouth and Bill Espie. They expected, quite rightly, that they be afforded a measure of independence, but Wilson and his wife, whom the boys dubbed 'Turtle', never worked out where they were going wrong.

The nickname Turtle came from Mrs Wilson's squat, dumpy figure. The boys saw Mrs Wilson not as a serious manager of young men, but as a comical figure. Vince Copley recalls the day a youngster named Murray Walker came to St Francis House.

'We all rushed up the corridor to the main door when Walker arrived. That was a bit of a no-no. The boys weren't supposed to be where we were and that act in itself must have annoyed Turtle who was quickly on the scene. Just after Murray knocked at the front door, Charlie Perkins turned to Turtle and asked, "Is he a good boy?" All hell broke loose. As Turtle lashed out smacking Charlie across the face with her open hand, she screamed, "He's a better boy than you, Charlie Perkins!"'

It seems the Wilsons had a penchant for slapping the boys. Any respect Mr Wilson had built with the boys suddenly disappeared when they learnt that one day the superintendent slapped McArthur across the face. Wally did not hit back. He said calmly, 'I will not retaliate because you are the superintendent.'

Before Wally McArthur came to St Francis House he was already a champion runner and a brilliant rugby league player. He became very much his own man, but the impact of having been brought up in an institution instinctively made him bow to the authority, no matter how unjust or inhumane.

At Mulgoa, Wally, James Stirling, Harry Russell, Jim Foster and Cyril Hampton played rugby league at Penrith and Mount Wilson secondary schools. Later, younger boys at St Francis House followed in Wally's footsteps. The boys tried soccer, rugby and Australian Rules. They discovered which football code they loved best and went with it.

During the reign of Superintendent Wilson, the South Australian Education Department sold off some of the land surrounding St Francis House for a large housing project. Hundreds of 'temporary homes' were constructed on the very turf where Port Adelaide Football Club played its first official match in 1870. Port Thistle Soccer Club was forced to find an alternative venue in Robin Road, about 500 metres away from the house.

The major shift for the soccer club was one thing; the other, which the boys very much enjoyed, was the sudden arrival of lots of young women living closer to St Francis house than ever before.

In 1955, Malcolm Bald, the handyman who had been an assistant to Wilson, took over as superintendent. Bald, the son of a fitter and turner, grew up in Largs Bay. His father worked for the Osborne Power Station. The second of three boys, all of whom gained employment as tradesmen, the Bald brothers were all members of the First Semaphore Boy Scouts.

The boys called Bald by his shortened first name and Mal rose to the rank of assistant scoutmaster. Some of the boys liked Mal, even Charlie Perkins, who was always suspicious of any white man in authority.

'I liked Mal Bald better than the others, but we didn't understand each other. We never seemed to hit it off and I thought he considered me a smart-alec type. Despite that I felt Mal was generally one of the rare good blokes.'

Gordon Briscoe didn't notice anything unduly unusual about Mal Bald until the year of the referendum on constitutional change for Aboriginal people in 1967.

'I then learnt that he was living with two young boys on an isolated farm between Murray Bridge and Karoonda in South Australia. I heard sometime later that between 1967 and the early 1970s he left South Australia for the west following two prison terms; and while there I heard his life was cut short in circumstances I leave for other historians to investigate.'

Gordon Briscoe said that in hindsight he could recall a number of incidents that were 'sexually inappropriate while he was in charge of us'.

'Mal would often take the younger boys out to Torrens Island and Outer Harbor where we would all swim. The mangroves were about 30 metres deep providing ample cover for Mal to sit on the bank and watch 15 or so young boys slide naked down the muddy bank of the Port River.'

There is no doubt that the boys at St Francis were as vulnerable there as at any other church-run institutions where priests and ministers abused young boys.

There were other incidents over the years where staff behaved inappropriately at St Francis House. Gordon Briscoe describes such acts as 'overzealous touching while supervising the boys at night' and, of course, there was the ever-keen Mrs Taylor casting her evil eye over the older boys when they were taking their morning shower. Staff at St Francis House were appointed by the church and state; people who were trusted to look after the boys' welfare, both physically and spiritually.

In late 2012 the Australian government established a royal commission into institutional responses to child sexual abuse. Given the extent of abuse in institutionalised life throughout Christian schools and hostels, perhaps it's not surprising that Max Wilson suffered abuse from several quarters at St Francis House.

'I was abused by the staff, the wardens and the boys. They used to call me "runt". The smallest and thus the most vulnerable suffer more than the others.'

Max Wilson was, by self definition, 'a loner'.

'I didn't like the home, the boys or the wardens. Being away from my family was a huge wrench. I hated the food and the people, all of them.'

The Boys from St Francis

Vince Copley recalls summer holidays at St Francis House and how an Anglican priest based in a parish in the Adelaide Hills would arrive, staying as a guest of the house, and would always join the boys for a daily swim either at Semaphore Beach or in the Port River.

'This bloke enthusiastically swam among us and his usual trick was to dive like a dolphin, and how amazing it was that the priest always surfaced between a boy's legs,' Vince says. 'He was the swimming monk we called "Submarine".'

Every one of those youngsters was vulnerable and open to abuse. In cases of sexual abuse at church-run institutions there appears to be a common thread whereby the alleged perpetrators get away with their evil deeds because their victims feel great shame and do not have the confidence to confide in their parents. In the St Francis boys' case they didn't have their mothers with them, and after Father Smith left the home there was no one on hand in whom they could trust. There has never been an inquiry about St Francis House.

Although he did not realise it at the time he was living at St Francis House, Vince Copley knows that one particular activity by one of the older boys was a form of abuse.

'We called him "the Masturbator". For a long time he'd jump into a younger boy's bed and do something to the lad that he didn't understand. He'd touch him down there and after a while the boy would jump out of bed and head for the toilet. The boy would think what he felt was a need to go to the toilet . . . but it was the other,' Vince says.

'It was all new to us. We didn't know what was happening and we didn't have our parents there to explain.'

Abuse in other forms was rife. When Squizzy Taylor was on the rampage, he'd dash up the stairs looking for a victim. The boys would hide under their beds. One time Vince was successfully hidden when another boy kicked him out from under the bed, straight into Squizzy's view. He was flogged with the rubber hose but, when Mr Taylor was catching his breath, Vince yelled, 'What about the boy under the other bed?'

Vince said his St Francis House experience was generally a good one. However, the ugly face of racism did materialise occasionally. When Vince was one of the champion footballers attending Le Fevre Boys Technical School, for example, a boy asked him to his house for tea with his family. Vince was delighted to be asked into a white family for a meal, however, what he didn't know then was the boy had done so to curry favour with him as the school's football team vice captain. Maybe by getting to know Vince he might just squeeze into the school team's best eighteen.

'The lad was selected,' Vince says, 'and that was the last time I was invited into his family home.'

Despite being unimpressed with institutional living at St Francis House, Max Wilson did enjoy his time at Ethelton Primary and Le Fevre Boys Technical School.

The high school headmaster Fred Vickery held that position from 1943 to 1969. He was universally respected and the boys from St Francis especially enjoyed his style. The boys liked the way Mr Vickery allowed them – no matter what their colour or creed – to sort out their differences in the schoolyard, between themselves. That suited the Aboriginal boys perfectly.

Mr Vickery was an accomplished sportsman and he enjoyed

outdoor pursuits such as bushwalking and gardening. He always arrived at school astride a little red motorbike.

All the boys liked Mr Vickery's sense of adventure and they admired his concept of fair play. His Australian Rules 'stab passes' were a treat and said to have been in the mould of Port Adelaide great Bob Quinn. Vickery encouraged student participation in all sports and he introduced soccer, rugby, hockey and baseball to the school. A keen swimmer, he also liked surfing and taught his students to surf on a flat ironing board.

He also mentored a number of St Francis House boys, giving them a chance to play for the Port Adelaide Football Club. Among these boys were Vince Copley and Malcolm Cooper.

When Max Wilson arrived at Le Fevre he and his friends got wind of a scheme whereby the school prefects planned to lure the new chums to a spot behind the classrooms and thus out of Mr Vickery's gaze for the purpose of roughing them up.

'We were tipped off that the prefects were setting us up for a hiding, but we were ready and eager to take them on,' Max smiles.

'When we finished with that lot there wasn't one prefect left standing. They rolled about nursing their wounds and we triumphantly strolled back into class. As we knew how to use our fists and we always engaged in "scraps" in the streets and on the beach, we clobbered them, dusted ourselves off and wandered back to class as if nothing had happened.'

Max played soccer for the South Australian under-17 team, visiting other states and often performing in front of a big crowd before an international match.

'We all loved the game because through soccer we gained

respect. Academically we might not have been too brilliant, but in soccer, Australians Rules, rugby league and cricket we ruled the playing fields.

'Through soccer I got to meet the great England player Stanley Matthews, but soccer in those days was very much in its infancy. There wasn't much of a future in Australia as to making a living out of the game, so you looked to other things. But I played club soccer later on after playing for the state under-17s, although that experience playing soccer for my state here and in other parts of Australia was the best thing that ever happened to me. Sport generally was good to me and for me.

'I got to swim locally with John and Ilse Konrads and with Dawn Fraser at the Adelaide Swimming Pool (now replaced by those 'tank traps' next to parliament house) and at Semaphore.

'We used to have some good fights with Dawn and her bunch of girls. She was gorgeous and a damned good scrapper. Dawn gave the boys as good as she got. Those girls could sure swim and they could fight.'

When Max was about 14 he received a telegram from a family friend in Alice Springs. His mother was gravely ill.

'I approached the superintendent for permission to go home to be with my mum, but I was told, "No, Max, you cannot do anything medically to help: go to school."'

Then three weeks later another telegram arrived.

'My mother had passed away. Again I asked for permission to travel to Alice Springs, but I was told "Max, you can't do anything to help. They will lower her into the ground and cover her in dirt ... now, go to school."'

The Boys from St Francis

Poor Max Wilson was not allowed to attend his mother's funeral. He said it would have given him some comfort, a feeling of closure.

'I cried for weeks,' he lamented. 'And now at the age of 73, after all this time, I still mourn the loss of my mum.'

Max regarded himself as a rebel during his time at St Francis House.

'I didn't like St Francis House and made few friends there, but after a while I got to know a group of young people called "bodgies" and "widgies".

'They used to congregate at Semaphore Beach, near the clock, the bodgies in their stovepipe pants, leather jackets, rubber-soled or pointy shoes and slicked-back hair, dripping with Brylcreem or Californian Poppy hair oil, and the widgies in their jeans and wearing short cropped hairstyles.

'I got to know them. The boys were very good to me. There was no racism, nothing like that; they accepted me as a fellow human being. And their mothers were terrific. They taught me all about life. They taught me about sex and they always took time out to help me with a problem at school.'

Society itself wasn't quite ready for the bodgies and widgies phenomenon. The front page of the *Sydney Morning Herald* on 1 February 1951 carried this important message:

> What with 'bodgies' growing their hair long and getting around in satin shirts, and 'weegies' cutting their hair short and wearing jeans, confusion seems to be arising about the sex of some Australian adolescents.

'The mothers of Semaphore's bodgies became my surrogate mothers. They were beautiful people,' Max adds.

Sunshine and shadow

Max was sceptical about talking about his experiences when I interviewed him, but afterwards he said he enjoyed talking about his life: a cathartic release.

Vince Copley, the man who asked me if I would write the story of the boys who grew up at St Francis House, was born at the Wallaroo Government Hospital on 24 December 1936. His parents were Fred Warrior and Kathleen Winifred Edwards. Vince was the last born. First came Winnie, then Colin, Valda (who died very young), Maureen, Josie then Vince. Fred Warrior died when Vince was just two years old.

One day when Vince was about five he answered a knock on the door. There stood a tall man, resplendent in suit and tie, wearing a bowler hat and carrying an umbrella. Vince left the man at the door and rushed into the kitchen and said breathlessly, 'There's a *goonya* (white man) at the door.'

The white man was Alan Copley, with whom his mother had a relationship. In later years Vince learnt about a sensationalist story that appeared in the Adelaide *Truth*, which was nothing short of defamation.

'After my dad died my mum and other ladies she knew would date white military men. But the story which appeared really hurt my mother and her friends because it depicted her as a woman soliciting men.'

In those days Aboriginal people had no redress. They couldn't afford legal representation and they were at the mercy of a racist system.

Vince excelled at Australian Rules football and became a leader of the community in sport and politics. In the Queen's Birthday 2014 Honours List, Vince was awarded an AM (Member of the general division of the Order of Australia), acknowledged for his tireless service to the Indigenous community as an advocate for the improvement of social, legal and economic rights and cultural identity. His award delighted his many admirers.

An all-round good bloke with a great sense of humour, Vince was a brilliant sportsman and a role model for his community. What a life he has led.

High achievers

'When we got to the hospital, staff turned us away. "We don't want your kind here. You are not welcome."' – Vince Copley

Most of the boys from St Francis were high achievers. Their success in business, politics and sport came from their basic instinct to work hard and learn. They reflect the spirit of Thomas Jefferson, who said: 'I'm a greater believer in luck and I find the harder I work the more I have of it.' The boys from St Francis found acceptance at school through their being exceptional athletes. It seems that even in racist Australia during the 1950s it didn't matter what colour or creed a boy happened to be if he could bowl a ball and swing a bat better than most, or was brilliant at soccer, rugby or Australian Rules.

Vince Copley lived his early life with his family at the Aboriginal reserve at Point Pearce, 120 km north-west of Adelaide. The sister reserve to Point Pearce is Point McLeay on Lake Alexandrina, near Hindmarsh Island at the mouth of the River Murray. Many of Vince's people – related by tradition and blood – hail from this region. When Vince's mother became ill he went to live in Alice Springs with his sister Winnie. It was there that the family learnt of the good work of Father Percy Smith and after a short time in the Northern Territory Vince went to St Francis House. Gordon Briscoe sometimes calls Vince 'Fat Tarzan', although mostly he's known as 'Cop.'

The Boys from St Francis

Vince's sister Josie married a famous South Australian footballer, Fred Agius, who played for West Adelaide. Although his other sister Winnie died at a relatively young age, she was instrumental in establishing the forward momentum for the 1967 referendum and made a significant contribution to Aboriginal politics on the national stage. Vince had just turned 10 years of age when he was taken on holiday to spend a few days with his older sister Winnie in Ardrossan.

'I was supposed to be collected at the bus stop in front of the general store, but no one turned up. Apparently they didn't have a enough money to put petrol in the car. Eventually all the people at the bus stop were collected and I was left there sitting at the bus stop in front of the store. So, I'm stuck. We cannot communicate because I don't know their number. As I sat on the seat I overheard the bloke who ran the shop on the phone. This bloke Tucket is ringing the police, "Listen ... we've got some nigger trouble here!"

'I will never forget that phone call. I had heard the word "nigger" before but there I was looking about me, "Where's the nigger?" Then it hit me. I was the "nigger" Tucket was talking about. So the police came and they were good and kind and they took me to the police station and made up a nice bed for me and I spent the night in the cell at Ardrossan Police Station. Next morning I had a good breakfast, including porridge, so the experience was not a bad one. My sister eventually turned up and I was okay.'

Vince Copley grew up with a sense of belonging and achieving. He had suffered verbal abuse almost on a daily basis but he did not cower from discrimination; it made him more determined to make a mark on society. At St Francis House he learnt to be independent and developed a strong work ethic. He also was a staunch ally; a loyal and honest friend.

From an early age Vince said to himself, 'I am not going to be a drunk and I am not going to wear second-hand clothes. And I am going to drive a Fairlane.'

At the age of 11 Vince was on holiday in Ardrossan when he was suddenly struck with a terrible abdominal pain.

'The pain was unbelievable. Uncle Cliff knew that it was something bad, so he fired up his old T-Model Ford and we set off for Ardrossan Hospital. When we got to the hospital, staff turned us away. "We don't want your kind here. You are not welcome." Same thing happened when we got to Maitland Hospital. By now I was screaming in pain and Uncle set off for Wallaroo Hospital, more than 60 km away. We finally got to the hospital and thankfully they accepted me. I was rushed into theatre. Apparently it was touch-and-go for I had acute appendicitis and if the thing had burst I was in serious trouble.'

Vince Copley is a quiet and patient man but he has never forgotten the staff at those two hospitals – Ardrossan and Maitland – where he was refused entry because he was Aboriginal.

'You know, I am not vindictive, but I wish I could find something to get back at those two towns,' Vince smiles.

By the time Vince had reached his teens, football wasn't all that occupied his thinking. Hormones had kicked in and suddenly he saw girls in a whole new light. All the boys round Vince's age liked what they saw when they set eyes on Judy Almond, the daughter of Jim and Jingle Almond. There were, of course, lots of girls nearby at the migrant houses, but Judy was right there in front of them at St Francis House. They all wanted to take her to the tower, where the door was usually shut but if left ajar was the perfect spot for a 'ticklebelly' session. One long weekend Judy invited a girlfriend to stay and the boys were right on to it. It was a balmy Saturday night when two of the boys whisked Judy and her girlfriend up into the tower. The boys from St Francis had a keen network and within minutes the place was abuzz with the news, 'There's two girls in the tower ... who's with them?'

Vince decided to investigate. He climbed a nearby pine tree and from his vantage point he could see quite clearly what was going on. Vince had been up the tree for a good 10 minutes when he heard a voice behind him: 'Move yer bloody head, will ya? I can't see.'

Many years later, Judy Almond would marry David Woodford, another boy from St Francis House.

Girls were one thing, but the passion Vince had for Australian Rules football won out and it wasn't too long before fate took him on a long football journey in the country.

At the age of 16 while playing for Port Adelaide he won the coveted Tomkins Medal, fairest and best player in the SANFL under 19s. He was already into his second year of a boilermaker apprenticeship at the South Australian Harvest Board in Port Adelaide.

'I'd work all day, then go to trade school at night. It seemed the normal thing to do.'

It was that very year that his mother died.

'At 16 I was without a mum or a dad. I guess at that time of my life I was just kicking a bag of air about. Football was my love and I thought I could make a bit of money playing the game.'

The young rover-cum-centreman was strong, tough in the

High achievers

clinches and possessed lightning speed. He was sure-footed and an accurate pass by hand or by foot. Vince found it difficult though to marry sport and everyday life. During the football season he was content because the clubs he played for provided a job and accommodation, but the summer months were a bit of a lost cause. He teamed up with two cousins Bradley Graham (brother of Sturt and South Australian champion footballer Michael Graham) and Spencer Weetra.

'We couldn't get a job in summer, so we went to Port Adelaide and bummed around, sleeping wherever we could, usually under a bridge,' Vince recalls.

'It was a tough time. Bradley and Spencer were always looking about for a drink, a wine shop, but I didn't want to go down that path. After six months in the Port we went to Barmera to pick grapes. I hated that job. The vines were in tall grass, infested with spiders and snakes.'

Vince decided their best option was to leave Barmera and go back to Adelaide. They got aboard a grape truck and were dropped off in Nuriootpa.

'We had little money, so we slept under a tree in Nuri and next day set out to walk to Adelaide. Happily when we got to Lyndoch a bloke offered us a ride to Adelaide.'

Vince could see then how young Aboriginal men slide down a sad and slippery slope. No hope of a job soon eats at anyone's self-esteem. And in the 1950s racism throughout Australia was rife. It was a major factor for the Indigenous young not being able to find meaningful employment. And so their self-esteem plummeted and so they opted for the demon drink, if only to feel good when depression lurked.

Port coach Fos Williams had agreed that Vince could play in

The Boys from St Francis

Playing for Port Adelaide, 1953. Second-to-back row: second from right, Malcolm Cooper. Seated front row: far left, Vince Copley; second from right, Ken Hampton. Photo courtesy Port Adelaide Football Club.

the under 19s if he didn't make the league side in 1955. There was nothing in writing from Fos, or Port secretary big Bob McLean, but a deal is a deal and Williams and McLean went back on the agreement. Vince was asked to play seconds, not under 19s, but he didn't want to do that; he knew playing seconds was fraught with danger as most of the players were not skilled enough to go any further and too old for the under 19s. In the wake of Port reneging on the deal, Vince signed with West Broken Hill. From there he got an offer to play for Fitzroy.

'There wasn't much money in the game in those days, but Fitzroy must have been keen to get my services for they made me a terrific offer. I had run up a bill for clothes and living costs leading up to the offer. It was a big amount, more than £1000

High achievers

and they said they'd pay all my bills if I signed. I signed on the spot. Back at Port Adelaide they paid match fees to players who had 50 or more matches under their belt. Such a player might get up to a £5 match fee. That was in addition to the 10 shillings we all got if we turned up to training. Fitzroy paid my £1000 debt, provided work and accommodation and a salary of £13 a week.

'One time I stood former Fitzroy great Normie McDonald, the first Aboriginal to play VFL football. He was a great but he was well past it when I stood him.'

Vince's pace and skill must have greatly impressed Fitzroy, for his offer to play for the club was brought about under the coaching watch of Bill Stephen and Len Smith, brother of the legendary Norm Smith. The Victorians might not have given South Australia a big rap regarding the standard of their football, but they knew talent when they saw it and Vince Copley oozed football talent. While Fitzroy had generously offered to pay Vince's huge debt to acquire his services, the only dampener was the realisation that he had to serve a three-year qualification to play in the big league. Three years is a long time in a footballer's life. Vince's first game was not memorable. He played for Fitzroy against Sydney and was knocked out in the first quarter.

Vince had one VFL season with Fitzroy then returned to Adelaide. One man he got to know really well was Doug Nicholls, a former Fitzroy footballer. When Vince was in Melbourne Doug was the curator at Northcote Oval. Doug was a Yorta Yorta man. A professional athlete, Churches of Christ pastor, South Australian state governor, ceremonial officer and a pioneering campaigner for reconciliation, Doug was a great role model for all Australians.

'Doug Nicholls took me under his wing. He made a huge

The Boys from St Francis

impression on me. Here was this man, a great footballer in the VFL and a man of the cloth, a kind and popular man with everyone. But he was tough, a boxer in his time and like a lot of Aboriginal people he had to fight to lead a good life.'

Vince was sad to leave Doug, but he had made up his mind to go back to Adelaide and there he was approached by officials of the Curramulka Football Club, in the Southern Yorke Peninsula Football League. He signed the contract with Curramulka by candlelight in the barley lumpers' quarters at Pine Point. The contract was for £20 a game; good money in the 1950s. Vince initially signed for one year.

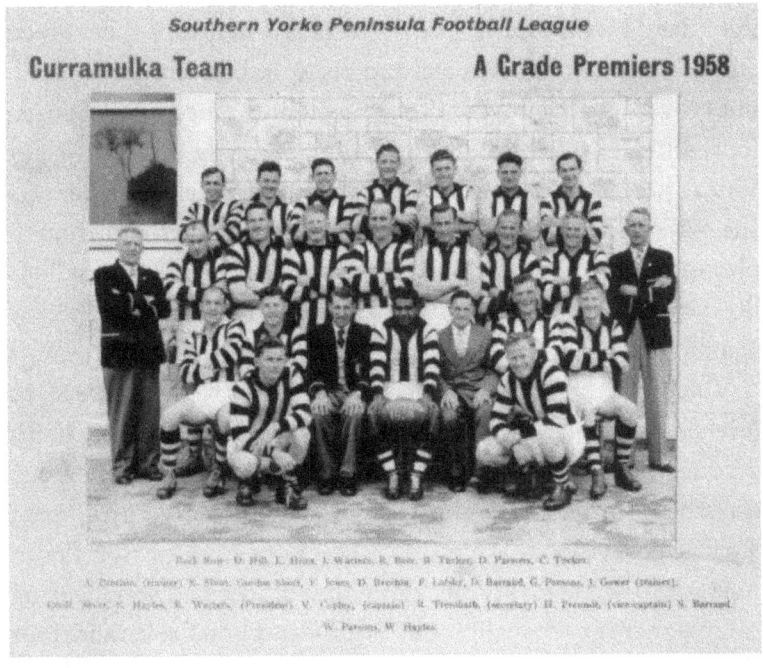

Curramulka Football Club A-grade premiers, 1958. The captain, Vince Copley, is seated at the centre, holding the premiership football.

High achievers

'I wondered about this town. Would the people be like those who refused me at the hospitals in Ardrossan and Maitland? How would I be received at Curry?'

There was no need for Vince to be concerned.

He'd been at the club for just a day or two when a teammate said, 'Would you like to come over to our place for dinner tonight?'

'I couldn't believe it. In my experience you'd play the game, then it was "see ya later" until the following night's training or match.

'"I haven't got a car. I can't get to your place," I said.

'"That's okay, Vince. We'll pick you up and drop you back to where you are staying after the meal. No worries."'

A week later another club man invited Vince to a dance.

'I can't dance,' Vince blurted.

'That's okay. We'll teach you.'

'I couldn't believe it. The whole town were so accepting of me. I guess I just wasn't used to being treated so well by any community. It was a different world.'

During that first year at Curramulka Vince worked at nearby Curran Two, a 1000-acre mixed farming property run by husband and wife farming team, Watkins Holmes Thomas and Alice Esther Thomas (nee Clift). Vince carted hay, mended fences, threw fleeces in the shearing shed and toiled hard as a willing hand. Life was good: good, that is, in the winter months. The farming Thomas family couldn't afford to employ him all year so in summer Vince had to find other work and accommodation.

'I could see then how young Aboriginals fall into hopelessness. Having experienced the feeling of hopelessness in not being able to get a job and not being able to afford accommodation and then meeting Doug Nicholls I came to a logical conclusion about my people's lot. Either they became a priest, a minister of religion or they became a drunk.'

One day a farming friend associated with the football club asked Vince, 'Can you play cricket?'

'"Yeah," I said straight away. "Yeah, I can play cricket."'

Vince believes playing sport year-round saved his life.

'I was employed full-time in winter at Curran Two and in summer I'd play cricket and the club got me accommodation and I found work every harvest; I sewed bags and worked as a roustabout during the shearing months.'

He believes his experience at St Francis House helped make him strong and proud. He had a great belief in his sporting ability and while hurt by racist taunts throughout his young life, he wasn't going to let that get in his way. He would overcome whatever obstacles he faced.

The town of Curramulka embraced Vince Copley. At the time he signed with Curry, Vince was the only Aboriginal player in the competition. When Vince first came to the club, Rex Watters was president. Recently Rex said of Vince: 'Immaculate ball skills, rover-centreman, faster than Shaun Burgoyne.'

At just 21 Vince Copley was made captain-coach of Curramulka. His tender age alone made people sit up and take notice, but the most remarkable aspect of his appointment was that a bunch of white blokes were being mentored by a young Aboriginal man who wasn't even allowed to vote in his own country.

'When I got to Curry, footy was just the high mark, the long-drop kick, then have a chat to your opponent about how seeding was going,' Vince recalls.

High achievers

'I planned to change these blokes: make them play for the town, turn them into a harder playing group.'

It didn't take long for the entire district to embrace Vince Copley. He was a tremendous footballer and coach. Most of all he was a decent, hard-working human being. One night the club staged a fight in town. 'An emerging champion was invited to box against a formidable opponent in the Curramulka Town Hall,' Vince said, 'I was also on the bill, fighting some lesser bloke in a supporting bout. The main man was Norm Peterson. I remember him from high school. Then he was a little, fat kid and was always pushed around. Now he was 6'4" and three axe handles across his back.'

Vince's opponent that night failed to show, so too Norm Peterson's opponent, so the organisers asked Vince if he'd take on Peterson. After copping a left to the face early, Vince decided that the best form of defence was to attack.

'For a few minutes I was on top of him. Peterson's seconds were yelling out for the fight to stop and, according to amateur boxing rules, I should have been awarded the fight, but we fought on. Next round he floored me,' Vince laughs.

Norm Peterson became a Labor politician, representing the seat of Semaphore. He became speaker of the house from 1990 to 1993 in the Bannon Labor government.

Vince patched up his differences with Fos Williams, formerly of Port Adelaide, and played for him at South Adelaide in 1960. That season he would visit Fos and Von Williams at their home.

'I remember bouncing baby Mark on my knee,' Vince laughs. 'He was a happy little baby and Fos was delighted to have a son, but Fos was all serious when it came to footy. If you didn't get the ball you were no use to him. And he expected you to burrow

The Boys from St Francis

Vince and Brenda Copley on their wedding day at Curramulka Anglican Church, 26 June 1971.

in and make every effort to get the ball. I took Fos's ideas and values to Curramulka. The club and the players gave me the respect they would show any top footballer. The results came. The town got a lot of pride.'

Life was good for Vince Copley. He had found good employment year-round, he was greatly respected in both football and cricket circles, and he had fallen in love with Brenda Thomas, the daughter of Watkins and Alice Thomas, at Curran Two.

'One day I was sitting on the tractor looking back at my life and thinking how good life had become for me: utopia. But then I thought of how things were at Point Pearce, the reserve where my relatives lived and were still doing it tough. They still had to sign exemption forms to go to and from the reserve. The form

High achievers

which effectively states that you are "an honorary white" for the time you are absent. I thought then that I must do something more meaningful with my life. I wanted to help my people.'

Marriage to Brenda and becoming a project officer with the Department of Aboriginal Affairs in Canberra was to come.

In 1972 Vince received the welcome news that his great friend and mentor Doug Nicholls had become the first Aboriginal person to be knighted. Then four years later, on 1 December 1976, Sir Doug Nicholls was appointed South Australian governor. Over many years Doug was active in helping pave the way for better health and education for his people. Sadly he was suffering ill-health and within weeks of accepting the governorship his health deteriorated to such an extent that he was struggling to perform his official duties. In March 1977 Doug was to have hosted the Queen and the Duke of Edinburgh at Government House during their Adelaide visit, but he was too ill to do so. In Doug's absence, Sir Walter Crocker, a highly respected envoy who had served nine years as lieutenant-governor of South Australia, hosted the luncheon. But Doug wanted the royals to interact with some of his people so he called Vince.

'I was used to going to Government House. While Doug was governor I went there almost every day for morning tea.' He laughed.

'To attend the function, I asked two aunties, Mrs Gladys Elphick and Maud Tongene. Gladys accepted immediately, but Maud wasn't too keen. "Oh, I'm second best, am I, Vince?" She wasn't too happy being the second person I invited.'

Vince and Brenda Copley sat either side of the Queen.

'As it was a lunch and not a formal dinner, I had to change my mode of dress,' Brenda says. 'I had this very long blue gown, so at the last minute I hurriedly shortened my dress by cutting it off just below the knee and I sewed it with red cotton.'

When the Duke enquired about Australian beef, Vince told him that all the choice cuts of Australian beef were exported... to the UK.

He says the royals were 'very gracious, warm and friendly'.

During that short period when Doug Nicholls was South Australian governor I asked him why it was rare to see an Aboriginal play cricket, while many Indigenous youngsters play Australian Rules football. Was it a throwback to cricket being the 'white fella's sport'?

'No,' he said. 'It gets down to affordability. If an Aboriginal boy goes to a big club to try out all he needs is a pair of shorts and singlet. And if he shows a bit of promise the club will provide him with a pair of boots. Cricket is different. A player needs creams and shirt, boots, socks, a protector, pads and a bat. That's too much for the average Aboriginal family to afford.'

When playing for Fitzroy Vince attended a meeting at Portland where Pastor Doug Nicholls was the keynote speaker. 'I'll never forget how Doug spoke about his idea of reconciliation,' Vince recalls. 'Doug opened up with, "You can't play a piano without using both the black and the white keys."

'When Doug was appointed South Australian governor he pleaded with Premier Don Dunstan to have me as his aide-de-camp, but Dunstan refused. You know Doug was hardly ever at Government House. He was usually meeting and greeting in Rundle Mall; a man of the people. Near the end of his life I'd visit Doug at the Royal North Shore Hospital in Sydney and he'd always welcome me with, "Glad to see you. Glad you could come."'

High achievers

Most of the boys from St Francis achieved in life. Men such as soccer international and legendary activist Charlie Perkins; soccer star, designer and activist John Moriarty; history professor and author Gordon Briscoe; and Harold Thomas, the man who created the Aboriginal flag, were all high achievers. They were, perhaps, the most high-profile achievers among the boys who grew up at St Francis House. Their stories are all different, but always there's that mix of sadness and joy.

When Max Wilson was 10 years old the warden at St Francis House called Max to his office. There he was introduced to a white couple and their son John.

'The priest – his name was Smith but it wasn't Father Smith – said, "Now, Max, these good, kind people are going to adopt you."

'I looked at the couple and their son and I set my gaze on the priest and I said bluntly, "No one adopts me" and walked out of the warden's office.'

Max says the new few weeks were a living nightmare.

'I was flogged for my "insubordination" and "rudeness toward this lovely white family."'

A few years later, Max was selected in the South Australian state under-17 soccer team. While soccer was the 'highlight' of his life, Max recalls how he had to get written permission from the Australian government to travel interstate.

'All that was to do with the assimilation policy. I got permission okay, but they insisted that I must travel with a chaperone in tow.

'Did they think that this 14-year-old kid was going to run away? Where the fuck was I going to go?'

Max bought a motorbike when he was barely 15, but he

somehow hoodwinked authorities and successfully acquired a licence. The strategy worked wonders because Max found work as a telegram boy, skipping across the sand hills daily on his way to delivering telegrams to people in the vicinity of Estcourt House in Semaphore Park.

'My bike was big and cumbersome, but I got used to it and I needed it to get the job, for which I was paid 14 shillings a week; good money. I bought all my motorbikes with the money I earned as a telegram boy.

'When I was about 14 or 15 I got a job at Roy Angel's garage. But that didn't last long as they went bust; then a few months later I was called up to the warden's office, along with Gerry Tilmouth and Robert Hampton. We were told that we needed to get work straight away and find alternative accommodation. I asked if we could be sent back to Alice Springs to our families, but the warden refused and repeated his demand that we "find work and go away".'

The trio found work in a well-established Port Adelaide-based business, Globe Timber Mills. Max became a storeman. The boys found lodging at a boarding house in Robin Road, close to St Francis House. They moved in on a Monday, spent the night there and next morning arose early for work.

'After the day's work we arrived back at the boarding house only to find all our belongings strewn on the front lawn and in the gutter on Robin Road. To our horror the owner said, "We don't want any black niggers here!"'

The boys had to find accommodation somewhere, so they returned to St Francis House, told the warden of their predicament and he agreed that they could stay until they found suitable alternative accommodation.

High achievers

'He agreed that we could stay, but at a price: for each of us he doubled the usual amount we had to pay for rent. I guess all these events built the anger in me.'

The boys were accommodated in the converted flats in what was once Captain Hart's coach house, at the rear of St Francis House. They stayed at the home for a few months until they found board with some people in Dale Street, Port Adelaide.

Max can't remember the name of the people who took them in, but he says they were 'lovely people' always willing to help them and to advise them in a caring and constructive way.

The Colebrook girls

'One day Matron approached me and said, "Millie, you can do a lot better in life than cleaning and washing." So I became a nurse.' – Millie Glen

Colebrook Home was an impressive two-storey building situated on the lower slopes of the Adelaide Hills, on land fronting Shepherds Hill Road, Eden Hills.

The home housed young Aboriginal girls who were brought from cattle stations in the state's far north, where their parents sometimes lived and worked. They hailed from a diverse range of language groups including the Arrernte, Arabana, Antakarinia and Pitjantjatjara. As with the boys from St Francis some of the girls at Colebrook Home were placed there by their parents so they could receive a better standard of education in the city, while others were forcibly removed from their families under the federal government's 'assimilation' policy. These children were part of the horrendous reality we now all recognise as the Stolen Generations.

There was also an impetus by missionaries, even by good and well-meaning men of the cloth such as Father Smith, to remove children for a 'religious' upbringing. Colebrook Home was established by the United Aborigines' Mission (UAM). It opened in 1924 and was initially called the Oodnadatta Children's Home, under the supervision of missionary Annie Lock. Partly due to problems with a consistent supply of good water, the home

The Colebrook girls

was moved to Quorn in 1927 where it was renamed Colebrook Children's Home, named after T.E. Colebrook, the first president of the UAM. The home was relocated to Eden Hills in 1944.

Under the care of two women, Matron Ruby Hyde and Sister Delia Rutter, the home flourished, gaining a good reputation for care and discipline for the children living there.

In 1952 Hyde and Rutter retired in the wake of much political turmoil with the UAM. Colebrook Home was closed in 1981; the impressive old home on the site was demolished and replaced by a 'return to nature', the Colebrook-Blackwood Reconciliation Park, opened by former residents. In front of where Colebrook Home once stood is a group of bronze carvings, one the poignant *Grieving Mother* sculpture. Colebrook Home's heyday seemed to coincide with St Francis House and every month or so a group of Colebrook girls would travel across town to meet up with the boys at St Francis.

All the boys were keen to see the girls, although the older boys weren't so interested in the girls buying them an ice cream or baking them a cake as was the case with the younger fellows. Those older boys wanted a date with one of the girls; perhaps take her to the pictures or for a ride on the back of his motorbike to the Semaphore Beach sand hills. Among the regular visitors, especially in the summer months, were Lowitja O'Donoghue, Faith Coulthard, Millie Glen, Grace Lester, Mona Paul, Rose Foster (Jim Foster's sister) and the four Brumby sisters, Aileen, Murial, Rose and Nancy. 'These girls weren't much older than the younger boys,' Vince Copley observes, 'but we looked upon them as older sisters, almost surrogate mothers. We found that if something was worrying us we wouldn't go to the priest, we would confide in one of the Colebrook girls.'

The Boys from St Francis

A number of the Colebrook girls became prominent figures in Australian society. Lowitja O'Donoghue became a key Aboriginal advocate and leading public servant. In addition to her outstanding public service, Lowitja was a wonderful role model for Australian nurses.

Born on 1 August 1932 in the remote Aboriginal community of Indulkana, Lowitja (born Lois) was the fifth of six children to Tom and Lily O'Donoghue. Tom O'Donoghue was a stockman of Irish descent and Lily was a member of the Yankunytjatjara nation of north-west South Australia. Initially the O'Donoghues lived at Everard Park, near Adelaide, where they had two children. They then moved to Granite Downs, a large cattle property east of the Stuart Highway in the far north of South Australia. Concerned for the welfare of their children and educational opportunities in particular, Lowitja's parents took all of the children to the Baptist Church-managed UAM in Oodnadatta. From here Lowitja was moved to the Colebrook Children's Home in Quorn. Lowitja was happy at Colebrook, where she received a good education in the home itself and at Quorn Primary School. The girls at the home experienced little discrimination during their time in Quorn. Indeed, the community actively encouraged children from the home to participate in local events and held busy bees to help maintain the home.

In 1944 fate changed the future of Colebrook. The children were brought to Adelaide for a holiday, since Quorn was in the middle of a drought and water was scarce. Although Adelaide was the acknowledged driest capital in Australia, the driest continent on earth, the city had a reasonable supply of fresh water and water became the catalyst for Ruby Hyde to look for an alternative site. Lowitja loved the new home they found at Eden Hills. She attended Unley High School and passed her intermediate certificate and studied right up to leaving certificate standard, but did not sit the examination.

At Colebrook Home the older children looked after the young ones. At 16, Lowitja, who also loved seeing the youngsters at St Francis House, got her first job as a nanny looking after six children. She worked for this family at Victor Harbor, 100 km south of Adelaide. Lowitja must have made some impression for while attending a Baptist Church service she was persuaded by the matron of the South Coast District Hospital to pursue a career in nursing. From 1950 to 1953, Lowitja worked as a nursing aide at Victor Harbor Hospital. However, there was no comprehensive training course for nurses at the hospital and, with strong support and encouragement from the matron, Lowitja decided to train at the Royal Adelaide Hospital.

There had been a long-standing policy at the RAH to take only nursing students who had obtained their leaving certificate, so initially the hospital would not countenance accepting her application. Fortunately for Lowitja the RAH introduced a more flexible scheme allowing deserving students to be admitted to the training course without the necessary educational qualification. In 1954 she was among the first intake of students without a leaving certificate to train as a nurse at the RAH. She qualified and worked at the Royal Adelaide until 1961, becoming the first Aboriginal nurse in South Australia.

A year later, though, Lowitja changed jobs to work as an Aboriginal liaison officer with the Education Department of South Australia. She then moved to the South Australian Department of Aboriginal Affairs as a welfare officer, based at Coober Pedy.

The Boys from St Francis

In 1967 Lowitja joined the Commonwealth Public Service as a junior administrative officer in the Adelaide office of the newly formed Department of Aboriginal Affairs. After eight years in that post she became the department director, responsible for the implementation of Aboriginal policy nationwide. Various administrative roles led to her state government appointment as chair of the Aboriginal Development Commission. In 1979, she married a medical orderly called Gordon Smart, whom she first met at the Repatriation Hospital in 1964.

In 1991, she, Alf Bamblett and Steve Gordon became the first Aboriginal people to attend a federal cabinet meeting. Lowitja used this occasion to put the position of the Aboriginal and Torres Strait Islander Commission (ATSIC) forward with regard to the government's response to the royal commission into Aboriginal deaths in custody. In 1992 she became the first Aboriginal Australian to address the United Nations General Assembly during the United Nations International Year of Indigenous People.

When Lowitja retired she added the name Lowitja to her existing legal name, Lois O'Donoghue Smart, to emphasise her Luritjan heritage. After the publication of the *Bringing Them Home* report in 1997, she said she preferred the word 'removed' over the word 'stolen' for her personal situation, because when she was taken to Colebrook Home her mother was not informed of the move. It was 33 years before they were reunited.

Australian of the Year in 1983, as well as the recipient of an OBE, AC and various other honours, Lowitja O'Donoghue did Colebrook Home proud and, by association, so too St Francis House.

As with most of the girls from Colebrook Home, Millie Glen

The Colebrook girls

Millie Glen on her return to Rainbow Town, pictured with Albert Namatjira, c. 1949.

has a long and interesting story to tell. She doesn't know much about her mother, only that at the age of two ('according to Aunty Liza, Brian Butler's aunty') she was brought from Rainbow Town (at the Gap in Alice Springs) to the Bungalow.

'There I was treated well,' Millie recalls. 'It was run by a Mr and Mrs McCoy. While I don't know much about my mother, I do know that my father was Fred Raggatt. My mother was working as a domestic at Glen Helen Station. I was the product of that liaison. Very early on I was taken to Rainbow Town and there I remained until being relocated at the Bungalow.'

The Boys from St Francis

Millie's father, Fred Raggat, died at Strathalbyn on 28 August 1946. He hailed from England and was the second owner of Glen Helen Station, the vast cattle run near Alice Springs. He was a hard man living in a harsh and unforgiving environment, however, he smiled on the environment, ensuring that a large plot of land on the station became a nature reserve, allowing the bush to grow unmolested by introduced fauna and encouraging indigenous animals to flourish.

Port Elliot's newspaper at that time, the *Southern Argus*, carried this obituary on Thursday, 5 September 1946:

> The death of Mr Fred Raggatt, at Strathalbyn on Wednesday evening of last week, removed a widely-known far northern personality. He was 86 years of age and came to Australia in 1870 with his brother and settled at Wilmington (Beautiful Valley). After a short stay there he took up cattle droving, and his first big trek was for the late Judge Gordon, taking a mob overland to Queensland (Brisbane). He continued in the droving business for some years, then returned to Alice Springs, when that township was surveyed, and he purchased the first block of land, on which he erected a store, a big interest in which is still retained. Later on he purchased Boss Springs Station, which he afterwards disposed of to take over Glen Helen Station where he bred horses and cattle. He was also one of the first to take sheep to the far north, this being done after one of the disastrous droughts, sheep recovering more quickly than horses and cattle. Apart from two trips to England, he spent the whole of his life in the interior, and he told some most interesting stories of the north. A year or two ago he came south and for about 12 months has been

The Colebrook girls

living with his cousin, Miss Hannah Raggatt. He was married 46 years ago, but was left soon after with a daughter, now Mrs F.T. Clements of Semaphore. The funeral was conducted in the Strathalbyn cemetery on Friday last, Pastor Stow officiating at the graveside.

Millie was among the many hundreds of Indigenous Australians who were evacuated in the wake of the Japanese bombing of Darwin. Along with the likes of John Moriarty, Jim Foster, Wally McArthur and many more, Millie was taken by truck, then train, to faraway Mulgoa, situated at the foot of the Blue Mountains in New South Wales. She attended Mulgoa Primary School, but never got the chance to start her secondary education. At the age of 14, she began working at Ashford Hospital, run by an English woman who became her guardian and mentor.

'One day Matron approached me and said, "Millie, you can do a lot better in life than cleaning and washing." So I became a nurse.'

Rose Foster, who was also part of the Stolen Generations and was evacuated to Mulgoa along with her brother, Jim, and Millie, was a life-long friend.

'During holidays we used to visit the boys at St Francis House, but Rose and I were destined to do good works elsewhere. We loved nursing and when we qualified we went back to Sydney and took up positions at Richmond Hospital, near Penrith, New South Wales.' She also met Dr Charles Duguid. 'Oh, what a brogue he had; the possession of as broad a Scottish accent as you would ever likely hear. Soon after we arrived at Richmond Hospital, Dr Duguid opened a girls' hostel in Millswood, Adelaide, and he

The Boys from St Francis

Rose Foster, c. 1960. Photo courtesy Jim Foster.

asked me to help run it. The hostel housed some 15 girls. They attended Unley High School where they developed a sense of identity, but we never knew the actual day we were born.'

Millie Glen's ambition was to complete her nursing studies and become a midwife with Rose Foster. However, Dr Duguid wanted Millie to stay on at the girls' hostel in Millswood. So she did. Meanwhile, Rose completed her midwifery course at Queen Victoria Hospital.

After spending seven years at the Millswood hostel, Millie and Rose travelled throughout Australia.

'While Rose always worked in nursing, I diversified once in Perth, looking after two little boys, children of a couple who were both doctors. And I even tried my hand as a cook. Soon after my cooking experience I became a cook at St Francis House. There

The Colebrook girls

I met up with Aileen Cooper. The boys were always coming into the kitchen pleading for me to give them some bread. They were so sweet; they had me wrapped round their little fingers. A few of us ladies were like surrogate mothers to the boys, especially the younger ones, and we'd listen to their concerns and take them on outings, to the Alice over Christmas and occasionally a weekend trip to the Adelaide Hills.'

Most of the St Francis boys who came from Alice Springs would spend their Christmas holidays there, however the older boys who came to the home from Mulgoa spent their holidays on the river, at Barmera or Berri. Vince explains that the Mulgoa boys left their mothers when they were toddlers. They didn't know whether their mothers were dead or alive, let alone how to contact them. The infamous Mal Bald used to take the boys to the river in his old, battered truck.

Millie and Vince vividly recall the earthquake that hit early in the morning of 1 March 1954. It was the worst earthquake in South Australia's history and the second worst in Australia.

'Nearly tipped me out of bed,' Vince recalls.

No one was killed by the earthquake, which registered 5.25 on the Richter scale, but it caused widespread structural damage to buildings around Adelaide. Many houses were cracked and heavy pieces of masonry fell from parapets and tall buildings in the city. The tremors went on for five or six minutes. St Francis House escaped any major damage, perhaps due to its sandy foundation and solid stone construction. One odd happening was the Mount Barker Creek, which had been bone dry for months, suddenly started to gush water, flowing at 25,000 gallons an hour.

On 18 May the same year a huge storm blew away a section of

The Boys from St Francis

Mrs Evans (right) with Jingle Almond in front of the south side of St Francis House, c. 1948.

the Semaphore jetty and destroyed the miniature railway track. It smashed jetties along the coast from Outer Harbor to Glenelg leaving a trail of destruction in its wake. Some of the roads along the beach were so badly undermined by the surging waves that road closures became the norm for months to come. At St Francis House the storm brought down two large pine trees, one of them the tree where Vince had watched the goings on in the tower years earlier. Such was the velocity of the wind that it caused the heavy slate tiles on the roof of the main building to fly off and crash to the cobbled courtyard below. One of the

The Colebrook girls

cooks at St Francis House, Mrs Evans, wasn't deterred by the hail of heavy slate tiles when she rushed from the kitchen in the main house to her room in the renovated unit at the rear of the property, because she wore her tin helmet, courtesy of the British government during the early years of World War II. Mrs Evans survived the nightly waves of Luftwaffe bombers during the Blitz, thanks to her stoic nature, a big dollop of luck and, of course, her tin helmet.

Millie Glen smiles when she hears Vince talk of Mrs Evans and her tin helmet, for Mrs Evans was also a good cook and she taught the others to make raspberry and plum jam and good old English-style marmalade. Millie confesses that she couldn't resist making little treats for the boys.

'Although it was frowned upon by the warden, I used to make some sneaky scones,' she laughs.

Many of the Colebrook girls became nurses, including Faith Thomas. She made her name, however, as our first female test cricketer.

Faith

'Matron stood us outside in the corridor and told us to get back to Alice Springs and "nurse your own people". I thought then that I would not let my friends fight this battle alone. It sounds like a goodie. I'll chuck my commercial art job and go with this mob.' – Faith Thomas

St Francis House produced many top-flight sportsmen, but none of them played cricket for their state or country. The girls from Colebrook Home also excelled at sport, and one girl – Faith Thomas – became Australia's first Aboriginal female test cricketer.

Women's cricket began in Australia in the 1920s, and in the 1934/1935 summer a visiting English women's team played a Queensland eleven that included two Aboriginal women – Mabel Campbell and Edna Crouch.

Edna's niece Thelma Crouch became a prominent player and represented Australia in the junior cricket team against England in 1949. There were some early gains in women's cricket for Aboriginal people, but only one made the big time: Faith Thomas (nee Coulthard). Faith said the kids at Colebrook in Quorn never thought of playing cricket, but they did enjoy a game which was 'a bit like a cross between cricket and rounders. We had a stick for a bat and we threw stones at the girl holding the stick.'

They also had fun, as a lot of children did in the 1940s and 1950s, chucking stones at the lights atop electricity poles. The kids with the fastest, most accurate throws could easily

Faith

knock out a street light. And what fun it was for the successful thrower; the light bulb exploding before their very eyes. More importantly the games with the sticks and stones helped them hone extraordinary hand–eye coordination. When the girls moved to the new Colebrook home at Eden Hills they played the same crude form of cricket, but the equipment was far better: a proper bat replaced the stick and an old ball, often a tennis ball, came in place of a stone. However, stones weren't cast aside altogether for there was a daily battle between a handful of combatants. Their game was simple. One kid threw a stone at another kid who protected herself with a sheet of corrugated iron.

Faith was born at Nepabunna Mission in the Flinders Ranges of South Australia. The daughter of an Adnyamathanha woman, Faith was taken as a babe in arms to the Colebrook Home in Quorn.

'Mum did not abandon me. There was no support for her at that time. A single woman, Mum had just given birth and her only way of earning a living was working in hotel kitchens. Mum reckoned a pub kitchen was not the sort of place for a baby, so she turned to Colebrook. You know, the first time I met my father was in 2000 in the Ceduna Nursing Home. Dad had just celebrated his 100th birthday,' Faith says.

Life after the European invasion in 1788 has, right up until recent times, been hell on earth for many Aboriginal women, often used as sexual chattels. Secret liaisons between white bosses and Aboriginal servant girls were commonplace. Faith doesn't deny her heritage. She is proud of it, and is in no way angry or resentful toward the white man, despite hardship through the years.

How did Faith track her father down?

'Persistence,' she says joyfully.

Faith enjoys a laugh and is unafraid to laugh at herself. Her mother kept in contact with her through the years and Faith has never considered herself to be a 'stolen child'.

'Colebrook Home was a real home away from home for me. Mum took me there because she knew that I would be well cared for and have lots of children about me. The people I grew up with at Colebrook were (and still are) my extended family.'

She says that as a 'kid growing up in Quorn we did not know we were any different. It wasn't until we went to live in Adelaide and the Education Department refused to let us attend schools that we realised we were different and would be treated differently to non-Aboriginal kids.

'But we overcame that and those barriers were broken down. Discrimination really hit home when a couple of the Colebrook Home girls wanted to go nursing.' Another Colebrook girl had studied nursing interstate. 'We always wanted to know why she trained at Bethesda Hospital in Melbourne. It was because she was refused by all the hospitals in South Australia because she was Aboriginal.

'Round 1950 Lois O'Donohue had found a job as a nursing aide in Victor Harbor. However, four other Colebrook kids also wanted to pursue a nursing career.

'At the time I was working in Lush Studios and I thought at lunchtime I would go along with them and support them at the interview. I had no intention of becoming a nurse, but I went with the girls to see this old matron at the Royal Adelaide Hospital, who didn't even invite us in to her office.

Faith

'We were told the correct procedure by Nellie ... to bow and scrape, stand with our hands behind our backs and say "Yes, Matron" this and "Yes, Matron" that. Matron stood us outside in the corridor and told us to get back to Alice Springs and "nurse your own people". I thought then that I would not let my friends fight this battle alone. It sounds like a goodie. I'll chuck my commercial art job and go with this mob. We went straight to see the Protector of Aborigines and Dr Charles Duguid, a Scottish-born medical practitioner and Aboriginal rights activist.

'They had a meeting at the Adelaide Town Hall which was well attended and included many old sisters. They told us if we girls wanted to go nursing to go and start in country hospitals and two years later to transfer and the matron would be unable to knock us back.'

Dr Duguid's interest in Aboriginal rights was sparked by an incident near the Coniston cattle station in the Northern Territory. In August 1928, dingo hunter Frederick Brooks was killed by Aboriginal people at a remote place known as Yukurru or Brooks Soak. The murder sparked a savage response from cattle-station owners and police. Official records state that 31 Aboriginals were shot and killed in the police search for murder suspects between 14 August and 18 October 1928. However, as is usual for records concerning the First Australians, the number of people killed was more like 170, mainly Warlpiri, Anmatyerre and Kaytetye. The massacre is the last-known officially sanctioned killing of Indigenous Australians.

In 1935 (and later between 1951 and 1961) Dr Duguid became president of the Aborigines Advancement League. Dr Duguid also, in 1937, helped found Ernabella Mission in the Musgrave

The Boys from St Francis

Ranges of South Australia. Having Dr Duguid on side was a comfort to the Aboriginal girls who wanted equal rights in their quest to pursue a nursing career.

Fate took Faith by the hand one night at the Royal Adelaide Hospital where she was on duty as a night duty nurse. Fay Beckworth had just finished her shift and sighed relief at Faith's appearance saying that she now had to get to cricket practice. Somehow all those days mucking about with bat and ball came to the fore in Faith's mind. The game of cricket appealed to her and she told Fay that she was interested in the game. Fay immediately invited Faith to practice, explaining that they were keen, but lacked players.

'That was the beginning. We practised in the north Parklands during the week and I was picked in the team for the following Saturday. And there I stayed. At Colebrook the game we played with sticks and stones was sort of rough-hewn cricket and it fired my interest. But it was only when Fay mentioned training that I showed my hand.'

'My new training ground was in the north Parklands. There were lots of large gum trees and dozens of grazing cows. Nevertheless it was an oval. We had to shoo the cows away from the joint and get out there with a shovel to get rid of the dung off the pitch before we started applying ant powder where the stumps were pitched at each end. There were always great ant nests thriving.'

Faith bowled in the manner of Jeff Thomson; a few shuffles in and then let fly. She had watched people in Blackwood play cricket and copied their bowling styles. Faith insists that as kids they bowled and didn't throw when they played their impromptu games of cricket.

Faith

There was no television in those days, no means to study and copy. You had to really know yourself and perhaps the times helped people develop their individuality more fully and more rapidly than they might expect to today.

Faith got a hat-trick for Windsor in her second match, taking 3/4 to help Windsor dismiss Olds for 28. In reply Windsor finished with 5/180, state vice-captain Aileen Daley scoring 80. That same year Faith took 6/0 to demoralise the Adelaide Teachers' College team.

Vic Richardson, the ex-South Australian and test captain, was unimpressed with the few shuffling paces in her approach. Faith got no formal coaching, but Vic suggested to her that she add a few paces.

'He said, "Faith, you need to take a run and point your feet where the ball's going or you'll rip your cartilage to pieces. You need more balance."'

Faith accepted Vic's advice and added six paces to her approach.

She found the new run-up far more energetic and she was able to better utilise her body at delivery, instead of relying almost exclusively on shoulder power. Faith also loved, like all fast bowlers, to knock down the stumps.

'No one ever told me about the subtle things like swinging away for catches in the slips. I always tried to bowl them out. They encouraged me to bowl to the slips but no one explained the positions on the ground. They'd say, "go to cover" and I'd stand there and where they pointed I went. There was no sitting down, talking about tactics and things like that, or when bowling to slips saying "this is where we want you to put the ball". If they said they'd set a field and wanted me to bowl to it, it didn't mean a thing to me.'

The Boys from St Francis

The extraordinary upshot of all this is that when Faith Thomas played for Windsor, then South Australia and then Australia she did not know all of the fielding positions.

'They had it all worked out, but no one ever told me. I only began to get the idea of all the field placings years later when watching the big cricket on the television.'

Faith was born on 22 February 1933, round the time Harold Larwood was taking his Bodyline attack to the likes of Vic Richardson and Don Bradman. Educated at Quorn Primary School and later, when the children moved to Eden Hills, Unley Girls' Technical School, Faith passed her leaving certificate in 1950 and began her working life as a commercial artist with Lush Studios. But art would soon be left in the wake of her nursing career.

Faith trained at the Soldiers' Memorial Hospital in Murray Bridge. She nursed at Queen Victoria Hospital from 1954 to 1956, and completed her midwifery training at Queen Victoria Hospital in 1958. This was the time of her best years in cricket. In the summer of 1956/1957, Faith scored 28 for South Australia against the visiting New Zealanders, then took a remarkable 9/15. Just before her test selection, a little item appeared in the *Eden News*, a local newspaper that covered events in Eden Hills, on 1 February 1957.

> A credit to Colebrook is Sister Faith Coulthard, who has not only succeeded in her chosen career of nursing, but has also made good on the cricket ground, being under consideration for the all-Australian team. This popular lass will be remembered by many Edenites.

Three of the South Australian players in 1957/1958 had medical backgrounds: Ruth Dow was a qualified medical doctor,

Faith

Barbara Orchard was studying medicine and Faith was nursing. That summer the national championships were held in Adelaide. New Zealand also took part, with South Australia the only undefeated side.

In January 1958, delegates from England, Holland, South Africa, New Zealand and Australia met in Melbourne to form the International Women's Cricket Council. Faith was selected for the test series and on the train to Brisbane she recalls having to lie in the pack-rack to get some sleep. At the famous Gabba, Faith's spirit soared for there were three Aboriginal men clapping her every move.

'I literally played for those three old fellows,' she recalls.

How they cheered when Faith clean bowled the England captain, Mary Duggan, with a searing yorker that sent her leg stump flying. The stump actually flew high over the wicketkeeper's head, the only time Faith has ever seen a stump do that. The Australian captain was Joyce Christ and when Mary Duggan saw the name 'J. Christ' on the scoreboard she exclaimed:

'How in the hell are we supposed to win ... look at that on the scoreboard!'

Faith played two test matches against England and was made 12th man in the match at Adelaide. She played at the Gabba in Brisbane and in Melbourne, the test in Sydney being washed out. Adelaide Oval was the venue for the fourth test and it was just half an hour or so before the first ball was bowled that Faith was told that she was to be 12th man. Bitterly disappointed, Faith was even more saddened because all her family had travelled from the far north of South Australia to watch her bowl in a test match. She was more than a bit peeved about having to carry the drinks instead, so she decided upon a plan of non-cooperation. She would spill the drinks, 'accidentally-on-purpose'.

'I was determined to make an impact. I walked onto the Adelaide Oval carrying the drinks in a low-sided wooden tray. Halfway to the wicket, I tripped and fell headlong over a blade of grass.' Faith throws her head back and laughs. 'And every time I walked on to that field in that match I fell over that same blessed blade of grass. On each occasion my "fall" caused every drink to spill; there was not a drop to be had. But I managed to hang on to the salt shaker. Ruth Dow used to get us to take a handful of salt instead of salt tablets, but there was nothing to wash it down.'

Faith stops talking. After a long pause, she begins to giggle again.

But she was destined to never again play for Australia, although spilling the drinks in Adelaide was not the reason her cricket career ended abruptly. Faith was offered a place in the test touring side to England and New Zealand in 1960.

She reluctantly withdrew from the selected side because she had completed nine months of a year-long midwifery course and did not wish to repeat the year. At least, that was how Faith rationalised withdrawing from the tour. In reality it was only one factor. 'To be perfectly honest I was afraid of the travel. We would go by ship, second-class cabin. I was afraid I would have been claustrophobic. I simply hate being closed in. There I was, a girl from the desert about to sail the ocean. It did not appeal to me at all. I'm sure Matron Carroll, my boss at the Queen Vic., would have made allowances for me if I had gone to England. Later the matron asked me why I did not go on the tour.'

When Faith was first selected for Australia, the press moved in like sharks in a feeding frenzy. They saw Faith as a 'novelty'

Faith

and were after every conceivable angle. Team management closed ranks and protected her.

'I'd run away every time I saw a reporter,' Faith says. 'We were referred to as "natives". It was "native nurse" this and "native nurse" that. This goes back to the days of being under the control of the Protector of Aborigines. We were natives, the protected Aborigines. At the time there was a song on the hit parade called "Freight Train, Freight Train Going So Fast"; well, the opposition used to try and put me off by singing it. Racist no doubt, a freight train being big and black.

'But it had the reverse affect. It resulted in things flying everywhere. I got my ire up a bit and bowled faster and more accurately that I thought I could. As far as the press were concerned the management told reporters that they were supposed to be reporting on the cricket, not "novelties".'

Faith believes that Aboriginal sportsmen and women do not experience the same ratio of racism as other Aboriginals in other walks of life because they can compete on the same level. 'I think a lot of Aboriginal people create their own little problems. They expect to get a game when they turn up but don't practice and they don't put in the dedication. Not that I did to any great extent, but then my employment stopped me from getting to training and that was more or less accepted in those days.'

Faith played good quality hockey and squash, too, and her sporting career brought her in contact with Vince Copley's great friend Doug Nicholls, football legend Fos Williams, and East Perth and Carlton footballer Syd Jackson.

Faith served as a nursing sister at Point McLeay Aboriginal Reserve (1957–1958); she was a welfare officer with the Department of Aboriginal Affairs (1958–1959); nursed at Alice

Springs Hospital (1959–1961) and worked as a medical patrol officer at Amata Aboriginal reserve in 1967.

She patrolled a huge area in the far north of South Australia from Amata, Indulkana and Oodnadatta to Wratinna Station, and Mimili. Her job also involved following groups on walkabout to provide medical care, plus the extra duties of distribution of child endowment, pension cheques and rations.

From 1967 Faith was a nursing sister at Point Pearce Aboriginal Reserve in charge of health and hygiene, with particular emphasis on maternal and child care. She also worked a couple of periods as a domiciliary nursing sister with the Family Planning Association.

In 1961 she married Bernard Thomas, the son of Alfred Thomas, a former conductor of the Birmingham Symphony Orchestra, and in 1963 they had a son, Stuart. Faith was always keen on music and was a foundation member of the Aboriginal Youth Orchestra, which later became the Centre for Aboriginal Studies in Music at Adelaide University. She played double bass and her son, Stuart, played clarinet.

Ever bright and sporting a happy smile, Faith was always a popular visitor to St Francis House.

'I'll never forget Faith turning up to see us on a number of occasions of a Saturday night,' Vince Copley recalls.

'In the summer months she invariably wore her white cricket attire, as she had come straight to the house from wherever she had played that day. We saw her at the home in her cricket gear, but never really went to watch her play.'

In 1997 Faith was awarded an Aboriginal and Torres Strait Islander Sports Lifetime Achievement Award. Faith said (in part) in accepting the award, 'back in those days of assimilation

Faith

there was no support of any kind. It was really lonely. The sporting fraternity had no idea how to communicate with an Aboriginal. I was treated as a curiosity. What do they call us? Black diamonds. We had to be hard as diamonds and learn to roll with the punches. We had to shine brighter than the rest to be accepted.'

The flag

'The colours of the Aboriginal flag have a specific symbolic meaning. Black represents the Aboriginal people, red represents the red earth and the spiritual relation to the land and yellow represents the sun, the giver of life.' – Harold Thomas

From the time he first held a pencil, Harold Thomas loved to draw. He was fascinated by all the wonders of nature; the glory of a spring sunrise to the harsh reality of a seeming never-ending drought. One of 13 children, Harold was born in Alice Springs 'in the mid or late 1940s'. Sadly his family did not all live under the same roof. He laments that 'we were removed as children at different stages.' At the age of seven he came to St Francis House, but my research into Harold's experience there ground to a sudden halt in Humpty Doo one humid March day in 2015.

The previous day I had been in Darwin, admiring the magnificent Adelaide River war memorial and the abandoned Pine Creek gold mine. The war memorial is beautifully maintained, a fitting memorial to the men and women who lost their lives during the heavy Japanese aerial bombardment of Darwin in World War II. At the site of Pine Creek's open cut mine, we peered down at a massive gorge filled with water. Long closed, the Enterprise Pit had been carefully filled with water to prevent the acidic build-up of dangerous toxins. The site was used in October 2014 for an episode of the UK television program *Top Gear*.

The flag

Trevor Woodhead, a good mate of Vince Copley, was driving me from Darwin to Katherine to interview two other St Francis House 'old boys', brothers George and Freddy Kruger. We had left Darwin's Central Hotel at 6 am before our brief stopovers along the Darwin–Katherine highway, proving an invaluable history lesson. After a little over three hours – and 316 km – we drove into Katherine. It was pleasantly warm. Trevor stopped at the police station.

We needed precise directions to locate George Kruger, a man I had met at a reunion of old boys from St Francis House in Adelaide two years earlier. From what I remembered George was tall and strong with a splendid moustache, the type you associate with an RAF Spitfire pilot. We arrived at George's front gate, but the yard was seemingly impenetrable, strands of barbed and razor wire fixed over old, rusty cyclone. An angry dog barked, the odd snarl the only change in his tone.

'Go inside and knock on the door,' I volunteered.

'No way,' Trevor laughed. 'Have you seen that dog?'

Maybe George was asleep. We considered chucking stones on the tin roof, but thought better of it and retreated into town. We made a few visits; the third time his son came to the gate. Happily we spoke through the wire.

Yes, George was taking a rest.

'Come back in an hour or so.'

We did.

Over coffee George gave us an insight into his life at St Francis House and his work with Professor Fred Hollows. Here was another St Francis House success story.

Later we tracked down George's brother Freddy Kruger in a caravan park. At 70 Freddy was still coaching youngsters in the gentle art of boxing. Apparently Aboriginal kids take to boxing readily. I think I know why this is so: throughout their growing years as children, well into adulthood, they have to dodge racist jabs and endure a never-ending stream of verbal and non-verbal taunts.

While I was happy with my talk to both brothers, I didn't realise why they were so difficult to find in Katherine. It turns out that there had been whispers about rednecks lurking in the area; even suggestions of clandestine meetings of an Australian version of the Ku Klux Klan in and about remote parts of Katherine. Maybe the whispers were just that, whispers. However, Aboriginal people know, as do all thinking people, where there is smoke there is usually fire. For my own part I found no evidence of the KKK in Katherine, although the wire and dog at George Kruger's house might be testimony to something untoward.

On the drive out, Trevor stopped at a delightful little waterhole on the outskirts of Katherine. There was a bunch of happy children splashing in the warm water. The place was idyllic, warm; the leaves of the gum trees on the banks of the river waved rhythmically, as if in tune with nature itself.

'I guess there's no crocs about?'

The big bloke smiled: 'This river is teeming with crocodiles.'

According to a particular aspect of Aboriginal Dreaming a crocodile carries the spirit of a dead person. Any crocodile attack is therefore directly related to 'payback;' or the traditional 'eye for an eye' justice delivered in the wake of some wrongdoing.

Trevor pointed to an embankment on the other side of the stream.

'That's a perfect spot for a crocodile to sit in the sun and

The flag

wait for the chance to slide into the water in the hunt for prey.'

Trevor knew his sport, having played cricket and rugby union as a schoolboy. His cricket journey spanned 30 summers. He served as the inaugural Indigenous director on the Northern Territory Cricket Board for 10 years, liaising with Vince Copley on the National Indigenous Cricket Advisory Committee to Cricket Australia to develop and implement the National Indigenous Cricket Strategy. One day Trevor had the chance to take ex-South Australian and test fast bowler Jason Gillespie, Australia's first male Indigenous international cricketer, on a fishing trip. Since the shooting of crocodiles was banned, their numbers have multiplied at an alarming rate and nowadays all the creeks and streams within the Darwin and Katherine area are crawling with these huge reptiles.

'It was a few years ago now,' Trevor recalled. 'We set out in a long narrow boat and Dizzy loved being up the front, looking for all the world like a famous ship captain taking the long boat to shore. We stopped at the foot of a wide, sandy steep embankment. Jason looked out, but not up. When I alerted him to what was at the crest of the slope, he jumped backwards. There above us was an enormous salt water croc, sunning itself, with both eyes glued on the juicy fare below.'

Afternoon tea at the waterhole was perfect and again I learnt more about the Top End environment; how danger walked hand in hand with the stunning beauty of the bush. I couldn't help thinking how pristine Australia must have been before the white man came with their weapons, their grog and their greed.

We soon left the children happily splashing together in the crocodile-infested stream and set out for Darwin. I instinctively knew Harold Thomas would prove difficult to track down for an interview. It turned out that the Krugers were nothing compared to Harold.

I rang Harold when I arrived in Darwin. We had a short telephone conversation, then he agreed that he would drive from Humpty Doo to Darwin and meet me at the Central Hotel at the specified time of 2 pm.

But Harold didn't show.

I made dozens of phone calls to his home in Humpty Doo but didn't get through. I was in the Qantas lounge at Darwin Airport when I thought I'd try a last time. A woman answered the phone.

'Just a minute.'

Harold was apologetic.

'Ashley, sorry about not meeting you. I had a re-think. Frankly I didn't have a good experience at St Francis House. There are many bad memories. I don't wish to talk about it.'

I respect that, though Harold did spend a few years at St Francis House. I thought it would be better if he could have told me his experience in his own words, rather than finding his story told in snippets of information from others. There is of course plenty of material in the public domain about Harold Thomas, the artist, too.

A Luritja man from central Australia, Harold is an acclaimed artist, specialising in oils, watercolours and acrylics. He is very much his own man and hasn't followed the modern tradition of Aboriginal art, but he demonstrates through his images a connection to the land through what can only be described as poetic vision.

And Harold Thomas created the Aboriginal flag.

One of South Australia's best footballers was Sonny Morey. Sonny spent three years at St Francis House from 1957. He knew

The flag

Harold Thomas and was a member of the Ethelton Primary School soccer team that Harold captained in 1959. Sonny says Harold Thomas was forever sketching on bits of paper.

After Harold Thomas read a copy of the first print of *The Boys from St Francis* I received a telephone call from him. Sitting by his easel in Humpty Doo he said: 'I've just read the book and I loved it. I read it out to my wife and she loved it.'

He had decided he wanted to tell his story, and he talked enthusiastically about how his art began.

'At St Francis House one of the boys (Gerry Tilmouth) was studying to become a sign writer. I used to watch how he drew and managed to get some idea of colour and the illusion of colour. Gerry really inspired me to draw. I drew on scraps of paper, bits of cardboard, whatever. The concept of the Aboriginal flag came later, much later, but it all began at St Francis.

'Some of the boys at St Francis used to play table tennis. There was no rubber on the face of the bats, but on one particular bat was drawn the face of Father Christmas. Jamie (Jim) Bray was the artist and this magnificent drawing further inspired me.

'When I was about 12 or 13 the warden called me to his office. "Now, Harold, I want you to meet Reverend Donald Wallace and Mrs Wallace. They are going to be your foster parents."'

The warden gave him sixpence for a bus fare to the city to meet the Wallaces.

'"Get off at the corner of East Terrace and North Terrace where your new family will meet you. Make sure you behave yourself."

'I got off the bus and there was no one to be seen. After a few minutes a man appeared from behind a bush and asked: "Is that you, Harold?"'

Harold found his foster parents to be kind and caring, and they encouraged him to pursue his dream in art classes at Willunga High School and later at the South Australian School of Art.

Harold's early art included illustrating stories of World War II prisoners of war and a variety of other poignant topics. For a time he studied under the watchful eye of renowned New South Wales-based artist Reg Campbell.

'Reg taught me how to do watercolour. At school a rather eccentric teacher, Remus Degallous, advised me to paint under the Russian name Dowsky, as Harold Thomas, he said, was "too Anglo".'

After his time at St Francis House Harold won a scholarship to study at the South Australian School of Art. At art school Harold found his niche. While he is clearly pained by his experience at St Francis House, Harold loved his time at art school.

After graduating with honours in 1969 and armed with his diploma of fine arts, Harold applied for a job at the South Australian Museum, becoming the first Aboriginal to be employed in a museum in Australia. The South Australian Museum possessed the largest collection of Aboriginal art and artefacts in the world and Harold, with free access to these cultural treasures, was in his element. It was here that he first began to get a sense of the power of his people's culture and how it begged to be expressed in some way.

He embraced the history of art and created a list of famous artists who had influenced him the most: Caravaggio, Goya, Delacroix and Turner. Turner captured for eternity some of the most magnificent skies at Margate in the United Kingdom; sunsets to behold, sunsets of the gods. Interestingly, the seaside town of Largs Bay, a couple of miles from St Francis House, was once listed to be called Margate. The idea was axed when Governor Hindmarsh decreed that the suburb be named in

The flag

honour of one of the colony commissioners, Sir John George Shaw-Lefevre, and the largest and deepest waters in the British Isles, Largs, on the Firth of Clyde.

Just as the Scots knew every inch of the Firth of Clyde, the boys from St Francis knew every minute detail of the seafront from Semaphore to Outer Harbor, including Largs Bay. Drawing the sea, the sand and wildlife became a daily habit for Harold Thomas while he was at St Francis House.

Harold set out to design the Aboriginal flag during the land rights movement of the early 1970s. No one could have imagined how much of an impact it would have on all Australians. The strength of the colours and the message it conveyed made the flag the success it is today. Harold has said that he never needed 'to promote the flag, or flog it. It just carried itself from person to person.'

There is a strong, symbolic meaning to the flag. Black represents the Aboriginal people, red represents the red earth and the special Indigenous spiritual relationship to the land and yellow represents the sun, 'the giver of life'.

In 2001 I was coach to a group of Aboriginal cricketers who flew to England to play 10 matches. It was a part re-enactment of the first Aboriginal cricket tour to England in 1868, Australia's first international sports tour abroad. During the 1868 tour King Cole, or Bripumyarrimin, fell sick with a heavy chest cold. His last match was against MCC at Lord's on 12 and 13 June, in which he wasn't called to bowl and was dismissed for seven. The summer of 1868 was hot. Hay fever abounded, so too chest complaints. However, King Cole's illness was anything but minor. The great worry in those times was for a chest cold to worsen.

He developed a combination of tuberculosis and pneumonia and died in Guy's Hospital, London, on 24 June 1868.

The Boys from St Francis

It was arranged that my 2001 team would visit the cemetery where King Cole was interred. Team manager Grant Sarra said, in part: 'Sadly King Cole played only seven matches. But he played at Lord's and he experienced the joy of being treated as an equal in England: a courtesy he was never afforded in his home country. This makes today especially poignant for the 2001 team. This ceremony represents a culturally important and spiritually significant occasion. Sharing, caring and respect is paramount for people and the environment. In traditional society Aboriginal people believed – and we still do believe – that the land is our mother. We come from the land and we go back to the land. Through our birth we have a very special and unique place and will always remain connected to the land we call Australia. The Aboriginal belief is that the land and all things are part of a vast network of relationships – created by the great ancestral beings of the Dreaming. They created the rivers, the streams, the plants of the landscape and the animals and we, the people. Before settling back into the land, the great ancestral being laid down the laws for our people to live by. The land is our mother.'

King Cole lies somewhere in Meath Gardens (known as Victoria Park cemetery at the time of King Cole's death). The exact location of his grave is unknown. During the great cholera epidemic of 1866 as many as 800 bodies were buried on any given day at the cemetery. They are buried at varying heights and it would be impossible to identify King Cole without taking DNA samples of the half million bodies buried there.

The Aboriginal elders who accompanied the 2001 team brought ochre (the mother) to England. The ochre was lovingly crushed to fine powder by members of the 2001 team, and ATSIC field officer John Tatten sprinkled the powder on the plot of land

The flag

thought to be where King Cole lay. Grant Sarra said: 'As a sign of respect today we bring part of the mother's spirit to lie with the spirit of her child – King Cole.'

Imagine the scene when young Harold Thomas sat down to create his masterpiece. Before him is a blank sheet of paper. He wanted to highlight the three colours he had chosen. Black is the colour of his skin. During the 1960s and 1970s there was American pride among the blacks who were still fighting for equality. Black, to Harold Thomas, was not just skin colour. Harold's black on the Aboriginal flag was as much to do with pride of being black in Australia than anything else. His take on the black was a political inclusion rather than a spiritual, Aboriginal concept.

'At that time in the late 1960s, early 1970s, black pride represented being black in Australia,' he said.

A year after the 2001 England tour I was in London where a hard-copy version of my book on the 1868 tour was published. *The Black Lords of Summer*, published by University of Queensland Press, was the Australian title, but it got a different tag in the UK, *Lords Dreaming*. Independent publisher Ernest Hecht (Souvenir Press) said frankly: 'We can't have the word "black" in the title. Mention the word black in London and you are in for a contest. Elsewhere also. Ask for a short black in New York and you'd get a bunch of fives.'

Harold Thomas's choice of colours for the flag is simply magnificent for it conveys a powerful message, a unifying symbol of struggle, spirituality and love. His design has an immediate and lasting impact.

The flag was first flown at Victoria Square on National Aborigines Day, 12 July 1971. (Nowadays National Aborigines Day is known by another name, NAIDOC Week.) However, the flag was not recognised by the federal government as the official flag of the Aboriginal people until 1995. This national recognition was precipitated by Cathy Freeman's actions at the 1994 Commonwealth Games in Canada. After winning the 200-m and 400-m finals, Cathy draped herself in both the Australian and Aboriginal flags during a lap of honour in both events. The images were beamed throughout the world and became the catalyst for official Australian recognition.

To gain this status the government needed to proclaim the flag under the Flags Act. At this time Harold's design became public property, but Harold wanted to reclaim the flag's copyright. He took his grievance to court.

It was something of a landmark case, for Harold found 'people coming out of the blue to say that it was their design'.

'I wanted to prove that I was the creator of the Aboriginal flag.'

After a seeming interminable time fighting for his rights, Harold won his case. In 1997 the Federal Court of Australia officially recognised Harold Thomas as creator of the flag.

The court battle probably steeled Harold against all outsiders. His world is one of recluse. He loves to paint and exhibit his works, but few people know where to find him. He has also been shortlisted for the annual David Unaipon Award for unpublished works by an Aboriginal or Torres Strait Islander.

Harold has said the journey for Indigenous Australians continues. 'Today you can be a doctor or a lawyer, but you also need to maintain your identity. You have to bring your mob with you. Too many people forget who they are.'

Today, Harold's pseudonym of 'Dowsky' is long forgotten. He paints under his real name and his work sells on a global scale, commanding good prices.

He is something of a legend in the art world.

Their hero

'Wally was showing her off, but really he sought our approval. We loved him because he was so honest. He cared for us. He was our protector, our dear brother and our hero.' – Vince Copley

More than 170 years before the boys arrived at St Francis House, Thomas Jefferson addressed congress and uttered the now-famous line, 'that all men are created equal, that they are endowed by their Creator with certain unalienable rights'.

That quote came on 4 July 1776, Independence Day, 12 years before Captain John Hunter sailed HMS *Sirius*, flagship of the First Fleet, into Sydney Harbour. Aboard the *Sirius* was Arthur Phillip, the first governor of the new colony.

And so began more than 200 years of terror, disease and discrimination for the Indigenous people of the great Southern Land. By the 20th century Australia's Aboriginals knew all about this word called 'equality'. They knew, as the boys from St Francis would learn soon enough, that some men 'are more equal than others'.

Even winning the right to vote in 1967 did not bring true equality to the nation's Indigenous people. St Francis House proved to be an extraordinary breeding ground for top-flight sportsmen. But acceptance in a general sense was never forthcoming. When it came to non-sporting pursuits, such as a walk down the street with a white girl, they were given the cold shoulder.

On a wet September day in 2015, Wally McArthur was put to

rest. The funeral took place at Morphettville Race Course, where former St Francis House residents were pallbearers, among them Sonny Morey, John Moriarty and Vince Copley: 'The race course was appropriate, for Wally liked a punt ... and he was always first past the post.'

Wally leapt from the pages of *Boy's Own Annual*. Instead of cowering to Australia's White Australia Policy, Wally put everything into his running.

In recent times we have seen what has been described as the overt hostility of crowds toward Sydney Swans champion Adam Goodes. Was Goodes booed by large sections of the crowd because of his colour, or was it generated by the opposite team's supporters to try and throw him off his game?

All the boys from St Francis have experienced all manner of racism: the clandestine kind and open hostility. Back in the early 1950s when Wally McArthur strove to become an athletics star, discrimination was more up-front; as obvious as the nose on your face. McArthur's ambition was to become a champion international athlete, but no Aboriginal athlete was chosen for Australia in the Olympic games until the 1960s. Years later – decades after his brilliant athletics and international rugby league career was over – he reflected on a lack of opportunity.

'I wasn't bitter about being left out of the Olympics. No doubt I could have run for Australia, my country. And I probably would have taken at least one gold medal at Helsinki.'

In 1999 journalist Peter Hackett wrote a poignant article about the 'betrayal of Wally McArthur'.

'I have no idea how many records I broke in my athletics career,' Wally told Hackett, 'I just ran because I enjoyed it. What I did as an athlete didn't win me much recognition.

Their hero

Semaphore Rugby Club. Back row, far right: Wally McArthur. Middle row, second from left: Harry Russell. Front row, second from right: Jim Foster.

'As a little kid back in Borroloola fishing in the waterholes you always had to be on the lookout for crocs. You had to be fast on your feet. There was also this emu that used to hang about the cattle station and he always went for me. He frightened the hell out of me, but I learnt to out-run him!'

Wally learned to play rugby league at Penrith High School, too. When he and other boys such as John Moriarty and Jim Foster were moved from Mulgoa to St Francis House in 1948, rugby league became a great interest for all. While South Australia was not a strong rugby state, Semaphore had its own team – one of only five in the state. Rapidly Wally forged a reputation for being fast. He'd get the ball and take off, running and twisting past all opposition. In such circumstances there was only one outcome; another McArthur try. Semaphore cruised through the

The Boys from St Francis

1950 and 1951 seasons undefeated and in 1952 Wally McArthur was voted the South Australian Rugby League's best and fairest player. In his time at Semaphore Wally is said to have scored in excess of 900 points.

Wally's experience with racism in athletics gave him a reason to choose rugby league as his main sport. He realised that in rugby league he would be judged on his football ability, not the colour of his skin. The Rochdale Hornets in the UK were keen to sign him, but they had to tread carefully. Australian rugby league players were held in high esteem in the United Kingdom and international transfers had been banned across the sport in 1947 due to fears that Australian players would be poached to play in the more lucrative English league.

Rochdale's strategy previously had been to persuade Australian rugby league players to switch to the amateur rugby union for a few matches, thus bypassing authority: all legal and above board. This time around, Rochdale declared that Wally had decided to move to England to find suitable employment and to secure his engineering ticket. Ironically the Australian Rugby League Board of Control, forerunner of the ARL and NRL, turned a blind eye and the deal was completed without incident.

Wally flew from Sydney to the United Kingdom in 1953. The *Daily Express* reporter Jack Bentley wrote that McArthur might play for the Hornets against Leigh soon after his arrival in England. Leigh's new signing from athletics, Macdonald Bailey, the 100 metres bronze medallist at the 1952 Helsinki Olympic Games and joint world record holder, was due to play in that match. Bentley said spectators could expect to see 'two black flashes in action – one on each side!'

Their hero

Wally arrived to a hero's welcome at Rochdale. The local press gave him positive coverage, listing all his athletic feats, and a former Leeds player, Jack Lendill, who had emigrated to work and live in Adelaide, was quoted as saying of the new signing, 'Wally McArthur is probably the fastest winger in football boots.' Lendill went on to say that McArthur would prove a sensation in English football.

I played for Railways against Wally's team in a league final in Adelaide. It was all thanks to Wally that we were beaten. It was simply impossible to catch him. He certainly didn't need much room and, as regards tackling, on those granite grounds in Australia he could bowl a man over with terrific strength and power.

Wally's four-year contract with the Hornets stipulated that he be paid £200 per year, plus match fees and return airfares. They arranged for him to continue his engineering apprenticeship at Rochdale's Thomas Holt Ltd. The English press paid little attention to the colour of his skin. The tag 'black flash' was rarely used after Jack Bentley's article in the *Daily Express*. There was a brief reference to Wally's origins published in the *Rochdale Observer* a few day after he arrived in the UK: 'From boyhood Wally McArthur has been in the midst of one of the greatest Christian and social experiments ever attempted in Australia. Wally appears to be one of many proofs of the success of the experiment,' it claimed. Interestingly the writer failed to point out that this 'great' Christian and social experiment also involved seven-year-old Wally McArthur being taken from the bosom of his family and driven thousands of miles to a strange institution. It was 55 years before he again set eyes on a family member.

The Boys from St Francis

His debut for the Rochdale Hornets was against Salford on 12 December 1953. To the astonishment of teammates, opponents and spectators, Wally scorched across with lightning speed, twisting and turning through the packs to score three goals. In thick fog he scored a hat-trick against Whitehaven, and in August 1954, Wally stunned all and sundry with a club record-equalling 25 points against Blackpool – scoring three tries and kicking eight goals. McArthur's brilliance attracted big crowds. For the first three months of that 1954 season, home crowds averaged more than 10,000.

Never before or since has the club experienced such big crowds and they came almost exclusively because of Wally's brilliance. But within a few months inconsistency set in. Wally was brilliant one day, average the next, and club officials complained to the local newspaper that there were 'rumours aplenty' that some supporters were telling Wally that 'he would be better off somewhere else, at a club that could make better use of his talent'.

A few months after Wally arrived in Rochdale his fiancée, Marlene Newchurch, joined him. Vince Copley tells of the day Wally first brought Marlene to St Francis House.

'Wally was showing her off, but really he sought our approval. We loved him because he was so honest. He cared for us. He was our protector, our dear brother and our hero,' Vince says.

'There might have been a bit of good-natured banter that day. I can imagine some of the boys teasing him, "Oh, come on Wally, you're too good for her. Let me take her off your hands," because Marlene was a stunner. We liked her instantly. The couple got engaged before Wally flew off to England.'

They married as soon as Marlene arrived in Rochdale. Wally

Their hero

had been led to believe the club would find them suitable accommodation, but the club claimed that as he was single when he arrived they had provided appropriate housing for him. Wally was offered up for sale with a price tag of £2500.

Fiercely protective of Marlene, Wally stood his ground against the club. The *Rochdale Observer* reported:

> The idol of thousands of Hornets rugby fans 21-year-old Wally McArthur was set to leave the town and possibly even Britain because he was 'fed up to the teeth' with the way the club had treated him. He even spoke about returning to Australia and going back to professional sprinting.

From 1953 to 1959, Wally played for four English rugby league clubs: Rochdale, Blackpool Borough, Salford and Workington Town. He didn't limit his sport to rugby league, either, finding time to continue to run competitively. In 1957 he was the North England sprint champion, taking both the 100- and 220-yard titles. He also won the 100-yard sprint in the 1957 Highland Games. Wally missed meeting the Queen, patron of the games, but was pleased to have been introduced to the Duke of Edinburgh.

Historian and lifelong Salford fan Graham Morris was a youngster when Wally joined the club. He remembers the fans' excitement about the new recruit: 'Tall and slim, Wally had the look, grace and speed of an outstanding athlete. His speed and agility, combined with a classic side-step, made him a great crowd-pleaser. Wally scored 29 tries in 46 matches for Salford. He was undoubtedly, until the arrival of David Watkins in 1967, the most exciting player seen in a Salford jersey since World War II.'

In 1958 Workington Town bought him from Salford for

The Boys from St Francis

Jim Foster (right) watches hay being cleared at Wigan Rugby League Club, 1956.

£3000. The club struggled both on and off the field and Wally believed that he was owed £800 when his time with Workington Town came to an end.

Eventually Wally applied to the national rugby body, the Rugby Football League, for a clearance certificate to allow him to play professionally in Australia. Wally McArthur's international career was over, but he was the torchbearer, blazing a trail for other Aboriginal Australians to showcase their skills in Britain. In fact, Wally's cousin Jim Foster sailed to England in 1956 and played rugby league for Blackpool and Wigan. It was at Blackpool that Jim teamed up again with his old St Francis House mate.

'I'd burrow in and get the ball and Wally would yell, "Jim, give to me, give to me!" Then he grabbed it and took off in a flash.

Their hero

Give him the ball and he'd outrun them all. He was amazing,' Jim Foster laughs.

Jim spent more than six years in England. He played rugby league in winter and cricket in summer. He was saddened when Wally decided to return to Australia.

Upon returning to South Australia in 1959, Wally and Marlene moved to Port Adelaide, where the champion sportsman found work as a fitter and turner. They later shifted to Whyalla where he worked as a welder on the shipyards.

For a time Wally worked for Australian National Railways as a ganger on the Nullarbor Plain, helping maintain the Indian Pacific line. It was there in 1977 that a workmate got his leg jammed in the braking assembly of a railway cart sitting in the path of an oncoming train. Wally freed the man with moments to spare, and suffered terrible leg injuries when he leapt from the cart himself. Both of his legs were badly broken, so too his feet.

Thereafter he could only walk with the aid of a stick, and his physical disability left him unable to find work. In the 1970s there was little or no occupational health and safety for any workers, let alone those who toiled in heavy, manual jobs. Wally received a pittance in workers' compensation.

Wally displayed similar courage to policeman Bill Espie, who saved a motorist's life by pulling him from his burning car. Unlike Bill Espie, Wally wasn't awarded a bravery award, but his actions epitomised the quality of the man.

Instinctively, the boys who attended St Francis House yearned to be the best they could be at sport, and Wally McArthur was faster than them all. But he was also a courageous and good man, and a hero to many.

To the boys of St Francis he was theirs alone.

Charlie

'Evonne Goolagong [Cawley] is a heroine now [circa 1975], but what about later? She will be just another darkie like us. People protect her now but what about when she no longer can make money from playing tennis?' – Charlie Perkins

St Francis House produced an amazing array of heroes, including Wally McArthur, but also Charlie Perkins, who became a hero both to his people and the soccer community.

While his peers said Charlie studied hard and got on well with all the boys, he didn't like his experience at St Francis House.

'After Father Smith left the home, the atmosphere changed,' Charlie wrote in his book, *A Bastard Like Me* (URE Smith, Sydney, 1975). 'We had various other people in charge there. Discipline was severe and we were punished quite harshly, often for what seemed to be fairly minor offences.'

Charlie had seen inequality in Alice Springs. Never could he forget the image of his grandmother at the wire, trying in vain to get into the compound to see his mother and hug him. He found that an Aboriginal could find some sort of equality in becoming a champion sportsman, however, equality both on and off the sporting arena seemed a dream too far away for the young Charlie Perkins.

'When football games are over the blacks go their way the whites go theirs. Evonne Goolagong [Cawley] is a heroine now [circa 1975], but what about later? She will be just another darkie

Charlie

Charlie Perkins on the grounds of St Francis House, c. 1949.

like us. People protect her now but what about when she no longer can make money from playing tennis?'

What Charlie predicted for Evonne in 1975 hasn't come to pass, but it took her to excel in her chosen sport to win acceptance in society.

Sport came naturally to the boys who grew up at St Francis House, which became obvious when they tried a new sport for the first time – such as the fateful day they tried soccer for the first time.

'We must have been about 13 at the time,' Charlie recalled in later years. 'They invited us to play against them in an impromptu game. That was the very day our St Francis House eleven beat the under-18 state intermediate team 10-nil!'

At the age of 14 Charlie joined the Scottish soccer club, Port Thistle. There was something special about soccer and the people it attracted. Most of the players were migrants or sons of migrants who had fled Europe in the wake of World War II. Charlie was delighted to find that all of the people associated with Port Thistle 'treated me like a human being'.

'It was the first time in my life I felt truly free,' he wrote. 'The players would talk roughly to me and that was fine because I knew exactly where I stood with them.'

In 1950 Port Thistle won the second division championship and was elevated to the first division. However, to qualify for promotion the club needed to field teams in the junior division. There was enough local talent in the area to easily fulfil the condition. Port Thistle managed to straight away have two underage teams: a full juniors team and a senior colts squad to complement the senior eleven.

St Francis House boys filled the junior team. Others in the junior eleven were Ernie Perkins (Charlie's brother), Gerry Hill and John Moriarty. All the St Francis boys played Australian Rules football too, and Charlie could have excelled at either or both games, but he chose soccer because he believed the players and officials exuded a different attitude to the white Australians.

Gordon Briscoe also believes Charlie chose to strive to excel at soccer as a way of dodging the bullies at St Francis House and his frustration over Father Smith's decision to leave the boys because of a 'new job and title'. He also said years later that 'Charlie's preference for soccer over Australian Rules was almost entirely due to his resentment of the prejudice he confronted by those who played and organised the game.'

Charlie

It was during his first season of senior football with Port Thistle that Charlie left St Francis House.

'I got an apprenticeship as a fitter and turner at British Tube Mills,' he recalled. 'I had to ride my bike 12 km to and from work from my boarding house. There was the odd good bloke at the boarding house, but most of them were drunks. And my wages were £3/10- a week and I had to fork out £3 a week to stay there. That left me 10 bob – 10 bloody bob – left to buy food and necessary books to study toward getting my apprenticeship.'

By the time Charlie successfully completed his fitter and turner apprenticeship he was 21. He was playing soccer for Budapest, South Australia's top club, and was one of the highest paid players going around.

Soccer meant the world to him. Work was what he called an 'inconvenience' to his soccer career.

He was paid £8 a week playing for Budapest and really embraced the club's social activities. There was then even enough food to go around for a fit and strong young man used to burning lots of energy, after having always been hungry during his time at St Francis House. Charlie's big luxury of any given week was to buy a packet of sultana biscuits, washed down by the contents of a large bottle of Coca-Cola. He also liked to go to the pictures, but could rarely afford it.

At work he met one of the nicest characters of his experience, Scotsman Bill Orr. When the two men first struck up a conversation, Bob said, 'You are not a white Australian, are you?'

'No,' Charlie said, 'I am an Aboriginal.'

'Thought so. You have some pretty big problems in this country?'

For a time Bob Orr became Charlie's confidant and mentor.

The Boys from St Francis

Calm and wise beyond his limited schooling, Bob was street smart, a good reader and a good listener.

Charlie absorbed Bob's sage advice with great enthusiasm. Theirs was a natural relationship as they bounced ideas and talked many and varied subjects. If Bob thought his younger friend had overstepped the mark in what he did or said he'd tell Charlie in no uncertain manner. Their bond was built on mutual trust and respect.

Eventually Bob returned to his native Scotland. He was instrumental, however, in winning Charlie a contract to play for Everton in Liverpool. Charlie was fascinated by the accent ('half English, half Irish') of the people known in that part of the world as 'Scousers'.

It wasn't a luxury trip to England for our intrepid traveller. Charlie sailed on an Italian liner, 'the cheapest possible class'. Money was scarce and he had few decent clothes to wear. The only white shirt he possessed was missing the left sleeve. Sailing through the heat of the tropics and the Suez Canal Charlie covered his shirt with a coat. When the ship docked in Genoa, he caught a train through Europe to Paris, arriving early one morning. Accompanying Charlie on the journey were two Arabs. Charlie thought they could become friends, for they didn't question his heritage and their skin was much the same hue. The men offered to carry Charlie's luggage across the road from the station, which Charlie thought was helpful. But they hurried across the road and disappeared. Charlie never saw those two Arabs again, nor his luggage.

He finally crossed the English Channel and arrived at Victoria Station in London. A few weeks before he had sent Bob Orr a telegram asking him to meet him at 'London Railway Station'.

Charlie

Somehow Bob figured it out and turned up at Victoria with a huge grin on his face and as the two men shook hands on the platform, Bob laughed, 'You're a real bushy, Perkins.'

In later years, Charlie would often think of his playing days at Everton, remembering the supreme skill of his teammates. In Australia he was used to training for just two days of any one week, whereas in England they trained six days every week, with match day every Saturday. The Everton players could pinpoint their passes with exquisite precision, for good and ill. He found that his teammates often passed the ball nearer the opposition than himself or they deliberately lofted the ball over his head, making him seem slow in the first instance and unable to read the pace of the game. Once he challenged a teammate for deliberately setting him up, but he was ignored. One cold winter's day the coach yelled from the sideline, 'that sort of thing doesn't happen' and Charlie threatened to flatten him. But Charlie realised that the Everton players were not racists, they were professional footballers where you were either in or out of the 'inner circle'.

Charlie got a job in the shipyards at Cammel Lairds on Liverpool's famous Mersey River. There a West Indian worker introduced him to unionism. A fitter, Charlie could never get close to the white workers. They seemed to resent him, as well as the West Indian union representative. One day one of them dropped a red-hot welding rod from high above where Charlie was welding. It just missed his head.

It was around that time Charlie decided he would leave the Everton club.

Fortuitously he bumped into promising youngster with the Wigan Football Club, Gordon Tilley, who suggested he move from Everton to play with Wigan, the pride of that little town near Liverpool. Gordon was about to begin his national service and offered Charlie board at his parents' home.

'Mr Tilley, a miner, and his wife treated me grandly, like a son,' Charlie recalled later.

He found a job as a miner and stayed with the Tilleys for most of his time in England, although he did live for a time with Wally and Marlene McArthur in Leigh, a small village near Wigan. Wally was by then a rugby league legend in the north of England.

Shortly after Charlie's arrival in England, the football world had learnt the shocking news that an aircraft carrying the Manchester United team had crashed after a fuel stop at Munich airport. A total of 23 people perished in the tragedy, including eight Manchester United players. Charlie was shaken by the disaster and he had many a chat with Wally about luck, opportunity, and how fate can ruin lives in an instant.

Catching up with Wally at Wigan was something of a godsend for Charlie. One night they chatted into the night at a pub and found they had consumed their bus fare. It was a good hour's walk home to Wally's place, enough time to concoct an unlikely story about broken-down buses. They eased into the McArthur house and were confronted by Marlene.

Charlie looked at Marlene and began, 'Well, it's like this Mrs McArthur—'

He stopped short and ducked as she threw a dinner plate over his head with the speed, if not the precision, of one of his Everton teammates deliberately kicking the ball out of his reach on match day.

Charlie then moved to Bishop Auckland, the top amateur team in the world at the time. Bishop Auckland is real Geordie

Charlie

country, on the Scottish border near Newcastle. Like the Wigan people the players and the fans embraced Charlie, a complete contrast to the treatment he experienced in Liverpool. He mixed socially and found not a hint of racism or discrimination.

Life was good. Some of the top players were getting match payments of up to £25, good money to greatly complement the workday pay. One day Charlie played a match against Oxford University and he marvelled about how he, an Aboriginal, could be playing against 'all these university characters'. The experience fired his ambition to gain a decent tertiary education and go to university.

Then a bolt from the blue. Charlie received a letter from John Ferguson, a good friend based in Adelaide. He had been in contact with the Croatia Soccer Club in Adelaide, and they wanted Charlie. He told Ferguson if they paid he would return home to play for them.

Charlie loved his involvement with both the Wigan and Bishop Auckland teams. He even had an English girlfriend for a time. Life was good. However, he believed if he could gain an education, an opportunity might arise in Australia – a chance to use his knowledge and education to help his people. In early 1960 Charlie Perkins's mind was made up, and he prepared to say goodbye to his English friends.

Just before Charlie was due to return to Australia, though, Manchester United manager Matt Busby approached him with an offer to join the famous club's elite playing group. Busby had sustained terrible injuries in the Munich Air disaster, but he returned as the club's manager and eight years later he would built a super team to take out the European Cup in 1968.

In pure football terms this was the chance of a lifetime. From those childhood days playing soccer at Ethelton Primary School, Charlie had always yearned to become the best he could be and to play top-level professional football.

But his view of the world had changed. The decision to forego the generous and tempting Manchester United offer was difficult. He was homesick for Australia, the Aboriginal people, sun and open spaces.

The two-year experience in England was good for Charlie in many ways.

'The greatest benefit I got from spending time abroad was that I found I could relate to myself and I gained belief in my ability to do a variety of things.'

He also developed an almost obsessive urge to study hard and gain a university degree. Charlie was still passionate about football, but the game no longer dominated his thinking. Charlie envisioned a more fulfilling future away from the football pitch.

He was going home.

Home

His mind returned to Saturdays at the Odeon Theatre on Semaphore Road, where the white girls were perfectly content to sit and hold hands with the Aboriginal boys under the cloak of darkness, but were afraid to be seen in the public gaze, walking down the street with one of the boys.

In the wake of a long sea voyage from England, the SS *Orsova* docked at Outer Harbor. Charlie was glad to be home, back to country and his people. As he walked from the ship he saw the smiling faces of two people he knew well, John and Yvonne Ferguson, and he noted a group of men in suits, which he took to be officials of the Croatia Soccer Club. The officials wasted no time and within days Charlie was on the training track. Matches began almost immediately and Charlie revealed what he had learnt about soccer in England. The South Australian state selectors saw in Charlie Perkins a ready-made potential champion. He was selected in a state trial, turning out for the 'Possibles' against the 'Probables'.

From the names given the two opposing sides it's likely 'Probables' were regarded as the better squad. Charlie soon put paid to any such theory, slicing through their ranks with amazing agility and none-too-little aggression. The state selectors were delighted with Perkins, who was named as the vice captain for the South Australian team to play Victoria in Melbourne the following week.

Charlie loved playing for Croatia in Adelaide. He was well paid and whenever he scored a goal the club secretary handed him a crisp £10 note. Whenever he dined at a restaurant the club took care of the bill. Life was good, but girls were on his mind.

Charlie never got to mix much with Australian girls. Those he dated were usually 'new' Australian girls, those who had emigrated from Holland, Ireland, Scotland, Denmark, Sweden or Germany. Up until the day he met the love of his life, Charlie maintained that Australian girls were boring and 'a bit snooty'.

The exception was Eileen Munchenberg, whom he met at a soccer function at the Hilton Hotel – not one of the flash chain hotels, but a small establishment of the same name situated on South Road, Mile End.

'Charlie was 24 and I was 21,' Eileen recalls. 'We clicked immediately and within a few months we were married.'

The daughter of a staunch Lutheran couple, Eileen says there was never any discrimination shown 'by anyone within my family toward the Aboriginal people'.

'However,' she adds with a smile, 'my parents did discriminate when it came to religion. They always said, "Whatever you do, don't marry a Catholic."'

Charlie also remembered his first meeting with Eileen.

'I went along to the Hilton with my cousin Gordon Briscoe. There I was dancing about with this dumpy girl with long hair,' Charlie wrote in 1975.

'She had just returned from New Zealand and was about 2 stone overweight.'

A few extra pounds weren't going to put Charlie off and he asked Eileen out for a meal.

'I'd love to, Charlie. Pick me up at home,' she said.

However, Charlie's experience with white Australians had affected him greatly. His mind returned to Saturdays at the

Home

Odeon Theatre on Semaphore Road, where the white girls were perfectly content to sit and hold hands with the Aboriginal boys under the cloak of darkness, but were afraid to be seen in the public gaze, walking down the street with one of the boys.

'Oh, no. Can't I meet you somewhere?' he asked.

The day Charlie arrived at the Munchenberg home Eileen introduced him to her parents. Eileen's family were all welcoming and genuinely interested to meet Charlie, who was blown away by their warmth.

There is no doubt that Charlie's upbringing in Alice Springs and subsequent events at St Francis House affected him and undoubtedly created doubt in his mind as to the motives of some people, especially white Australians. Some might say he developed a chip on his shoulder; others might assert that it wasn't a mere chip, it was a tree trunk. However, discrimination cuts deep. Before he went to England to play soccer, Charlie played cricket for the Acorn Cricket Club in Port Adelaide. After a day's play the cricketers adjourned to a pub for a drink. The barman demanded Charlie show his 'pass'. In those days an Aboriginal wasn't allowed to set foot in licensed premises if he did not carry a ticket complete with his photograph, fingerprints and two references to confirm that he was a 'fit and proper person to walk the streets and to go in public places'.

Charlie refused to stoop to agree to such demeaning conditions. As he entered the bar, the barman said: 'Listen darkie, you know you don't belong in here. If you don't get out I'll get the copper on ya.'

Charlie went outside where a teammate found him and offered to bring him a beer. Charlie refused, saying, 'If you brought me a beer that would cause trouble. Anyway, I'd prefer a lemon squash.'

The Boys from St Francis

After that time with his cricket mates, Charlie would look at even the roughest pub in Port Adelaide and, because he was not allowed inside, it appeared somehow very grand.

The most obvious difference to Charlie living in England compared to Australia was the social life. He could walk down the street with a white woman and he was served in cafes and restaurants without question. If there was an argument, he could do so on equal terms in that his Aboriginality was never an issue.

Brenko Filipi, the Croatia fan who brought Charlie home from England, was delighted with the club's new star. The pair developed a close father-son relationship, similar to that between Father Smith and Charlie before the clergyman suddenly left St Francis House in 1949. Filipi remembered Charlie's influence.

'He'd always talk his players up and after his half-time pep talks they all came out like lions.'

While Perkins was the 'master tactician', his former St Francis House teammate John Moriarty was also making great progress with Croatia. The pair were among the five best players at the club and were regular state representatives.

Before the Ampol Cup in 1961 Perkins was described in an article under the heading KING SOCCER.

> What a complete player Perkins is – recognised as one of the leading wing-halves in Australia, he can move to centre-forward, inside-forward or centre-half and operate in a most efficient manner.

However, midway through the 1961 season Charlie found that soccer was no longer the all-consuming priority in his life.

During Charlie's two-year absence abroad, there was a lot

of disquiet in Adelaide as to the continuing treatment of the Aboriginal people at home. While Charlie had been playing soccer in the winter snow, three Indigenous leaders met with a group of interested people in the sweltering heat of Adelaide.

The three Indigenous men were Jeff Barnes, represented the South Australian Aborigines Advancement League; Pastor Doug Nicholls, a good friend of Vince Copley, who was then field officer of the Victorian Aborigines Advancement League; along with Bert Groves, president of the Aboriginal-Australian Fellowship in New South Wales. They wanted to do something to combat the injustices of the ludicrous conditions for Aboriginal people under the South Australian Aborigines Act. The meeting proved a great success, with the formation of the Federation of the Advancement of Aborigines (FCAA). The name of the body was later changed (Federal Council for the Advancement of Aborigines and Torres Strait Islanders, or FCAATSI). The formation of such a representative Indigenous body had been mooted for years, however, little was done until the London Anti-Slavery Society moved to approach the United Nations on behalf of Australia's Aboriginal population to seek a swift pathway to equality for the downtrodden Aboriginal people.

A number of old boys from St Francis House – Malcolm Cooper, John Moriarty, Vince Copley and Gordon Briscoe – got involved with FCAA. By the time Charlie Perkins arrived back in Australia there were already moves by the body to address several important issues, including a campaign against the South Australian Aborigines Act.

The South Australian Act was as bad as any in the land. Aboriginal people could be kept forcibly on any reserve, which could be created, altered or abolished without warning. They could be removed from any town or fringe-camp, or anywhere else the chief protector declared prohibited. Drinking, gambling and disobeying a manager's instructions were prohibited. All Aboriginal children under 16 were declared to be in the minister's care and liable to be institutionalised. It was an offence for Aboriginal people to 'consort with' or have sexual relations with non-Aboriginal people. An exemption certificate system enabled an Aboriginal person 'by reason of his character and standard of intelligence and development' to apply for exemption from the regulation. The Act was so worded that Vince Copley was not allowed to visit his family at Port Pearce, although he never complied.

In 1960 the South Australian branch of FCAA formally opposed the Act. Branch president and state Labor opposition leader Don Dunstan was aiming to introduce a private member's bill into state parliament abolishing its worst excesses. He believed that the mood of the people was such that there was an urgent need to change public opinion. Thanks to the efforts of the FCAA and the Aborigines Advancement League, chaired by Dr Duguid, a petition was drawn up in favour of Dunstan's bill.

The committee's target was to collect in excess of 20,000 signatures. They envisaged that migrant communities and people who had witnessed blatant discrimination against Indigenous Australians would be sympathetic to their cause. Charlie Perkins, John Moriarty and Gordon Briscoe were the main protagonists in 'Operation Migrant Support'.

In an exhaustive seven-week campaign amid much publicity, more than 14,000 signatures were collected. Some members of the Labor Party were uneasy about certain aspects of Dunstan's bill, which was narrowly beaten on a technicality. Premier Tom Playford's Liberal Party was also lukewarm over certain proposed changes. One Liberal member went so far as to say, 'The granting of Aboriginal citizenship rights was like handing detonators to five-year-old children.'

However, wiser heads in the Playford government prevailed and a year later, in October 1962, Attorney-General Colin Rowe introduced the government's own bill. While the bill was perceived to be steeped in assimilation philosophy, the worst features of the old Act were repealed.

They wanted the federal government to establish a referendum to remove two discriminatory clauses from the Australian Constitution. One of the clauses prevented the government from legislating for Indigenous Australians and the other excluded Indigenous Australians from being counted in the periodic national census. Oodgeroo Noonuccal, known at the time as Kath Walker, had argued passionately for Indigenous people to take control of their own affairs. Together with Doug Nicholls she helped establish the National Tribal Council, a body that would seek Indigenous representation from all states to be run by and for Indigenous Australians. Though it started positively, this body lasted less than three years.

In 1973, FCAATSI finally became an Indigenous-controlled organisation. By this time, however, with the number of Aboriginal and Islander grass-roots organisations expanding and the formation of both a Department of Aboriginal Affairs and a National Aboriginal Consultative Committee, FCAATSI struggled to be a truly federal umbrella body representing a diverse constituency. When the federal government cut FCAATSI's funding in 1978 it was forced to wind up its affairs. But nothing would prevent the momentum for real change in Aboriginal affairs.

Charlie and Eileen Perkins (nee Munchenberg) on their wedding day, Adelaide, 1961. From left: Isabel Smith, Father Percy Smith, Eileen and Charlie Perkins, and Eileen's parents. Photo courtesy John Smith.

By this time Charlie Perkins was already well known on the national stage. He was heavily involved in activism for his people, he was still playing top-flight soccer and on 23 September 1961 he had married Eileen Munchenberg. Eileen was patient, encouraging and committed to being a good wife, an understanding and supportive friend and she proved to be a shrewd advisor. Charlie instinctively knew that he needed a calming influence in his life, because he had a volatile personality.

Having worked so hard toward getting a fairer Aborigines Protection Act placed on the statute book, Charlie became dissatisfied with opportunities in South Australia. He considered accepting work in Darwin, but Sydney proved too big a lure. It offered a greater platform to get his message across, and it had far greater work opportunities than Adelaide. Charlie also harboured a desire to earn a university degree.

The problem was money. If Charlie and Eileen were to settle in Sydney, they needed enough money to find suitable accommodation and to fund Charlie's university place. He knew he needed to win a place in a good soccer club to take care of finances, and Prague Soccer Club interviewed him, but no contract was on offer.

Then fate took a hand.

As Charlie walked despondently from the interview to the hotel where Eileen was waiting, he literally bumped into an old friend from Adelaide, Hungarian-born Les Suchanek, then coach of the prestigious Pan Hellenic (Sydney Olympic) soccer team.

'Charlie, why don't you come out next Saturday and trial with us?

Charlie, of course, jumped at the chance. And he didn't miss the opportunity. He played with what Suchanek saw was renewed vigour and dash, obviously derived from his two years of professional football in England. At the final whistle Charlie had blitzed the opposition with his ball skills, scoring three goals and winning a contract on the spot.

Here was a man who always somehow found a way to win the big moments.

A year to remember

The fiery black woman then began calling out the names of white men the Aboriginals believed had been molesting their daughters. As the burly man made a hasty retreat, the black woman yelled, 'You bastard. You are nothing but a gin jockey.'

Charlie Perkins had an extraordinary year in 1965.

By then he had become a familiar figure within the Aboriginal activist movement, which included Indigenous Australians and many sympathetic white supporters. Reverend Ted Noffs saw great potential in Charlie and he arranged for the young firebrand to undertake a course in remedial English at the Metropolitan Business College; the catalyst for Perkins starting a Bachelor of Arts at Sydney University.

In 1965 he gained his degree, significantly the first Indigenous Australian to do so, and in February he was the central figure of the student Freedom Ride to north-western New South Wales, which first brought him to the public gaze.

Charlie was by no means a gifted student, but if determination alone was given a tertiary mark, he got a high distinction every time. During his years of university Charlie studied political science as his core subject every year. In addition he studied psychology, anthropology and sociology.

'I was not brilliant academically, but I was a real slugger. I worked hard all of the time. I never wasted an hour in my study schedule throughout any one of my university years. Eileen was an inspiration. She sacrificed much for my studies. We were a good team.'

A year to remember

From the outset of his university life Charlie suffered from self-doubt. He didn't believe he possessed enough knowledge to keep up with the others. A noun or a verb was to him some sort of foreign language and much of what the lecturers uttered went over his head. There was Charlie Perkins sitting right up the front of class, a dictionary in his lap, trying to figure out what the lecturer was saying. Eventually he found a way to understand and he blossomed. His strong work ethic was obvious, especially to fellow workers at the Sydney Council when he cleaned public toilets for work during university holidays. Perkins's toilets were the cleanest in Sydney. Just for the hell of it he would scrub the walls, the tiles and the floor. No wonder the council begged him to stay as a full-time toilet cleaner. Charlie also worked part-time with Mick Simmons Sport in George Street. There he stacked boxes, swept floors and dealt with the rubbish. Working menial, part-time jobs was good for Charlie's soul. He believed that it was good to keep your ego in check lest you start thinking that you were somehow superior. Charlie's graduation took place in Sydney University's Great Hall and, as would befit the first Australian Aboriginal to become a university graduate, he received the biggest applause.

A fellow named Perrin was also graduating that day.

'The worst thing I ever did was to have a name like yours,' he said at the time. 'Nobody even heard me. My mother and father did not hear my name called out at all!'

As the cardinal sat on stage in his impressive scarlet robes, Hetti Perkins looked about the Great Hall. Everyone seemed very dignified. She loved the ceremony and the history and was immensely impressed with the venue and the people in their university gowns and bright colours. Best of all for Hetti was to witness her son's graduation. She was so proud of Charlie. Eileen's parents were also present, delighted for Charlie and for their daughter. Two of Charlie's fellow old boys from St Francis House, John Moriarty and Gordon Briscoe, were also present. Both men were destined to follow in Charlie's footsteps and gain university degrees, too.

Civil unrest abroad did not escape Charlie's attention. During May 1961 student activists from the American Congress of Racial Equality (CORE) launched what was known as the Freedom Rides to challenge segregation on interstate buses and bus terminals. The activists rode on buses from Washington to Jackson, Mississippi, where they were confronted by violent opposition in the Deep South. Extensive media coverage eventually forced intervention by President John F. Kennedy. The campaign succeeded in securing an Interstate Commerce Commission (ICC) ban on segregation in all facilities under their jurisdiction.

In 1964 Charlie was among the leaders of a University of Sydney protest against racial segregation in the United States. However, some people among the Sydney community urged the students to 'look in your own backyard' if they wanted to draw attention to racial discrimination.

Inspired, Charlie was one of the key protagonists of the Australian Freedom Ride, a bus tour through New South Wales by activists protesting discrimination against Aboriginals in small country towns. The purpose of the Freedom Ride was to expose the terrible conditions Aboriginal people lived with in these towns. There were obvious discrepancies in living, education and health conditions for these people which Perkins and his colleagues hoped to expose. They targeted rural towns in

A year to remember

country New South Wales and concentrated on three – Walgett, Moree and Kempsey.

Walgett RSL was famous for entertaining the Aboriginal troops when they returned from action in World War II. Every Anzac Day most Aboriginal returned soldiers were allowed into the Walgett RSL, but not all of them. Some were refused entry even on that national day of remembrance. But every other day of the year all Aboriginals were banned from Walgett RSL. These men fought and died for a country that denied them basic human rights in many areas. The Aboriginal diggers weren't allowed into the hotels, either. If they wanted a drink they were sold cheap plonk through the back window at exorbitant cost, usually as much as three times the price the whites paid across the bar.

The 34 original Freedom Riders set up camp in Walgett's Church of England Hall. Armed with posters the protestors marched to form a picket at the RSL. Emblazoned across their placards were slogans like CIVIL RIGHTS FOR ABORIGINES, WALGETT RSL SHOULD NOT BAN ABORIGINES and ABORIGINES STAND UP FOR YOUR RIGHTS.

Soon after the protestors gathered in front of the RSL, white townsfolk began to congregate at the scene. Within hours hundreds of people arrived. The street was packed with a seething crowd, all yelling abuse, and some busting for a fight. Members of the RSL leaving the hall had to pass through the picket line. Some laughed nervously, others spat at the protestors or onto their banners. By mid afternoon the people of Walgett realised that the Freedom Riders were becoming an increasing embarrassment to them. Local Aboriginals also gathered at the scene. They interacted with the protestors and one wonders

The Boys from St Francis

what these people thought would be their fate at the hands of the whites once the Freedom Riders left Walgett. A couple of the local Aboriginals spoke with Charlie, who told them in no uncertain terms to do something about their lot in Walgett.

'Look, you blokes,' he said, 'stand up for yourselves. We are willing to do enough to stand here and protest, but you've got to from this week on. If you don't stand up and be counted your children when they grow up will be in the same position as you are now.'

When night fell the protestors broke up the picket line. Almost immediately there were verbal jousts with onlookers. The Freedom Riders were arguing with the town whites and the local Aboriginals were talking to the protestors and firing back at the whites.

One white man, a leading light for the Walgett Shire Council, declared: 'I know how to treat these darkies up 'ere. I always treat 'em real good. I employ them. They don't give me no trouble. You get a fair deal from this town, don't you?' The councillor directed his gaze at a black man before him.

Used to getting his way, the councillor expected the usual passive reply. Quick as a flash, though, the black man said in a calm voice, 'Fair deal? I don't get a fair deal, nor does any Aboriginal, man, woman or child in Walgett.'

It was a pin-drop moment.

The councillor was so taken aback by a black man taking him to task he struggled to catch his breath and slumped to his knees in the gutter, holding his head in his hands.

Harry Hall was the black man who dared to speak up; an impressive moment to all of the Freedom Riders, the local Aboriginals, and even many of the whites.

A year to remember

In the wake of the Freedom Ride in Walgett, Harry Hall continued to stand up for his people in the town. Although he lived a simple life, his home a tin shack on the river bank, Harry was a natural leader. He stood up to the white people in the town, the councillors and the police, never backing down and always seeking to get his people a better deal. Whenever he visited Walgett from then on Charlie always stayed with Harry at his tin shack on the river bank.

There were numerous other verbal confrontations during the Walgett visit by the Freedom Riders. At one point a black woman emerged from the crowd, followed by one or two others. Her eyes were on fire: 'Listen! You whites come down to our camp and chase our young girls around at night.'

There was silence other than a few murmurs when she pointed to a burly white man, standing with a cigarette hanging limply from a corner of his mouth, 'You were down there last night. I know you!'

The fiery black woman then began calling out the names of white men the Aboriginals believed had been molesting their daughters.

As the burly man made a hasty retreat, the black woman yelled, 'You bastard. You are nothing but a gin jockey.'

This courageous woman split the crowd. The whites scattered in all directions and the protestors were able to make their way back to the church hall. Many of the local Aboriginals returned to the hall with the protestors and a meal was prepared for all in the kitchen. However, the Anglican priest thought he was providing a group of university students overnight accommodation at the hall, not a big group of people including dozens of local Indigenous Australians. He was visibly horrified when he learnt that boys and girls would be sleeping in the same floor space.

He hurriedly telephoned a list of parishioners.

'This is disgraceful,' he said in a loud voice. 'We can't be associated with social action of this kind.'

The priest and members of the parish council asked Perkins for a word.

'We would like to know one thing, please. Are you young people intending to sleep together?'

Charlie told the church group that the protestors had their own individual sleeping bags and they all intended to sleep in the hall.

'We can't allow this,' the priest said. 'You people have got to leave town, now!'

Charlie jumped up on the stage of the hall and addressed the crowd before him: 'We've been asked by the church people to leave. They demand that we leave tonight.'

Perhaps the most upset among the crowd was the bus driver, who was still protesting under his breath when he drove off. There were some 50 cars and a handful of trucks in line behind the Freedom Riders' vehicle and most honked their horns in a friendly fashion. Just out of Walgett they came to a spot where the road is built up to a height of about 30 feet. The levee had been built years before to keep the road above flood waters.

In Charlie's words: 'We were travelling along this road a couple of miles out of Walgett and the cars were still streaming behind us. The next minute a big truck came out from amid the line of cars. We watched from the rear widow. Someone said, "They can't all be friends."

'We saw the truck roaring up on the outside. We were doing

about 40 miles an hour and were at the top of the levee bank. The truck pulled close in front of us and hit the front of the bus.'

While the bus driver fought to keep the bus from overturning, protestors were tossed about the cabin, luggage flying.

'The truck slowed down and we passed it. The driver yelled, "Look out, here it comes again!" Sure enough the truck hit us again. Its tray hit the front of the bus and we careered straight over the edge of the road and into bushes. We thought we were in for a fight, so I yelled, "Quick, everyone grab a bottle."

'A few of the cars following stopped and the people asked, "Are you alright?"

'The truck sped off, but some of the cars followed it and took the number. We later discovered that the driver was the son of one of Walgett's wealthiest graziers. This fellow was supposedly a friend of the Aboriginals. He would drive them from one place to another, to town to see a doctor, or take them shopping, and here he was trying to kill us.'

Perhaps the most revealing act of discrimination happened on 20 February 1965. Charlie and his party tried to enter the swimming pool at Moree, a council-owned venue that had barred Aboriginals for more than 40 years. When the Freedom Riders tried to go in, they were stopped by an angry crowd of several hundred people. The madding crowd pelted Charlie and his fellow riders with eggs and tomatoes.

During the angry confrontation white townspeople yelled abuse and alleged that the Aboriginals were unhygienic and their swimming in the pool would put the regular (white) swimmers at risk. Charlie and his supporters weren't about to go away. They continued to talk to the pool manager about their right to use the facility as it should be for all people in Moree.

The Boys from St Francis

Eventually the Moree mayor, William Lloyd, arrived at the scene.

Early in 1965 Graham Williams, a reporter with the nation's relatively new daily morning broadsheet the *Australian*, gave readers this fascinating insight into the Freedom Ride:

> As our aircraft banked high over Moree, a swimming pool two miles out of town glinted in the late afternoon sun, a pale blue brooch in the grey pastures and golden wheat-fields. The pool, as I found out later, is more than a landmark for this bustling town 400 miles north-west of Sydney. It is probably the only segregated swimming pool in Australia for Aboriginals.
>
> To the townspeople of Moree, this pool built by Apex at the government Aboriginal reserve is a practical solution to a problem of hygiene. To the Aboriginals of Moree it is the tangible symbol of their rejection by the white community, and an excuse to continue the colour bar at the town pool. This and other colour bars in country towns have a tremendously demoralising and degrading effect on Aboriginals.
>
> My tour of seven country towns with sizeable Aboriginal populations showed me not only that colour bars and discrimination operate extensively in swimming pools, hotels, picture shows and hospitals, but also that they have left a deep wound in the Aboriginals that may take generations to heal. And it showed me that as long as these colour bars exist, Asian nations can point the finger of apartheid at Australia.
>
> Of all the colour bars I encountered, those imposed by the Moree Shire Council and Kempsey Municipal Council at their town swimming pools are the most illogical. At Moree, the council has given a few town Aboriginals permission to use the town pool. A blanket ban used to cover all other

A year to remember

Aboriginals, until the high school obtained permission for its Aboriginal pupils to swim with their white classmates under school supervision. These Aboriginals are debarred at all other times. What once may have professed to be a hygiene bar is now more than ever a colour bar. At Kempsey, a North Coast dairying town of 8000 people 200 miles from Sydney, a similar and ludicrous position applies at the town baths.

Council officials in both towns were very reluctant to discuss the colour bars. The Mayor of Moree, Cr W.A. Lloyd, was evasive. 'I couldn't say Aboriginals are not allowed to use the pool,' he said. 'The manager has the right to refuse anyone entry if he thinks they aren't clean enough.'

Was the ban on Aboriginals on hygiene grounds? 'I can't say because I haven't got the text of the Council resolution before me.'

Did Cr Lloyd think Aboriginal children were clean during school hours and dirty afterwards? He replied that in school hours they were the responsibility of their teachers.

'I can't say anything further about the baths because I haven't got the resolution before me,' he added. Cr Lloyd told me later he had employed Aboriginals for many years. 'I've got no time for prejudice against them.'

At Kempsey the Mayor, Ald R. Melville, was informative about local Aboriginal problems until the colour bar at the baths was mentioned. He flushed slightly. 'When everybody's equal they will be treated as equals,' he said. Asked to explain what that meant, he said angrily: 'I'm not saying any more than that. A lot of people are trying to make this political. They're trying to shoot me down in flames because I've got Labor pre-selection for Raleigh.'

The Boys from St Francis

Later Charles Perkins, the Aboriginal student who, with the Rev T.D. Noffs, accompanied me on the tour, approached the baths manager and asked to be allowed to swim. The manager, Mr Neville Duke, politely but firmly said he could not admit him until he had gained the written permission of council.

Segregation still exists in hospitals in some towns we visited, despite a strong policy by the NSW Hospitals Commission that all hospitals be fully integrated. Moree Hospital still has its traditional McMaster Ward for Aboriginal patients and Wilcannia has two small wards for Aboriginal women. Aboriginals also told me that at two other hospitals, although there is no Aboriginal ward, they are usually put on verandahs away from white patients.

In several towns I visited, Aboriginals are barred from the lounge of some hotels and some barber's shops refuse to serve them. Several picture theatres are also segregated, the Aboriginals confined to the front rows of the stalls.

The colour bars and segregation are one side of the coin. What is the picture on the other side?

I found that hygiene, pride in personal cleanliness and habits, is a real problem with many Aboriginals in country towns. Most of the town Aboriginals are often cleaner than the whites. So are a few of the fringe-dwelling Aboriginals. But at the other end of the scale are many station and shanty town Aboriginals who rarely wash and have little idea of hygiene. This is part of the legacy of the depressed, ghetto environment they have known for decades. Most know no other way of life than a grossly overcrowded, three-room station cottage or two-room shanty that has no sink, bath or stove and often no water or electricity.

A year to remember

Here are a few examples of conditions at Aboriginal stations: Roseby Park station, 16 miles from Nowra: 116 people are crowded into 16 cottages, most of which have only two or three rooms. One family of seven sleeps in one large room. There are no sinks, baths or stoves – only tin fireplaces. One old man bathes himself in a garbage tin. Moree Aboriginal station: 430 people live in 39 houses. They crowd up to 12 and 13 in a house. Burnt Bridge station, Kempsey: 174 people live in 23 houses. There is no electricity. Water comes from a tap in the backyard. There are no sinks or baths, but there is a communal shower. Health often suffers in conditions like these. A teacher at one station told me that roundworm and hair lice are prevalent. 'The children take tablets for roundworm every six weeks but they can't seem to get rid of it,' he said. 'As for the lice, 27 out of my class of 30 really tried hard to get rid of it, but they couldn't in these conditions.'

At Kempsey, Sister Hack told me that young Aboriginal children are usually malnourished and lack stamina: 'This makes them prone to many complaints – pneumonia and bronchitis... tooth decay and a lot of hair lice and roundworm.'

Even taking into account the hygiene problem, white people are hard-pressed to defend the colour bar.

Those who are most aware of Aboriginal children's lack of hygiene fail to notice a similar failing in white children – just as they always remark on the Aboriginal rolling drunk around the footpath but ignore the white men lolling beside him.

Charlie Perkins adored his wife and he would not countenance her going with him on the original Freedom Ride. Eileen well remembers the time: 'I was pregnant with my first child and

Charlie was aware that anything could happen on this Freedom Ride. In 1961 during the Freedom Ride in the United States people were killed. Rioters burnt the bus with the people in them. So we didn't know what might happen. But to keep me safe Charlie insisted that I go back home to Adelaide. My parents and I avidly followed the news and there were some alarming reports in the newspapers. My dad said, "That Charlie has gone too far this time." Mum said, "No, Charlie's always right."

'Her comment buoyed me and I was pleased with the family support at this very worrying time.'

While Eileen was safe at home in Adelaide with her parents Charlie and his band of 'revolutionaries' were running a gauntlet of taunts and racial hatred.

A natural leader, Charlie encouraged the Aboriginal men and women of the towns they visited to stand up against the blatant discrimination they faced in everyday life.

'There was, however, the ever-present threat of danger,' Eileen says. 'And thank goodness, you know, there weren't any tragedies.'

Soon after they married, Eileen Perkins had accompanied Charlie to Alice Springs.

'I hadn't been there before and it quite shocked me. What really shocked me were the primitive conditions the Aboriginals had to endure. Having witnessed first-hand the situation his people faced on a daily basis alerted me to why Charlie was so committed and passionate to pursue his never-ending cause to bring dignity and respect to his people and I was just as determined to support him all the way. '

The Freedom Ride was a clever way to expose some of

A year to remember

these things that existed throughout Australia, for it received nationwide publicity.

There was public outcry over a number of unsavoury incidents, especially the near-riot at the Walgett RSL, the rebuff at Walgett Anglican Church Hall, the angry truck driver's attempt to run the protestors' bus off the road and the Moree Swimming Pool fiasco, all of which awakened Australia to its racist reality.

In a very large way, the Freedom Ride was a catalyst toward Indigenous Australians finally winning the right to vote at the 1967 referendum.

The year of 1965 was also pivotal for Charlie Perkins because it lifted his national profile to such an extent that he even won public support over his 'kidnapping' of Nancy Prasad, a young Indian girl at Mascot Airport. Nancy was about to be deported to Fiji.

In the wake of the 6 August 1965 incident, which took place as the aircraft revved its engines prior to take off, Charlie said calmly, 'I became a kidnapper unexpectedly.'

Kidnapped

The fat cop lost his hat in the melee, but while he put up a brave fight, he was no match for 25 young demonstrators hell-bent upon keeping him away from the 'kidnap' car.

In 1964 a story appeared in the national press which disturbed Charlie Perkins and his fellow students. A young Fijian-Indian girl, five-year-old Nancy Prasad, dominated the front pages of all the nation's leading newspapers. Exclusively because of the colour of her skin, Nancy was to be deported to Fiji.

Just weeks earlier Nancy's parents had been deported from Australia, however, her oldest sister Sandra Powditch and husband, Roy, desperately tried to adopt Nancy to prevent officials from deporting her. For weeks the case was dragged through the courts, but the Immigration Department stood firm. However, by August 1965 Nancy Prasad's predicament had caused so much controversy that there was widespread criticism of the government's application of the White Australia Policy.

The White Australia Policy came into being soon after federation in 1901. The basic policy was to exclude all but European whites from coming to Australia. In 1910 the Deakin government had a medal struck to commemorate the founding of the White Australia Policy. Emblazoned round its perimeter were the words, 'Australia for Australians'. In the centre was a map of the nation with the words, 'White Australia'.

Charles Bean, Australia's first official World War I historian, described the White Australia Policy as a 'vehement effort to maintain a high Western standard of economy, society and culture (necessitating at that stage, however it might be camouflaged, the rigid exclusion of Oriental peoples)'. History tells us of the fierce competition on the goldfields between British and Chinese miners and labour opposition to bringing in Pacific Islanders to work in Queensland sugar plantations. Effectively the policy gave British migrants preference over all others in the years leading up to World War II. During the war Prime Ministe John Curtin said in support of the White Australia Policy: 'This country shall remain forever the home of the descendants of those people who came here in peace in order to establish in the South Seas an outpost of the British race.'

In the wake of World War II and the plight of millions of displaced people in Europe, there was a change of heart by Australia, which welcomed the first British, non-white immigration. The White Australia Policy was dismantled in stages by the Menzies and Holt governments. In 1973 the Whitlam government passed the Racial Discrimination Act, effectively outlawing an individual or organisation making racially-based selection the criteria for emigrating to Australia.

But the White Australia Policy was very much at the fore in 1965.

On 6 August 1965, an hour before Nancy Prasad's aircraft was due to leave for Fiji, a hundred Sydney University students flooded into Mascot Airport. They carried slogans such as NANCY'S CRIME? COLOUR, DON'T DISCRIMINATE AGAINST RACE and A PERSON'S COLOUR SHOULD NOT MATTER.

Charlie wasn't thinking of doing anything silly. He knew that the deportation of five-year-old Nancy Prasad was very wrong and he believed that a passive protest by him and fellow students at the airport was their only real option to bring awareness to her plight and the concerns of all coloured people living in or wishing to emigrate to Australia. Some of the students were getting agitated, though. A group of them voiced the opinion that with all the Commonwealth police standing about it would be difficult for the protestors to do much more than stand about holding their placards. Then someone said, 'What if we kidnap her?'

Charlie thought the idea had merit. He figured that if Nancy was grabbed by one of them at the airport and whisked away, she could be taken to her sister's place. It seemed an idea that might just work. The police, immigration officers and security men would all be taken aback.

A plan was hurriedly hatched. While little thinking went into the plan it was brilliant in its simplicity. They needed someone with nerves of steel and a getaway car that wouldn't let them down. Before Nancy was taken into the terminal building, the plan was to snatch the little girl from her uncle's arms, rush to the getaway car and speed off.

No one rushed to volunteer for the job. Charlie looked about the group and made an instant decision. He would be the 'kidnapper'. At the time he thought little of the consequences and later on he realised how dangerous his thinking had been.

Quickly one of the students got word to the Prasad family circle. A 'kidnapping' was about to unfold at Mascot Airport and it would spark worldwide attention.

'We thought that it would be best to "take" Nancy on the outside, before she was carried into the terminal building,' Charlie later said.

'Most of the Commonwealth police were inside, but there

Kidnapped

was this one, huge burly man outside and no reporters or photographers. I was among some 25 demonstrators and the only obstacle between us and the revolving doors leading to the terminal building was this one big cop.'

Inside the terminal the Commonwealth police milled about and mingled with spectators, other demonstrators and the media throng.

'Because the police, apart from that one big fat cop, and other security staff were on the other side of the revolving doors I knew I could grab the girl and get her into the waiting car while my fellow demonstrators delayed the police at the doors and cramped the style of the big cop nearby.'

Nancy's uncle arrived, cradling her in his arms. Charlie walked up to him and said, 'I'll take her now.'

'Where are you taking her?' he asked, believing his niece would be safe, but a little worried that the students gave him so little detail about their 'kidnapping'.

'It's okay. Nancy will be alright. I'll take her to her brother-in-law's place and we'll look after her for a little while. Then you can come and get her. Now come with me, Nancy.'

And the brave little five-year-old dutifully walked over to Charlie and he took her hand and walked her to the waiting getaway car. The car – a vivid cadmium yellow Volkswagon – was not quite out of a spy novel. Charlie's fellow Sydney University protestors knew all about getaway cars from watching the crime gang series of the time, *The Untouchables*, and the engine was ticking over smoothly. The fat cop lost his hat in the melee, but while he put up a brave fight, he was no match for 25 young demonstrators hell-bent upon keeping him away from the 'kidnap' car. However, two policemen suddenly tore from the crowd and tried to block the car. The little yellow Volkswagen swung away from the kerb and Charlie saw the scene unfold in his rearview mirror.

'About 25 newsmen and photographers were trying to get through those miserable revolving doors at once. There they were, along with the police and security staff desperately struggling to negotiate the opening and there our lot were, pushing them backwards,' Charlie said later.

'One newsman from Channel 7 must have been tipped off. He was right on the spot and filmed the whole thing. We sped down the road and out through the entrance to the terminal car park. It was all too easy.'

Back at the terminal the scene was one of panic, disbelief and general chaos. People were running everywhere.

Charlie had told Eileen that he was going to the airport to see what was going on there and that he would be home in a couple of hours for tea. She was quietly sitting in the lounge room watching television when suddenly Charlie's profile filled the screen, accompanied by the TV presenter's voice: 'This man is wanted by police for questioning on a kidnapping charge.'

In mid 2015 I spoke with Eileen at Vince and Brenda Copley's Adelaide home. They had a good laugh about what happened at Mascot Airport that eventful day and Charlie's take on events.

'When I saw Charlie's face on the television and then the announcer talking about a kidnapping I just couldn't believe it. It was like the wild west!' Eileen said.

'Charlie said when he got to the getaway car it wouldn't start.'

Charlie's version of events was him at his embellishing best.

Vince Copley said, 'Charlie told me that he simply walked up to the bloke holding Nancy, grabbed her and took off. Then he said he rushed past the getaway car when he realised it wouldn't start and bullets were whizzing over his head.'

'In reality,' Eileen continued, 'the car had started and was idling when Charlie arrived with Nancy. However, it did happen to be facing the wrong direction in a one-way street.'

Nancy Prasad was driven to the family home of her sister. Then Louise, the student driver of the 'getaway car', dropped Charlie off at home in Glebe.

Eileen was still visibly upset over seeing Charlie's face on television and the shock of the Prasad 'kidnapping'. Within minutes of his having arrived home, police had surrounded the Perkins home. Police officers were knocking on the door and dozens of cameramen were looking through the windows.

'It was like an invasion,' Eileen recalled.

'Charlie said, "Eileen, we had better make some tea or something for these people."'

They would have needed a lot of tea; by then there were more than 50 people in the house. Included were people from the Freedom Ride in a celebratory mood and reporters clamouring for interviews. That they had successfully highlighted the racial discrimination and injustice in the Nancy Prasad case made it all worthwhile for Charlie and his fellow students.

'There was no maliciousness involved in the kidnapping,' Charlie said, 'Nancy was not frightened. In fact, she was asleep by the time we reached her home. She was calm when I woke her and told her it was time to go inside.'

The protestors had successfully prevented the deportation of five-year-old Nancy Prasad that day of 6 August 1965, but the authorities got their way two days later when the little girl was flown to Fiji. Charlie was disappointed with the attitude of Immigration Minister Hubert Opperman, whom he believed made a lot of rather silly statements. The *Mirror* called the case 'one of the most depressing examples yet of the Australian bureaucracy at its lumbering, insensitive, boorish, overbearing, pig-headed, undiplomatic, pompous bureaucratic worst'.

Perkins said the students' methods were crude, but 'what else were we to do to bring awareness to the public over what was a great injustice?'.

The Liberal and National Party members were not the only politicians raising Charlie's ire. He thought the Labor Party was just as bad – 'regardless of Al Grasby's verbiage'.

While the kidnapping was a short-term loss, it proved a long-term win when within a few months the intractable Mr Opperman announced that he would consider a 'greater intake of non-Europeans, especially those well qualified or who already had family in Australia'.

Historians generally agree that the Opperman statement was a significant change in post-war policy and the Prasad case a key factor in reformulating that policy. Charlie reckoned both the Freedom Ride and the 'kidnap' brought about change, which 'would have happened anyway, but we helped make things change about 10 years sooner'.

Interestingly Charlie had his own thoughts about 'coloured immigration'. He detested most aspects of the White Australia Policy, but he strongly believed that there should be 'no coloured immigration into this country until such time as the Aborigines are satisfactorily placed in Australian society'.

Vince and Brenda Copley, Eileen Perkins and I chatted over steaming mugs of tea, discussing discrimination and how the

Kidnapped

Eileen and Charlie Perkins with (left to right) Hetti, Rachel and Adam.

boys from St Francis House had coped over the years with this scourge. Also how discrimination impacted their wives and children.

'Well, you know this sort of thing is very subtle in Australia,' Eileen said.

'I don't know,' Brenda volunteered. 'It's very blatant here.'

Just as the boys at St Francis experienced overt racism from that little white boy sitting on the wall near the Odeon Theatre on Semaphore Road, so too have the Copley and Perkins family dealt with it over the years.

Vince often refers to the times he would regularly catch the O-Bahn bus into town from the northern suburbs of Adelaide.

The Boys from St Francis

'The bus was often full, but there always seemed to be one empty seat right next to me and there were people standing in the aisle rather than sit down next to a black man.'

All the protesting and work by FCAATSI in agitating for change brought about the Australian Referendum of 27 May 1967, called by the Holt government, approving two amendments to the Australian Constitution relating to Indigenous Australians. The referendum, which was overwhelmingly endorsed by 90.77 per cent of people and carried in six states, gave First Australians the vote for the first time.

But, as so often is the case in any democracy, change comes upon us like a slowly enveloping cloud, not with the raging speed of a hurricane.

Late in 1969 Charlie was still playing soccer, but despite his peak fitness from regular training and playing the game at the top level, he couldn't understand why he found himself exhausted at night. Often he struggled for breath.

Then one day Charlie collapsed on a Sydney street. Over a few frightening moments he lost his sight. Passers-by called for help and the police arrived.

'They (the police) took one look at Charlie and decided he was drunk,' Eileen said.

'Charlie told me he somehow got himself by cab to Biggo's (Gordon Briscoe) place in Fairfield,' Vince said.

'I asked Charlie why he thought Biggo could help him. He didn't know. Maybe he felt lost, and when he needed help he turned to the closest old boys from St Francis House. In this case it was Gordon Briscoe.'

The incident was frightening and Charlie knew something was drastically wrong with him, but let it lie.

Kidnapped

Then in July 1971 Perkins went to a rugby union match involving the visiting Springboks. A violently pro-Springbok crowd was at the game and Charlie was amazed at the threatening nature of the crowd toward demonstrators outside the ground. After the game, Springbok fans spotted Charlie and his group: 'Dirty niggers! Black bastards! Go back to South Africa where you belong!'

He wrote in the *Australian* afterwards: 'I really thought white people in this country and Aboriginals had come closer together in the past 10 years. Your personal integrity is never left alone from the time you're born to the day you die.'

Rugby union was the Afrikaners' sport in the republic of South Africa. As with supporters of the New Zealand All Blacks, rugby to them is more than a sport: it is a religion. The horrific apartheid policy of the Vorster National Party in South Africa, however, alienated countries and eventually caused a halt to all international sport.

At first South Africa did as the Boers did: they circled the wagons and retreated into the laager. However, after 20 years of international sport isolation and trade sanctions that crippled industry and crushed the rand, the black majority in South Africa found its voice.

In a way Australia's treatment of its Indigenous people was every bit as bad as that of South Africa. However, Australia's 'apartheid' was covert, implemented throughout society by stealth and deception.

When Nelson Mandela was finally released from prison and became president, he brought an amazing statesman-like quality to his land and to the world. Mandela didn't advocate hatred, but wanted peace and harmony.

The Boys from St Francis

During his reign as South Australian premier, Don Dunstan invited Vince Copley to accompany him to Sydney for a meeting with President Mandela. For more than an hour they sat and spoke to Mandela about the situation in the republic and how it compared with Australia's race relations.

President Mandela won many Afrikaner hearts when he donned the Springbok rugby jersey at the 1995 Rugby World Cup final at Ellis Park, Johannesburg. There stood the president, wearing the Springbok gear as he shook the hand of winning South African captain Francois Pienaar. Among most white communities in apartheid South Africa, it was taken for granted that Nelson Mandela was a terrorist who must remain behind bars. This attitude was drummed into the young Pienaar, who would one day welcome Mandela to his wedding and name him godfather to his two sons. At the 1995 World Cup final when the fair-haired Afrikaner shook hands with the black freedom-fighter-turned-president, they instantly forged one of South Africa's defining images of racial unity.

Australia's opposition to a South African rugby tour Down Under had grave ramifications for the Springboks. Soon after the disruption and riots during the rugby tour, the Australian Cricket Board's chairman Sir Donald Bradman announced the cancellation of the proposed 1971/1972 South African tour of Australia. That was the catalyst for the end of international sporting ties with South Africa while that country remained a rogue state with minority white rule. Charlie and his fellow protestors helped in no small way to change attitudes in South Africa toward the indigenous population, which hugely outnumbered the whites.

But in 1971 Charlie's main concern was for his health. He

couldn't continue the fight for his people if he was an invalid. One afternoon he came off the soccer pitch with a blinding headache. Eileen phoned a doctor, who took one look at him and said, 'You're sick, very sick.'

At the time he was living and working in Canberra, but he needed to go to Sydney for immediate treatment. His kidneys had collapsed. The immediate answer was to hook him up to a kidney machine. This occurred over a 10-hour cycle, three times a week. In those days kidney dialysis machines were crude and cumbersome. Blood had to be purified. Salts in solution were pumped into the stomach to absorb toxic waste and then evacuated. Initially the process was exacting: painful for Charlie and frustrating for Eileen. Charlie had a sense of foreboding and didn't think he would survive. Eileen was courage personified.

Brenda Copley says Eileen Perkins 'is the most remarkable woman I've ever known'.

Eileen had to make the incision for the needle connected to the dialysis machine. She helped in emergencies and had to endure Charlie's depression and ill-humour.

Brenda says: 'Charlie often gave her hell over the dialysis business. He got depressed and he called her all manner of names. I once said, "Eileen, I'd have that man's guts for garters if he treated me so badly." You know, Eileen said she loved Charlie and knew that he loved her and that it was only the depression which made him say such awful things. "Brenda, I'm here to help him. I know I could lash back but I want to help and I'll continue to help."'

In 1969 Perkins began his career as a public servant working as a senior research officer with the Office of Aboriginal Affairs. When Gough Whitlam led the Australian Labor Party to victory in the 1972 'It's Time' victory, Charlie was offered a more prominent role. Despite his suspension for alleged improper conduct after labelling the Coalition government in Western Australia as 'racist and redneck' in 1972, he would go on to more promotions.

Eileen said the final years of Charlie's job at the Office of Aboriginal Affairs were perhaps the toughest as his disease was worsening. The dialysis was certainly keeping him alive, but he need a kidney transplant. Every morning Eileen would tie Charlie's shoelaces and help him dress. Often he would sit on a chair between the main house and the garage for 20 minutes before driving to work. Halfway to the office he would stop the car by the side of the road and doze for 20 minutes, then continue. Once at his desk he would rest again for an hour. For lunch he ate a diet-approved sandwich then slept for an hour in the car. Trips to Sydney were confined to no more than 30 hours or he would have to arrange to use a dialysis machine while there.

Eileen said she was warned by people at the time they became engaged.

'I knew then of Charlie's kidney problem. People would tell me that I was marrying an invalid: "Think about it, he's sick, black and broke!"'

In March 1972 Charlie and Vince spent a few days in Alice Springs. He had completed dialysis in Adelaide 10 hours before, but it was not possible to start it again for 20 hours. Something was terribly wrong.

'I looked at Charlie lying there,' Vince recalled. 'He was all puffed up, like a big, fat bullfrog, his face and neck all swollen with his veins sticking out. Charlie was lying on his back. He opened his eyes: "Hey, Vince. Why don't you go for a walk?"'

Vince resisted. He knew Charlie was planning to do something and he didn't like the thought.

'No, Charlie. I'm not going away. I'm here with you.'

Next morning the two men showered, dressed and packed. They had a plane to catch. As they walked from the motel, Vince said: 'You were going to jump out of the window when I was gone, right?'

'Yeah.'

Vince burst out laughing.

'What's so funny?'

'Well, have a look mate,' Vince said, pointing to the balcony of the room they had just left.

'Jumping from the first floor wouldn't have killed you. If you had you'd still have trouble with the kidneys along with broken legs and arms.'

Charlie later recalled, 'It's a lonely sort of death, but most deaths are, unfortunately. I might have done it!'

After returning to Adelaide a few days later, Charlie got word that a kidney had become available for transplant. Charlie was so ill on the plane returning to Adelaide from Alice Springs that he had prepared himself psychologically to die. But the 'best message' in his life heralding the available kidney for transplant buoyed him.

After his transplant, Charlie was, in 1981, appointed permanent secretary of the Department of Aboriginal Affairs. Prime Minister Hawke once said of Perkins that 'he sometimes found it difficult to observe the constraints usually imposed on permanent heads of departments because he had a burning passion for advancing the interests of his people'.

Charlie served as the permanent secretary until 1988. A year later he became chairman of the Arrernte Council of Central Australia. In 1993 he was elected commissioner of ATSIC for an area of the Northern Territory. In 1994 he was elected deputy chairperson of ATSIC.

Before the transplant, Charlie lay in Queen Elizabeth Hospital's ICU, his thoughts racing. And all the while, quietly, consistently and lovingly, the one marvellous constant in his life, his Eileen, was there with him, by his side.

The power of education

'My mother had taken me to school and when she came later that day to pick me up she found that her four-year-old son was gone: taken away in an army truck. I was 15 before I saw my mum again.' – John Moriarty

By now dear reader you will have delighted in the extraordinary success rate among the boys who attended St Francis House between 1947 and 1959. There were varying degrees of achievement among the boys, however, to a man they all went on to better themselves and to become good citizens. Some of the boys, including Charlie Perkins, John Moriarty, Gordon Briscoe and Bill Espie, came to the belief early in their lives that education was the real power in this world. Charlie once said: 'Combine language with knowledge and you're unbeatable.'

John Moriarty revealed exceptional vision, both on the sporting front and in public life. His pathway in sport was similar to Charlie's. They both played for Port Thistle and John found, as Charlie had too, that sport was a great leveller in a society that frowned upon First Australians.

John was taken from Roper River Mission in the Northern Territory without his mother's permission and sent to Mulgoa in New South Wales. He was then four years old. Born on the bank of the McArthur River in 1938 to an Aboriginal mother who spoke eight languages, and an Irishman, John Moriarty, from Blennerville, County Kerry, John's allocated birthdate is 1 April 1938, although he later learned he was born in July, 1937.

The Boys from St Francis

'Rarely did the authorities correctly record the real birthdate of Aboriginal babies,' John recalls. 'Whenever I had to go overseas I had to contact Father Smith to verify my birthdate. It still shows on my passport as April 1, 1938, but a policeman told me years later that the actual date was 7 July 1937.'

At the time John was taken to Mulgoa he spoke only the Yanyuna language. His Aboriginal name is Jumbana and his ceremonial name is Kundareri. 'I do remember digging for water lilies in the billabongs at Borroloola and in the Roper River when I was little. I'll never forget the day the army truck came. My mother had taken me to school and when she came later that day to pick me up she found her four-year-old son was gone: taken away in an army truck. I had turned 15 before I saw my mum again.'

There were a number of boys and girls of different ages as well as mothers standing in the back of the truck. John remembers being given a pair of shorts and a short-sleeved shirt.

'The girls wore floral dresses. A few hours along the dusty trip to Alice Springs, a wooden crate landed on my foot. It left me with a bleeding toe and disfigured toenail, which still reminds me of the trip to this day.'

I speak with John at a coffee shop on Sydney's north shore at Miller Street, Cammeray, coincidentally about 200 metres from where I was struck down by a car crossing the road with my brother 63 years earlier.

'Some of the children on the army truck had their mothers with them,' John recalls. 'There was Marie Burke, who had two daughters; Topsy Glynn and her two girls; and Alice Roberts, who had a boy and a girl. Those mothers were wonderful in the way they cared for us. They helped me enormously in that they

The power of education

knew my family and my background. Through their love and understanding they brought me the knowledge I needed about family and culture.'

John spent eight years at Mulgoa. There he enjoyed school and found how to supplement his meagre diet by hunting with other boys from the Mulgoa home on regular field trips to Mt Wilson in the Blue Mountains. 'We caught rabbits, goannas, bush tucker berries and some types of birds. There were a couple of the boys' mothers with us and we learnt an enormous amount about country and culture from them.' Thanks to these Aboriginal women, John and his peers were educated in their rich cultural heritage hand in hand with their mainstream schooling.

At the age of 12, John, Wally McArthur, Jim Foster and a number of other boys were taken from Mulgoa to St Francis House.

'I was very sad to leave my schoolmates in Mulgoa. I especially missed two of my closest friends, brothers Brian and Ken Walker. But I kept in touch and years later when Ros and I and our kids moved back to New South Wales I got back in touch with Brian's daughter Sharon whom I now see regularly. Brian and Ken had passed on before we returned to Sydney.

'When we arrived at St Francis House Charlie was a bit rough toward me, but Wally and Jim looked after me and he soon got the message,' John recalls. 'Funny really, because later on Charlie and I got on very well.'

'I enjoyed the life there when Father Smith was running St Francis House. As in Mulgoa, even though we were well fed, we always seemed to be hungry, so we needed to supplement our diet.'

The boys knew how to find extra food. There was weekly

The Boys from St Francis

Sunday morning church with the breakfast treat there of an egg and bacon roll and in the warmer months there was the added bonus on the walk back to St Francis House of fruit, which was plentiful, growing on the overhanging branches of the neighbours' fences. Most households in the 1950s had a grape vine. The boys had also learnt how to identify wattle trees with sweet gum to consume. 'I suppose growing boys need plenty of food. We always seemed to be after more food. Even today my wife, Ros, says "Take it easy, John. There's another meal coming shortly."'

Soon after John arrived from Mulgoa, his mother sent him a beautifully crafted pandanus basket specially woven for him. John always kept the basket in pristine condition, along with the woollen dressing-gown Father Smith presented him when he arrived at St Francis House. These are now safely tucked away in the National Museum of Australia in Canberra, alongside other personal items including a soccer trophy, three state blazers, scrapbooks and photographs of John's early years. 'At Ethelton Primary and Le Fevre Boys Technical High School we excelled at sport. There was really no trouble with the white boys. Some of our bigger boys such as Wally McArthur and Jim Foster kept a close eye on our welfare, but they never looked for a fight. They were too busy beating everyone on the sports field.'

In Mulgoa the sports were cricket in summer and rugby league in winter. There was no soccer. Yet soon after leaving Mulgoa, John Moriarty played in that amazing soccer match in the ground near St Francis House.

That was their first tilt at the game.

'After the practice game a man asked me if I wanted to join the Port Thistle Soccer Club.

The power of education

'"No thank you, sir," I said.

'Later he approached me again to join them and before I could repeat the words "No thank you, sir", the man said "If you join our team I will buy you a new pair of boots."'

John was immediately sold on the idea. From then on, soccer was Moriarty's game.

Around the time John turned 15, he began his quest to find his mother. She had sent him practical gifts such as the woven basket, but they had not seen each other for almost 11 years.

'There was a lot of chasing up on my part and with the help of others, especially the superintendent at St Francis House. Eventually the welfare department brought my mother down to Alice Springs from Borroloola. However, no one linked me with my mother when she arrived. There I was staying at St John's Hostel and my mother was at the Bungalow.

'I was taken to the Alice, but there was no fanfare. In fact, I had no idea where she was in town. Then something incredible happened. Across the road this lady was looking at me with a very fixed look. And she strode across the road. I was similarly transfixed. She asked me where I was from and I saw, "I'm from Borroloola."

'"What's your name?"

'"John Moriarty."

'She said, "I'm your mother."

'We sat down in front of a hotel, on the kerbside, and talked about my grandparents and the family back in Borroloola. It was a wonderful reunion for me and such a relief.'

John married Ros Langham in 1982. Ros hails from Tasmania and her upbringing could not have been more different than John Moriarty's early life. 'I was taught to love and respect country, so I think I got it really. I was born in Latrobe, a little town outside Devonport in Tasmania. My parents were very strongly Methodist, so there was a strong work ethic in the family unit,' Ros says.

'When I was a little girl I had never heard of Borroloola, nor had I knowingly met an Aboriginal person.' Her working life drew her toward John Moriarty when she joined the Department of Aboriginal Affairs and a number of people pointed her in the direction of 'someone who knows the real bush stuff'.

John says of their first meeting, 'I first saw Ros at the base of the building where I was working and she walked by and I thought she was a stunning lady with a tonne of poise.'

'When I spoke to John I found him to be funny, sensitive and I guess it wasn't all that long when I thought … I fell in love with him really. I realised that he was very comfortable across two cultures, so while he was clearly deeply Aboriginal he was also an Australian who wanted to take his place in mainstream Australia.'

John cannot remember his father, whom he believes was a cook in Borroloola. He sailed from Ireland to Australia in 1928, where he met John's mother.

'Because my mother was black and my father was white I was classified "half-caste" and that's why I was taken away.'

John Moriarty visited Ireland on three separate occasions to try and track down his father. On the third try, he spoke to a man called Pat O'Shea for about 20 minutes at a house in Castlegregory.

'Your father was here 52 years ago,' the man told him, handing John a trout rod, with a little brass reel. 'He left this here 52 years ago for you.'

The power of education

That very day John met his uncle Eugene who told him that his father had died years before, but John slept better than he had for years finding great solace in having found his father's family.

Ros recalls: 'When John's mother told me for the first time that he had been born on a riverbank – and she was blind by the time I met her – she pointed in the general direction where she gave birth and told me the story of the day she took him to school, then came back to pick him up and he was gone. I felt dizzy. I couldn't assimilate how a mother would feel.'

Looking back at his life, John says that sport – especially soccer – played a pivotal role.

'I enjoyed all sport, but I thought soccer had the point of difference for me. You had to be physically fit and mentally alert and you didn't have to be a trundling ruckman or a small rover to get a position.'

He went on to play for Port Thistle and Port Adelaide (1956 to 1958), Juventus in Adelaide (1960 to 1965) and he also had a brief experience playing for Prague in the 1960s. Moriarty represented South Australia 17 times. His first match was also Charlie Perkins's first representative game for South Australia.

Their lumbering DC6B aircraft took six and a half hours to fly from Adelaide to Perth. Most of the team were European migrants: British, Hungarian and Yugoslav.

In a successful first state game, Moriarty scored two goals. He became an instant hero and he remembers the accolades and press reports, as well as sitting dumbstruck before a microphone in the studio of a Perth radio station. John's mentor at Juventus was Mick O'Malley, born in Scotland of Irish parents, who hailed from Donegal, lived much of his early life in Glasgow and found his first posting as a national serviceman in Malaya. O'Malley eventually emigrated to Australia, playing left-back for Australia. Mick and John both worked at the Osborne Power Station.

'I'd pester him,' Moriarty says. 'I don't know how he put up with me, because he also had his work and a young family. But he worked me extremely hard. He would say: "You didn't do that as effectively as you should," then he'd kick the ball miles away and I'd have to run, turn, dribble and pass it back. It was fantastic training.'

As a member of the Stolen Generations, John Moriarty found that he was accepted by European migrants in a manner completely foreign to how he was treated by some white Australians. The European migrants at the hostel which stood directly in front of St Francis House were the first example of this. Their acceptance was based on character and personality, not on colour. Almost certainly it was the influence of these migrants that led the majority of the boys from St Francis to choose soccer over Australian Rules football. Like the boys, the migrants were considered 'outsiders'.

'People would often ask me why I played that "foreign game".

'My reply? "I don't have any prejudice heaped on me. I am accepted as an individual. Anyway it's a fantastic game and it's international; the world game."

'Because I played soccer the football community looked on me as one of their own. The Italians called me Johnny Moratti! I felt totally at ease with them. Even today people will approach me in the street and say, "I remember that goal you scored." Ros can't get over it.'

The power of education

Moriarty says he still experiences prejudice against 'those new Australians' who played soccer.

'A cousin of mine, Wilfred "Boofa" Huddleston, who was at Mulgoa with me then St Francis House, played for the Port Adelaide Football Club, the Magpies.

'He introduced me to Port stars John Cahill, Geof Motley, Ted Whelan and Fos Williams, all of whom I liked.

'Then Boofa insisted I attend a Port club function. Bob McLean was then the Port Adelaide Fooball Club's secretary.

'I shunned alcohol in those days and I noted that those clubs had a lot of booze, a lot of smoking. "Big" Bob McLean, as they used to call him, walked into the clubrooms and Boofa said: "Bob, I'd like you to meet my cousin." McLean brushed past me and pushed Boofa aside. He ignored us. I said to Boofa, "I will not support Port Adelaide ever again."'

In 1961, John Moriarty was the first Indigenous Australian to be called up to the national soccer team, but just after he was selected for a tour of Southeast Asia, FIFA banned Australia, ending his international career before it even began. In 1961 the Australian Soccer Federation was formed as a potential successor to the former governing body for the sport. However, this association was refused re-admittance to FIFA until outstanding fines had been paid, which was done in 1963.

'You know, missing the chance to play for Australia was a great disappointment. We were scheduled to pay in Singapore, but the tour was cancelled. I didn't get a guernsey, not even a letter from the soccer administration. Nothing.'

Moriarty was said to be fast, able to kick with precision with both feet and he had a sharp sense of where the goals were and how to beat the keeper. Maybe if he had played Aussie Rules in another era he might have been a Cyril Rioli or a Chad Wingard, both of whom instinctively know where the goals are and how to nail a six-pointer.

'The Australian team chairman of selectors at the time told me I was the first player picked. It was said the ban on Australia was because of "transfer irregularities".'

By the time the ban was lifted Moriarty's career was over.

He was just 27 when he collided with a goalkeeper, wrecking his knee and ruining any chance of playing out what had been an outstanding career in the sport. That he never got that Australian guernsey still plays on his mind. It is one of his sporting regrets, so too his decision not to take up invitations to trial at Tottenham, Arsenal and Everton.

He went to England at the height of the season and recruitment was far from the minds of club scouts. Instead, he travelled in Europe and in northern Africa, then returned to Australia to play soccer and matriculate.

Aboriginal rights became Moriarty's life's work. He was in the Department of Aboriginal Affairs for many years, was on the National Indigenous Council and has written a book on his life called *Saltwater Fella*. Further to the cause, he and wife Ros established their own design studio in Adelaide, later moving the company to Sydney.

Ros Moriarty studied at the Australian National University, receiving a Bachelor of Arts in 1976. Her early working life was as an ABC radio journalist, and their studio Balarinji was established in 1983, a year after she and John married. Their first collection was launched in Melbourne by the Australian Wool Corporation. Ros has written ten books, including her

The power of education

The 'boys from St Francis' reunion at John Smith's Banksia Park home, 1977. Back Row: Ken Hampton, Vince Copley, David Woodford, Charlie Perkins, John Moriarty, Des Price and Les Nayda. Front row: Gerry Hill, Father Percy Smith, Ken Nayda and Wally McArthur.

award-winning *Listening to Country*, a memoir that includes details of Aboriginal life in the Northern Territory, especially in the area where John was born.

'It's about deep belonging, the basic humanity that Aboriginal people have nurtured on this continent for so long.'

In later life Ros learnt there was Aboriginal blood in her family.

'Cousins on my father's side, through marriage, were Aboriginal but we'd always been told that their skin was darker because they worked outside,' she says.

Ros and John Moriarty are a happy couple and are a formidable business and entrepreneurial team. Their most celebrated project was to paint five Qantas planes with Aboriginal motifs in 1994 and 2018.

The Boys from St Francis

It was Ros who woke one morning at 2 am and said: 'We've got to paint a Qantas jumbo jet.'

Moriarty told her to go back to sleep.

'Actually, John's words were a little different,' Ros Moriarty laughed during an interview with Peter Thompson on ABC TV's *Talking Heads* in 2010.

'I thought that Qantas was the perfect vehicle to demonstrate what we were trying to do through design, which was to say something new about being Australian. It was the first art aircraft and it was big, and it was out there. Just a huge buzz.'

John says the designs Ros and he created were reflections of the colours and shapes of kangaroos. 'You know their waterhole, the tracks that they've travelled on and the hills inside the landscape. So in my language it is kangaroo dreaming or "Wunala Dreaming".'

Soon after Ros's lightning bolt moment, the couple showed their idea to then Qantas chief executive James Strong in a lift. 'He was pretty well knocked off his feet,' says Moriarty. 'James took a step back and had another look at it.'

Thanks to Strong's enthusiasm, and that of his deputy, Geoff Dixon, Ros and John Moriarty were commissioned by Qantas to present their designs of Wunala Dreaming and have the image replicated on a Boeing 747-400.

'When I first saw Wunala Dreaming being wheeled out of the hangar, I thought it was all my emotions coming at once,' John says.

'I think there were a lot of jaws on the ground; it was just a euphoric moment. It was so emotional to see Australia heralding Aboriginal culture on such a flamboyant basis.'

The power of education

John and Ros Moriarty are all smiles standing in front of a jumbo jet sporting their design.

A year after Wunala Dreaming a second Balarinji team artwork – Nalanji Dreaming – was painted on a 747-300 jet, which has since been retired.

One of the most remarkable events in John's life happened aboard ship during his first overseas adventure in 1963. John met a woman who knew a Melbourne lady named Merle Griffin.

They chatted and John told her part of his story and how he was taken from his family at Borroloola at the age of four and found himself at two institutions in turn – Mulgoa in New South Wales and then St Francis House. When the woman got back to Australia she related John's story to Merle Griffin. When John returned home in 1964 a letter from Merle awaited him. They met and formed a strong bond when Merle showed him

The Boys from St Francis

John as a child, Borroloola, early 1940s, by Merle Griffin. E.M. Griffin Collection, John Moriarty Collection, National Museum Australia.

photographs of him and his family at Borroloola. Some of these photographs appeared with articles Merle wrote for *Walkabout* magazine.

One of the images depicts two-year-old John Moriarty on the banks of the McArthur River.

A black white man? Never!

'Because I was seen as a model Aborigine, had successfully completed an apprenticeship and was playing top-flight soccer, I was asked if I wanted an exemption. Become a black white man? Never!' – John Moriarty

Many of the boys who spent their formative years at St Francis House were publicly exposed to the illogical injustices of the Aborigines Protection Act. In 1960 when John Moriarty and Charlie Perkins were selected for the South Australian soccer team to play Western Australia in Perth, they found to their horror that to travel interstate with their fellow players they had to apply for written permission from the Protector of Aborigines. This demeaning regulation fired their resolve to break the government's control over Aboriginal people. The Act was the very antithesis of 'protection'.

At the time, Moriarty was incensed: 'I jacked up as a matter of principle when I learnt about having to ask permission to travel.'

Doubtless this was the catalyst for Moriarty fighting for Aboriginal rights.

'But I was clearly aware of injustice years before I played representative soccer. That time I had the chance meeting with my mother on an Alice Springs street I discovered that she was still regarded as a ward of the state and subject to all manner of restrictions and curfews,' Moriarty says.

'Sadly she was shunted from one area to another. Shortly after we met that time in Alice, she had to hurry away to be at her accommodation to beat the curfew.'

The Boys from St Francis

Aboriginal people lived and died at the mercy of the government and the welfare system. Moriarty learnt that there was a provision in law for an Indigenous man or woman to seek an exemption. While a successful application for exemption meant freedom of passage it smacked of bowing to authority.

'Because I was seen as a model Aborigine, had successfully completed an apprenticeship and was playing top-flight soccer, I was asked if I wanted an exemption,' he recalls.

'"Not on your life," I said, "I refuse to have one. My principles wouldn't allow me to say that I have obtained the standard of living equal to that of a white man and be treated as such from now on. Become a black white man? Never!"'

Moriarty became a founding member of the Aboriginal Progress Association (APA) in the early 1960s. Former activists with the Aborigines Advancement League such as St Francis House old boys Malcolm Cooper, Charlie Perkins, Gerry Hill, David Woodford, Harry Russell, Tim Campbell, Ken Hampton, Richie Bray, Wilfred Huddleston, Vince Copley and Gordon Briscoe also joined the APA.

Malcolm Cooper was the APA's inaugural president. A brilliant footballer, Cooper played alongside the legendary Fos Williams for the Port Adelaide Football Club in 1954 and 1955. Richie Bray, a brilliant half-forward, played 77 games for the Magpies, a three-time premiership player in 1962, 1963 and 1965. Bray is the only ex-St Francis House resident to play in a South Australian league premiership team and be named in the SANFL Indigenous Team of the Century.

In the formative days of the APA, regular meetings were held at 5 Talbot Street, Angle Park: the modest, welcoming home of Malcolm and Aileen Cooper.

A black white man? Never!

Malcolm Cooper leaning against the courtyard wall at the back of St Francis House, c. 1948.

Aileen was a former Colebrook Home girl. She worked as a cook at St Francis House and that is where she met the young man that everyone knew as 'Coop'.

Mary Williams, a fiery lady committed to the fight against injustice toward Aboriginals, would also attend.

'We called her "Aunty Mary",' Moriarty says. 'She had a hot temper. With me it was fine, but with Coop, it was like rubbing a match against a striker. Poor old Malcolm used to get frustrated with her and she knew how to get Malcolm off-side.'

The APA meetings were vastly different to the Aborigines Advancement League for the body collective was committed to fighting for justice for Indigenous Australians on the political front.

The Boys from St Francis

Reunion at St Francis House, c. 1968. Back row: John Moriarty, Richie Bray, Wally McArthur, Charlie Perkins, Brian Butler, John Smith, Vince Copley and Des Price. Front row: Max Wilson and Isabel Smith. The woman in the middle is unidentified.

John Moriarty, who was the APA's first vice president, says: 'We set about working toward land rights. A lot of Aborigines were alcoholics, so we needed to help them find a pathway to good health and find a purpose in life.

'A football team [the Nungas] was formed and we raised funds by way of running dances and fetes.'

Nunga is a term for an Indigenous person living in southern Australia. Vince Copley used to perform as captain-coach for Curramulka of a Saturday, then make the two-hour drive to Adelaide the next day to turn out for the Nungas. The team played matches against the police force, the army, even people connected with the Glenside mental institution.

A black white man? Never!

'We were mid-way through the third quarter against Glenside when a whistle sounded and all the opposition players walked from the field for afternoon tea,' Vince laughs.

Had the Nungas not had a heightened sense of sportsmanship, they might have kicked a cricket score while the opposition drank tea and scoffed cream cakes.

The APA began to increase its influence on the political landscape in Adelaide and within a few years the Aboriginal Legal Service was established. Up until the late 1960s many Aboriginal people attended court without any legal representation because they could not afford it. Eminent lawyer Elliott Johnston attended one of the APA's early meetings.

'Johnston regarded that meeting as one of the baptisms in Aboriginal affairs legal issues,' Moriarty says.

Johnston was a long-time member of the Australian Communist Party and in 1955 he had visited communist China at the invitation of Mao Tse Tung. It wasn't until the 1960s that Johnston realised communist China was just as flawed as Russia. When the cruelty and stupidity of Mao's Cultural Revolution became apparent Johnston was shocked, but he remained a committed communist. In 1969 he was put up for elevation to QC, but the application was rejected on 'political grounds'. A year later, in 1970, after Don Dunstan's Labor party rolled Steele Hall's Liberals to seize power, Johnston was appointed QC. He later played an important role in the royal commission into Aboriginal deaths in custody in 1988 and 1989.

Vince Copley says that it was around 1971 when he and others got together to establish the Aboriginal Cultural Institution, a forerunner to the Aboriginal Legal Service. Vince chaired that first meeting: 'Elliott Johnston came to our meetings, along with other legal men such as the man who would become South Australian premier, Don Dunstan, and two young lawyers, Andrew Ligertwood and Andrew Hodge.'

Three years after Dunstan entered the House of Assembly representing Norwood, he was invited by Aboriginal residents to look at conditions at Point Pearce. There he met, with other Aboriginal activists, St Francis House old boys Charlie Perkins, Gordon Briscoe and John Moriarty.

Forty years after he first visited Point Pearce, Dunstan said in a 1996 interview: 'I hadn't been aware, until that time, of just how serious and important was the Aboriginal question in South Australia. It wasn't an area which I had studied and it wasn't one, as I was doing my political studies at university, which really impinged on what we were doing. It was going to Point Pearce and just seeing the way which these people were affected by the protection laws; their rights as people were enormously restricted and they'd lived under the most appalling conditions in old stone cottages which had been built in the last century and there was one tap for the whole village! It was just dreadful. And they were living on a handout system which was inadequate so they were in quite dire poverty and some of them of course were pretty articulate about that, particularly Bob Wanganeen who was really the sort of leader of the Point Pearce community in those days. He became a great friend, and I went back to parliament and put on a tremendous turn and immediately started investigating just what was going on. I thought, "Well, this is a great gap in my knowledge, and also a great gap in the Labor Party's policy that we aren't doing anything about it".'

Don Dunstan stunned the Adelaide establishment when he appointed Reverend Doug Nicholls South Australian governor.

A black white man? Never!

'By appointing Sir Douglas we knew he would be a great figurehead for South Australia. I was delighted that Doug accepted the appointment and that he was here before the stroke which disabled him. He did a tremendous job: good because he was a good man and when he and his wife went anywhere in South Australia after a short period after their arrival here, everybody burst into applause when he arrived. He was such a lovable character. And it really was a tragedy that he suffered that stroke. Doug was a great unifier, determined in his opposition to discrimination, but he never did so in a provocative manner'.

One of the biggest Aboriginal cases in the 1950s was the murder charge laid against Gordon Briscoe's uncle, Rupert Maxwell Stuart (known as Max Stuart). In December 1958 Stuart was alleged to have murdered nine-year-old Mary Hattam on a remote beach near Ceduna in South Australia. However, the investigation was full of holes and the case became a raging political football that hit the Adelaide establishment like a firestorm. Found guilty, Stuart was sentenced to death on 24 April 1959. Subsequent appeals all the way to the High Court failed.

On Saturday, 20 December 1958, Mary Hattam disappeared near Ceduna. She had been playing on the beach between Ceduna and Thevard with her brother and their friend Peter Jacobson. The boys left Mary to collect a tub used as a boat, but they got distracted and did not return for more than a hour. When they came back Mary had disappeared. When night fell Roger Cardwell, who ran the local deli and was married to Mary's cousin, alerted police and many townsfolk sitting in the memorial hall watching a film, *Dial M for Murder*. (Later Cardwell became a prominent Adelaide-based television reader for Channel Nine.) Just after midnight on 21 December, Mary Hattam's mutilated body was found. She had been murdered between 2.30 pm and 8 pm on the Saturday.

Police brought in 'black tracker' Sonny Jim, who followed the tracks from Mary's body to a nearby rock pool, then retraced his steps. Harry Scott, a second tracker, was brought in and he came to the same conclusion as Sonny Jim: the footprints had been made by an Aboriginal from a northern Australian group who had spent time living with white people.

Max Stuart was then 27 years old. He was an Arrernte man living in Ceduna running a darts stall with a friend, 15-year-old Alan Moir, at a fun fair. Both men had been drinking on the day of the murder, and Stuart had been arrested for drinking alcohol at 9.30pm that night. He spent the night behind bars. Full-blooded Aboriginals were not allowed to drink alcohol, but in 1953 a federal ordinance was passed allowing 'half-castes' to drink, so long as they applied for a 'dog licence', as it was commonly referred. Stuart had not renewed his exemption certificate and when arrested for drinking he would normally have faced a jail sentence of up to 18 months.

On the morning of Sunday, 21 December 1958, Stuart was released without charge due to all police resources being dedicated to the Mary Hattam murder investigation. Next day, police picked up Stuart for questioning over the murder. Under interrogation Stuart admitted he had been drunk on the Saturday, but strenuously denied that he had anything to do with the little girl's murder. Police took Stuart outside and made him walk barefooted on the beach, after which the two black trackers were called in. They confirmed that Stuart's tracks matched those on the beach where the dead girl was found. According to the police, Stuart then confessed.

He signed a typed confession with the only English he knew: his name, written in block letters in the fashion his sister taught him, misspelling his first name as 'Ropert'.

On the strength of that signed confession Stuart was charged with first degree murder and his trial began on 20 April 1959. When he was arrested Stuart possessed 4/6½ (or 46 cents) and could not contribute to the cost of his defence.

A lawyer was assigned to him by the Law Society of South Australia, but there was no money to cover out-of-pocket expenses which would have been necessary to check Stuart's alibi, conduct forensic tests and consult expert witnesses. Max Stuart was a veritable lamb to the slaughter. The case was based on circumstantial evidence that a top-notch QC would have had thrown out of court. Given a prepared statement from the dock, Stuart was unable to read the document. Tellingly, the presiding judge Sir Geoffrey Reed refused permission for a court official to read the statement on Stuart's behalf. However, Stuart did make his own statement in pidgin English: 'I cannot read or write. Never been to school. I did not see the little girl. Police hit me, choke me. Make me say these words. They say I kill her.'

In the wake of Stuart's murder conviction, the prison chaplain, who was unable to communicate with the condemned man due to his lack of English, brought in Catholic priest Father Tom Dixon, who happened to speak fluent Arrernte, a skill gained while working on missions. Father Dixon had grave doubts whether Stuart was guilty of murder. He called upon the services of noted anthropologist and linguist Ted Strehlow, who was raised in Arrernte society and had known Stuart since childhood. Professor Strehlow also had his doubts. He translated

Stuart's alibi wherein Stuart claimed he had taken a taxi to the Thevenard hotel where he had paid an Aboriginal woman £4 for sex and had remained there until he was arrested that night.

Six policemen testified under oath at the trial, claiming that the signed confession was Stuart's 'literal and exact confession, word for word'.

Long after the trial, one of the policemen who questioned Stuart, Chief Inspector Paul Turner, confessed on his deathbed in 2001 that he and fellow officers had 'jollied' and joked the confession out of the accused. Once they had it, they bashed him. The other five policeman involved in the interrogation refuted Chief Inspector Turner's version of events. Stuart's execution date was set for 7 July 1959 but the case had attracted nationwide attention. The *Sydney Morning Herald* and Adelaide afternoon daily, the *News*, led the fight to have the Privy Council use its executive power to commute the death sentence to life imprisonment. The *News* editor Rohan Rivett was a forthright man, given to strong views, although his way of putting his case in print often polarised public opinion. People either hated his writing or loved it. Rivett's constant barrage in the *News* helped lead to a royal commission in regard to Max Stuart, the inquiry getting under way in August 1959. In December 1959 the commission concluded that 'Stuart's conviction was justified'.

Rupert Murdoch, who had been handed the *News* on a platter by his father, had much sympathy for Stuart. However, Murdoch believed Rivett's drive to right a great wrong for an uneducated Aboriginal man was increasingly hurting the paper. In 1960 the *News* and Rivett as editor were charged with seditious and malicious libel, with Premier Tom Playford describing the Rivett-led coverage as 'the gravest libel ever made against any judge in this state'. Dr John Bray, later chief justice and chancellor of the University of Adelaide, represented Rivett in court.

It was a good outcome for Rivett. The jury determined that the defendants had not committed an offence and the remaining charges were withdrawn. At the same time, Murdoch reckoned readers were being turned off by Rivett's relentless campaign to free Stuart and so sacked him. The fact that the *News*'s circulation was higher in 1960 when Rivett was fired than it was when he started in 1951 was neither here nor there with Murdoch. He was the boss.

Murdoch said later: 'There's no doubt Stuart didn't get a totally fair trial. Although it's probable that he was guilty, I thought this at the time. In those days – although less so now – I was very much against the death penalty.'

Murdoch biographer Bruce Page wrote of his subject's involvement in the Stuart case: 'It was the very brief period of Rupert's radicalism, which was a very good thing for Stuart, as it got him out of the hangman's noose. Murdoch galloped into action, but it was a bad fight for him. The truth is it scared him off from ever taking on governments again. He reverted to his father's pattern of toeing the line.'

Those brilliant young strategists who championed the Labor Party cause in its famous 'It's Time' campaign in 1972 would beg to differ with Page. Murdoch's daily broadsheet the *Australian* ran a relentless campaign to ensure Gough Whitlam won government.

Max Stuart was not executed, but remained in prison until 1973. His case alerted the world to the plight of the downtrodden in Australia. World-renowned human rights lawyer Geoffrey

The Boys from St Francis

Robertson QC said of the case: 'It was a dramatic and very important case because it alerted Australia to the difficulties that Aborigines, who weren't even counted in the census, encountered in the courts. It alerted us to that appalling feature of capital punishment of the death sentence that applied to people who may well be innocent.'

Joy and sorrow

'If you can fill the unforgiving minute
With sixty seconds' worth of distance run –
Yours is the Earth and everything that's in it,
And – which is more – you'll be a Man my son!'
– 'If', by Rudyard Kipling

An unbreakable, everlasting bond of friendship developed among the boys who attended St Francis House. They stuck together with the same measure of comradeship that surely prevailed in wartime POW camps. They closed ranks against the injustices of a number of cruel wardens at the home and they worked as a team to raid the St Francis House pantry in their on-going quest to satisfy their hunger. They were all determined to achieve in life: to get a decent education and to be treated as equals in a white-dominated society. As we have learnt, sport brought them a measure of equality among their school and club mates.

In the Preface I told of the time Charlie Perkins and Vince Copley flew to Kuala Lumpur seeking an audience with the great heavyweight prize fighter, Muhammad Ali. They sought to lure Ali to Australia in an effort to have the famous boxer speak to our Indigenous youth, encouraging them to work hard, play hard on the sports field and make sure they gain a good education, for Charlie and Vince knew all too well the power of knowledge. The pair spoke with Ali at his hotel on the day before his world

The Boys from St Francis

boxing championship title bout with England's Joe Bugner. Lionel Rose, the darling of Australian boxing, was also staying at the hotel. After their talk with Ali, Perkins and Copley knocked on Lionel Rose's door.

Rose wept at the sight of the two Australians framed in the doorway.

'I can't believe you'd come all this way to see me,' he sobbed joyfully, falling to his knees. Rose was one of Australia's greatest fighters and tough as nails in the ring. But at the sight of his two countrymen his emotions overwhelmed him.

Next night, 1 July 1975, Rose out-pointed Japan's Shoji Uchida in the supporting bout before the Ali–Bugner title fight. Charlie and Vince enjoyed their ringside seats, gifted to them by Muhammad Ali, watching first Rose win then Ali overcome a superbly courageous Joe Bugner.

This was a high point, but there were also many lows. Two of the boys from St Francis – Ernie Perkins and Peter Tilmouth – tragically died in separate incidents.

Ernie Perkins, younger brother of Charlie, was a smart boy. According to his peers at St Francis House Ernie was naturally inquisitive and quickly revealed his skill in fixing anything mechanical. When one of the older boys purchased a motorbike they immediately asked Ernie to check it out. During trips home to the Alice, Ernie would race his motorbike up and down Rainbow Town at midnight. He was a daring lad – he didn't hold a licence, or registration, insurance, mud-guards or brakes – and he raced without lights.

Sadly the institutionalised life at St Francis House left Ernie and his older brother Charlie somewhat distant. Ernie had become closer to Vince Copley. Then one night in 1968, after

Joy and sorrow

Ernie Perkins at St Francis House, c. 1949.

a few drinks at Henbury Station where he was working, Ernie must have become disorientated and stumbled into the bush. The police were notified about Ernie's disappearance but they shrugged their shoulders and took no notice. When the hours of his disappearance became days the police reluctantly took up the search. They found Ernie slumped on the ground in the desert. He was dead.

Peter Tilmouth was a bright, energetic lad. At St Francis House Peter had gained quite a lot of notoriety in Semaphore and further afield for his brilliant 'William Tell' stage performances. Apart from his acting abilities, Peter was intelligent and he worked hard at Le Fevre Boys Technical School before becoming

Malcolm Cooper and Peter Tilmouth at St Francis House, c. 1952.

a fitter and turner. He joined the navy and spent years in the service before settling down, working his trade at the Woomera Rocket Range.

Peter met his future wife, Faye Walker, a nurse in Woomera, while working at the rocket range and their love quickly blossomed. They were married by Father Percy Smith on 9 February 1963 and had three children, Margaret, Trish and Peter. Peter Tilmouth was a loving husband and father and a diligent hard-working tradesman.

Peter wanted to be his own boss and decided to purchase an opal mine. On 5 June 1973 he was killed in a cave-in. Peter was buried in a lonely grave at Andamooka later that month, but

Joy and sorrow

the family yearned for his body to be exhumed and returned to country – brought back to Alice Springs where he was born on 22 October 1934. The family finally got their wish nearly 40 years later, although it cost $15,000 to exhume the body and transport it to Alice Springs. On 20 April 2011 during a traditional smoking ceremony Peter Tilmouth was laid to rest at Olive Pink Botanic Gardens in Alice Springs: in cultural terms the son had been brought home to the bosom of the mother. His eldest daughter Margaret Mibus delivered the eulogy, while his younger daughter Trish narrated the immortal Rudyard Kipling poem 'If'.

In part it reads:

> If you can talk with crowds and keep your virtue
> Or walk with kings – nor lose the common touch;
> If neither foes nor loving friends can hurt you;
> If all men count with you, but none too much;
> If you can fill the unforgiving minute
> With sixty seconds' worth of distance run –
> Yours is the Earth and everything that's in it,
> And – which is more – you'll be a Man my son!

Brenda Copley well understands Kipling's words, especially the last line, for it was Brenda who came up with this line pertaining to the boys from St Francis: 'They came as boys and left as men'.

The surname Tilmouth was prominent at St Francis House. Apart from Peter there was Gerald, Colin, Ron and Richard Tilmouth.

Vince Copley vividly remembers the time Peter Tilmouth came back to the home after his first day working as an apprentice fitter and turner.

The Boys from St Francis

Gordon Briscoe receives his PhD in history at Australian National University, 24 April 1997, with Professor R. Spears, director of graduate studies. Photo courtesy John Smith.

'Truck sat down to his meal, took one mouthful then in mock disapproval he pushed his plate away – probably only a couple of inches. And before he could retrieve it four or five of us had already split up the booty and gulped the lot.'

There is joy and sorrow in all of their stories.

Most of the boys at the home pursued work as tradesmen. Gordon Briscoe considered himself a 'failed Aborigine' when he left St Francis House in 1956. 'I would have been homeless had it not been for Mrs McGee who offered me board in a room on the back veranda of her Semaphore South home,' Gordon recalls.

Mrs McGee knew the St Francis boys and how difficult it had been for them to find suitable accommodation after suddenly being thrust into the big wide world. Briscoe gathered up his meagre collection of clothes, his football gear and said goodbye to his two brothers, Dennis and Bill.

The kind woman, who then still worked as a washerwoman for St Francis House, was married to a man named Bill McGee. Bill was a ruddy-faced, heavy-drinking, ever-swearing wharfie who, along with his workmates, frequented the front bar of the Admiral Hotel at the Black Diamond corner in Port Adelaide every night of the working week. But sober or drunk Gordon thought him a good bloke and he was eternally grateful for the start they gave him. Soon Gordon passed his fireman's examination and continued to work in the South Australian railways. He was then still a ward of the Northern Territory and South Australian governments. It would be another 10 years before he became a full citizen of Australia. From that humble beginning, Gordon Briscoe, railway worker and top-flight soccer player, studied hard and became the first Aboriginal to achieve a PhD in history.

Another high achiever in the wake of his days at St Francis House was Les Nayda. A pre-eminent Aboriginal rights campaigner, Les became the trusted advisor to Premier David Tonkin on all things Indigenous in the state of South Australia in the early 1980s. He spent more than 30 years in the public sector. As with many of his peers at St Francis House, Les was one of the Stolen Generations. Until he attained the ripe old age of nine, Les enjoyed the love and support of his family at Rainbow Town, the Indigenous welfare cottage community at the Gap in Alice Springs. Les's grandmother Tilly Hale and mother Betty Sultan were both victims of the Stolen Generations. Sadly Les never saw his mother after 1954, the year he was sent to St Francis House. Betty died four years later – in 1958. He discovered many years later that he had seven siblings: six brothers and a sister. Les first trained to be a wood machinist, but his passion was campaigning for Aboriginal rights. Widely known as an unconventional bureaucrat, Les pulled no punches and took no prisoners in fighting for the welfare of his people. At Les Nayda's memorial service in May 2014, former Member for Barkly Elliott McAdam recalled serving with Les on Australia's first Aboriginal Task Force: 'I sat with Les on many a committee and many a South Australian public servant would come in shaking after an encounter with him. They never knew what he was going to do next, but whatever he did he always found an outcome; there was going to be a benefit and he was going to create something different.'

As director of the Adelaide branch of Aboriginal Employment Education Development, Les helped establish the Family Wellbeing Program – a groundbreaking concept in recognising the effects of colonisation on Indigenous health. In addition Les played a key role in the establishment of the Pitjantjatjara Land Rights Act in the early 1980s and was the first Aboriginal to be appointed to the South Australian parole board.

Les Nayda stood up to be counted on myriad occasions. He was fearless in his fight against any form of tyranny. While he was the first Aboriginal man to be appointed to the parole board, in 1987 he resigned in protest over the treatment of Aboriginals in prison in the wake of a spate of deaths in custody. A year earlier, Les rocked the Adelaide establishment to the core by boycotting the 1986 sesquicentenary celebrations, arguing with his usual gusto that Aboriginal people had little to celebrate. He took his protest to an alarming extent, threatening to burn down the Old Gum Tree at Glenelg. He turned down a Member of the Order of Australia in 1977 saying he was 'not going to be patronised by handouts from white Australian governments'. However, in 1995 he accepted an AM. His marriage to Ann, with whom he had two children, Shane and Sharon, ended after 30 years, but he found a new partner, Anne Ernst, a work colleague at the Aboriginal Employment Education Development branch.

His family and friends maintain that Les Nayda's life-long drive to make a difference sprang from his experience as a Stolen child. Les and his family returned to Alice Springs in 2006 and a year later he suffered a stroke from which he never recovered. He died on 15 May 2014, with his long-term partner Annie at his side. His memorial service was held at Glanville Hall (formerly St Francis House) and Les's brother William Tilmouth delivered the eulogy.

'He was the first of us to be taken away, and was always troubled by the sense that he was the only one in the family to be removed,' he said. 'Les was gone before some of us were even born and he didn't even know that he had six brothers and a sister until later in life.'

Commissioner for Aboriginal Engagement Khatija Thomas paid tribute to Les, saying he 'was admired by many for his work in housing, education, employment and land rights and the fact that he took direct action to address the suffering of Aboriginal people'. Another St Francis House old boy, Brian Butler, said that Les 'was a tiger when it came to standing up to the bureaucracies and the atrocities that Aboriginal people have faced. He would never let people forget; he believed there was still a need for more apology from government'.

The Boys from St Francis

Radio guru Peter Goers wrote a heartfelt short tribute to Les in his *Sunday Mail* column of 12 July 2014.

> Recently I attended a memorial service for Aboriginal activist Les Nayda. Many Aboriginal people from all walks of life spoke and not once was there a suggestion of self-righteousness. There was warmth, generosity, assertion, understanding, some anger, some laughs, some tears and a belief in human goodness and frailty and the knowledge that the journey is always long. From people who have suffered and continue to suffer so much.

Two brilliant careers

Seven-year-old Sonny Morey was taken from hospital, his left elbow in plaster, and driven at breakneck speed straight to the waiting Vickers Viscount aircraft warming its engines at the end of the runway at Alice Springs Airport. He never saw his mother again.

Kenneth Valentine Hampton was born in Darwin on 3 December 1935. He was one of 11 sons to miner Timothy Hampton and Sarah Johnson, both Alawa people from the Roper River district. When Ken Hampton was three years old he was removed from his family and taken, along with Wally McArthur and John Moriarty, to the Anglican-run home in Mulgoa, New South Wales. In 1947 Hampton was brought to a new life at St Francis House. As with most of the boys Hampton loved the warmth and care shown him by Father Percy Smith. Under Father Smith's care, Ken was taught to be proud of his Aboriginal heritage and, unlike most of the boys who endured church because of the bacon and egg rolls to be he enjoyed after the service, he always looked forward to the religious Sunday. The impact Father Smith had on Ken was to prove profound indeed.

Ken was an enthusiastic student at Le Fevre Boys Technical School. There he learnt a trade and became an apprentice fitter and turner, qualifying in 1956. He thought he might ply his trade for the navy, but he was rejected because he was a black man. The rebuff was all the more hurtful because a number of his relatives had served in both world wars. Disappointed, but unbowed, Ken joined the Commonwealth Railways at Port Augusta and later worked for Broken Hill Proprietary at Whyalla. In the mid 1960s Ken joined the South Australian Department of Aboriginal Affairs, working in Port Augusta and Koonibba.

Years before, just after he left school and St Francis House, Ken had boarded with the Clifton family at Ethelton. Sam Clifton knew a champion athlete when he saw one and in Ken Hampton was something very special indeed. Sam coached Ken in sprinting technique and encouraged the youngster to compete in South Australia's premier athletics event – the Bay Sheffield. Ken made five attempts to win the coveted event, getting to the finals three times before 1961 – the year he became the first Aboriginal to win. As with the champion runner Wally McArthur, Hampton had the pace and endurance to represent Australia at the Olympic Games, but he was denied, as was McArthur, any such chance because of his colour.

A note contained in an article by Judith Raftery in the *Australian Dictionary of Biography* (MUP, 2007) describes Hampton thus:

> He overcame a dependence on alcohol and a consequent propensity to act violently.

In all the interviews I have conducted with ex-St Francis House boys and their families, I have not found any evidence of Hampton being violent. Vince Copley described a football function where Ken 'turned a little worse for wear', but that's it.

Having married Daphne Sultan on 12 November 1956, Ken was divorced in 1976 and remarried Margaret Smits, an Aboriginal health worker, in August 1979.

In 1976 Ken became the first Aboriginal to be appointed a Justice of the Peace, and by the 1980s he became increasingly involved in the Anglican Church. It was a time when the church resolved to offer greater support to Indigenous Australians wishing to join the clergy. Ken became the archbishop's lay preacher to Aboriginal people in December 1982. He worked with alcoholics and prisoners, offering pastoral care to country-based Aboriginal people undergoing medical treatment in Adelaide. His work in the church and with Indigenous Australians was acknowledged with an OAM in 1985. A year later on 20 December 1986, Ken Hampton was made a deacon in St Peter's Cathedral.

Hampton had no formal religious training. Archbishop Keith Rayner, who was described as having a 'masterly presidential style', said of Hampton: 'This [Ken's appointment] was not the normal course of action, however, Hampton was the person whom God has raised up for ministry among Aboriginal people.'

Ken envisaged establishing a centre where Indigenous Australians could gather in an atmosphere which celebrated Aboriginal spirituality and culture, and this was partially realised in the Nunga Anglican Ministry set up on 30 August 1987. Ken was also a member of the Aboriginal executive of South Australia's Jubilee 150.

In 1992 Hampton co-edited and co-wrote with established local writer Christobel Mattingley *Survival in Our Own Land: 'Aboriginal' experiences in South Australia since 1836, told by Nungas and others* (Hodder & Stoughton, Sydney 1992).

Reverend Hampton struggled with illness for many years and underwent a kidney transplant in 1974, then five years later in 1979 he had a coronary bypass. He died on 11 September 1987 at Woodville South. Survived by his wife, two sons and five daughters, Hampton's sporting recognition did not materialise until December 2009 when he was inducted into the Bay Sheffield Hall of Fame. But Hampton and fellow St Francis House athlete

The Boys from St Francis

Wally McArthur both deserve to be inducted into the Australian Sporting Hall of Fame. Only their colour prevented such an honour for both men.

Ken's legacy of wisdom, generosity, care, passion and determination were characteristics he demonstrated throughout his sporting and public life.

Sonny Morey became a champion in another field – Australian Rules football. Born on 23 April 1945 to Nancy Panunga and Thomas Gorey, Sonny's surname was changed, from Gorey to Morey, 'maybe because my father was a bit worried about litigation and some sort of claim in future. My father owned two huge properties, one was Yamba Station, situated 80 km north of Alice Springs. I can tell that Aboriginal people have a great connection to the land, but we don't own the land, we belong to it.'

Sonny was born in a creek bed at Snake Wells.

'A midwife would heat sand in the creek bed after having fashioned a hollow. Then she'd lay the expectant mother gently onto her back when the birth was imminent. This is the traditional way of giving birth and has been for thousands of years,' Sonny says.

'The umbilical cord was soon removed and traditionally it was buried under a nearby tree. I don't know for sure what sort of tree, but I suspect it was a red river gum, which are plentiful along the banks of the river.'

Sonny stayed at Yamba Station with his mother until he was five years old. Then the family travelled to Alice Springs where Sonny was placed in care at the Bungalow at the Old Telegraph Station. He loved life at the Bungalow and recalls vividly how the children swam regularly at the water hole. 'We'd slide down the big rock at our favourite spot, splash and laugh together until dark.' It was the same favourite water hole that Charlie Perkins frequented more than 10 years before Morey and his mates.

When he was five a truck came to the Bungalow and Sonny was taken to St Mary's Convent some 5 km from Alice Springs.

'My first day at St Mary's was terrible. I felt so alone and I didn't speak the language. Out of my safety zone, without my family, I was so sad.'

Traditionally Sonny's people followed the trusted pathway which had served them well for thousands of years.

'The women look after the little ones. For the first seven years or so the women, your mother and aunties, teach you the language. I could speak it pretty much fluently, but I didn't understand a word of English. When I went to St Mary's I got little help from the teachers. I learnt bits and pieces of English from my peers. There were some 100 kids at St Mary's. I guess it was the survival instinct which kicked in; instinctively I knew that I had to learn English and speak it well to make my way in the world.'

He remembers going to an open air picture theatre in Alice Springs to watch a Tarzan movie.

'Next day we kids were playing up a tree and I was trying to emulate Tarzan, missed my hold on a branch and fell to the ground, badly dislocating my left elbow. I found myself in Alice Springs Hospital. It's all a bit hazy to me, but I suspect the nurses alerted the welfare people. The authorities were always on the lookout for half-caste children, whom they believed should be "assimilated". It was more than assimilation; it was segregation. The authorities set out to break up families. The assimilation policy was really a form of genocide for the authorities hoped that by taking the children from their mothers and placing them with white institutions or white families the Indigenous people would die out.'

Seven-year-old Sonny Morey was taken from hospital, his left elbow in plaster, and driven at breakneck speed straight to the waiting Vickers Viscount aircraft warming its engines at the end of the runway at Alice Springs Airport. He never saw his mother again.

'I always wondered why we didn't go to the airport in the normal way. Why would they do that ? There was no logic in it. There were three of us. Peter Butcher and Walter Gardiner were taken from St Mary's Convent and I was snatched from the hospital.'

Perhaps the powers that be wanted to avoid Sonny's relatives at the railway station. They certainly weren't interested in limiting the cost of transporting the three little boys from Alice Springs to a new life in Adelaide. Why?

Even today Sonny Morey still asks himself that question.

Sonny looked out of the aircraft window and watched the big propellers in fascination. When they arrived at Adelaide Airport Sonny, Peter and Walters shivered.

He isn't sure who collected the boys at the airport, but he says it was cold despite them landing late at night on a midsummer's day, 10 February 1957.

'It might have been Mr Wilson. Whoever it was it was one of the last or the last warden at St Francis House. I well remember that day because the warden drove a Jaguar, quite some car,' he says.

'It was freezing cold. A lot of strangers. As a comfort zone we just stayed together. It took us two to three weeks to get over the

Two brilliant careers

trip and to get used to the others and the routines of the house.'

At that time seven-year-old Sonny Morey could speak a modicum of English, but his understanding of schoolwork, especially English and mathematics, was poor.

At that time he could still speak the language of Arrernte Anmatyerre, which was largely unknown to other Indigenous groups let alone white Australians. However, Sonny soon lost his ability to speak his traditional language.

'Today I can understand certain words and phrases, but sadly I cannot speak the language. My cousin Margaret Heffernan, the well known Central Arrernte linguist, author, interpreter and translator, has compiled a book of more than 600 pages dealing with the different dialects. That book has helped me reclaim some of the language.

'I think the help I got speaking with my peers and all the reading I have done has helped me learn to speak English pretty well.'

Today Sonny Morey is very articulate, something which belies that tough, early start in life. One wonders what the nuns at St Mary's Convent were doing toward Sonny's education.

As with all of the younger boys at St Francis House, Sonny attended Ethelton Primary School, but unlike many of them, he didn't enjoy school or how the teachers 'just ignored us. They never went out of their way to lend us a hand with our schooling ... yet the other [white] kids were always helped out. That was one of my regrets, that I never was helped by the teachers. I suspect the prevailing attitude was, "Oh, the Indigenous people ... they wont get anywhere and soon they'll have died out."'

At Ethelton Primary School Sonny was regularly humiliated

by the teachers in class. He couldn't speak English and didn't understand a word they were telling him, so 'I was made to stand in the corner, facing the wall like some sort of dunce.'

Sonny often reflected about his family. He thought his father, John Gorey, could have helped him contact his mother. Gorey had the means and probably knew precisely what had happened the day Sonny was taken. Sonny's mother had little command of the English language and would have found it difficult to track down her son's whereabouts. Sonny had many moments of reflection over his being brought to Adelaide. He didn't understand it and thought his mother and father did not really care about him. If they did wouldn't they try and make contact?

'I suppose I was bitter and a bit angry, but I decided to think this way: if they didn't care enough to come and see me I might as well move on with my own life.'

After his St Francis House experience, Sonny was fostered out to a family living north of the city. He attended Elizabeth Boys Technical High School.

'The teachers there weren't much help to me. I remember the principal, Leo Kloden, who later became director of the South Australian Education Department, sidling up to me one day and saying, "Morey, you won't amount to anything in life."'

Sonny played soccer for Ethelton Primary School in the winters of 1958 and 1959. He played Australian Rules football for Gawler Centrals in 1961 and was recruited to play for Central District when the club was – along with Woodville – brought into the SANFL competition. In those days footballers had to find full-time jobs and Sonny began his working life with a five-year apprenticeship as a fitter and turner with the PMG's department, forerunner to Telecom Australia, now Telstra. Along with his

Two brilliant careers

Champion Central District and South Australian state footballer Sonny Morey in full flight. Photo courtesy the Advertiser.

sublime skills on the football field, Sonny continued his pursuit of knowledge.

But it was his football skills that proved his passport to acceptance in the wider Australian community.

Sonny began his career with the Central District Bulldogs as a creative half-forward and wingman in the tough, embryonic days of the club. He is credited with having the first kick in SANFL football by a Bulldogs player.

Sonny will never forget that first Saturday in the club's

league history, a match in which West Torrens (26.24 – 180) beat Central District (6.4 – 43), by every count a football lesson. However, the Bulldogs had one win – Sonny got that first kick of the game.

'Big Brian Kemp got the tap and I was playing half-forward. I ran on to it, turned and headed for goal and let fly with a torpedo. The ball was heading for a goal, what a dream start, but right on the line there was that little bugger Bob Gibson stretching up to mark the ball.'

Ken Eustice, a South Australian football legend, was Sonny's first coach. He speaks passionately and proudly of Sonny, describing him as 'one of the most natural footballers I ever coached and I didn't teach him much. He is a credit to himself, his community and the Central District Football Club, both for his efforts on and off the field.'

Sonny missed, through injury, the club's first and only win of the 1965 season. In the early 1970s, he reinvented himself as a dashing back-pocket player. He played under three coaches – Ken Eustice (1964 to 1967), Dennis Jones (1968 to 1971) and Tony Casserley (1972 to 1978).

Jones, who played alongside Ron Barassi at Melbourne in their halcyon years, was instrumental in transforming Sonny's game, from a wingman to a rebounding back pocket. He was the first Bulldog to reach 200 league games, a feat he achieved in 1976. He was also the first of a strong Aboriginal heritage that has blessed this club.

Sonny won the club's fairest and best trophy in 1970 and two years later in 1972 he was runner-up to Malcolm Blight for the 1972 Magarey Medal. And he was to be rewarded with four state games over two seasons – 1973 and 1974.

Two brilliant careers

Long-time Bulldogs CEO Kris Grant says: 'Sonny was humble about his natural sporting talent. He was a well-liked member of the playing group and a loyal friend. He returned to coach the under-17s and had a natural affinity with the kids and was highly respected. In the 1970s we actually named a lounge in the licensed club after Sonny. As a player he was our first 200-game SANFL league footballer, noted for his clean skills, tough and uncompromising approach to the football and his great understanding with mate Bill Cochrane in the last line of defence.'

After his retirement from league football Sonny went on to be a successful coach of Eudunda in the Barossa and Light competition. He coached the Bulldogs' under-17s to a premiership in 1985. He is the only known Aboriginal coach of a SANFL flag at any level.

Sonny is a life member of both Central District and the SANFL. In 2011 he was appointed the inaugural coach and player of the Indigenous Team of the Century. After a long association with football and Telecom, in 1992 Sonny was appointed the Aboriginal mentor for the Playford Council, which he added to his work in a father-figure role in normal policing for the South Australian Police Force. In 2006 he retired from SAPOL and started working for the Australian Crime Commission, a role which involved working on special Indigenous projects. In 2010 he was employed part-time with Harrison Research, interviewing Aboriginal people for the Closing the Gap program throughout South Australia. In June 2014 Sonny was appointed an Indigenous patron at the Police Academy Fort Largs.

Sonny Morey first met Carmel McSkimming at Pine Point. They were at a barbecue and both joined in an impromptu

The Boys from St Francis

*A reunion at Glanville Hall (St Francis House), 2014.
Left to right: Des Price, Vince Copley and Sonny Morey.
Photo courtesy Carmel Morey.*

football match. That first meeting was a little different as Sonny explains: 'I was about to take a mark and Carmel cleaned me up with a fierce bump.'

They married in 1971, with two daughters – Kim and Nicole – three grandsons and one great-granddaughter.

One chore at St Francis House has stayed with him all his life.

'At St Francis my job was to get up at the crack of dawn and stoke the boiler,' Sonny laughs. 'From then on I have never been able to sleep in. I have to get out of bed early.'

Rising from the ashes

Like a phoenix rising from the ashes of a stolen past, the boys from St Francis rose to high achievement in Australian society. Their heritage is a mix of the white fathers of a long-established European people and the black mothers of the most ancient culture on earth.

With all the achievements of the boys from St Francis, there are some, such as George Kruger, who forged successful careers away from the public gaze.

George was born in an internment camp at the Balaklava grandstand on 21 September 1943 after his mother was evacuated from the Northern Territory during the height of World War II, due to the real threat of a Japanese invasion. Later George was taken back to Alice Springs to St John's where he linked up with many boys who eventually found themselves at St Francis House.

Today George is still a strikingly tall man with a superb RAF wing-commander-like moustache. As we enjoyed a coffee on the main street of Katherine, George related his story.

His mother was an Aboriginal woman named Linda Carter.

'After she married my father, George Kruger, everyone called her Lilly Kruger,' George said. 'My dad was a fettler on the railway.'

At the tender age of four George was taken to St John's Hostel in Alice Springs and from there he was transferred to Balaklava where others such as Gordon Briscoe lived, before going to St Francis House in December 1953.

The Boys from St Francis

When George went to St Francis House he slept with 11 other boys in the area called the common room.

'As you got a little older, you got the privilege of sleeping upstairs.'

George maintains that St Francis House was spooked.

'Lady Glanville hanged herself from the flagpole in front of what was then called Glanville Hall,' George said.

'Did you ever see the so-called ghost of Lady Glanville?' I asked.

'No, but when we'd walk up the stairs to the rooms above you could clearly hear someone walking behind you. You'd stop and look back. There was never anyone there.'

The mischievous older boys at St Francis House did a brilliant job in scaring the living daylights out of the younger ones when George Kruger arrived in 1953.

'In the Christmas holidays we'd go out bush, to Sandy Creek and other places, where we'd hunt, chasing rabbits and collecting goannas.

'I remember the first time I saw a rabbit. It was squattin'. I had a big stick, but I couldn't hit it. One of the others yelled, "Why didn't you get it, George?"

'No, I couldn't . . . it was lookin' at me.'

One of the boys in George's group was Alex McEvoy. He was the son of one of the top bosses at Holden.

'He had blond hair and blue eyes, so he didn't look much like the rest. He lived nearby and came with us on trips away during the holidays. He was a bit crippled.'

Alex McEvoy may have been affected by poliomyelitis, the disease which had reached epidemic proportions by the early 1950s, however, it was Fred Turner who became so ill from the disease that he was quarantined and slept alone in an out-of-the way room at St Francis House. Sadly Fred Turner died during his convalescence at St Francis House on 4 February 1955. None of the old St Francis boys I spoke with could, or wanted to, expand on poor Fred Turner's life.

George Kruger well remembers his time at Le Fevre Boys Technical School, especially the fights.

'There was a bloke there called Foreman, a big boy. He used to pick on us, then one day we waited for him beyond the school front gate and we belted the shit out of him.

'His dad came looking for us. He didn't have a go at us for hitting his boy, just to tell us that he suffers from asthma and the belting really affected him. That boy we belted became one of our best mates.'

Joe McEvoy was a horse trainer in Semaphore Park and George worked in the stables. Sometimes he'd help walk the horses around the Saltbush Riding School track.

'We'd be up at the crack of dawn. I remember one day we were moving a few cows into a patch of lush lucerne and I heard this "tick, tick, tick" and I said to old Joe, "What's that noise?"

'"Oh, that's nothing son, just the wind blowing the wire on the fence to create a funny sound. Grab it and see what happens."'

That was George's first experience with an electric fence. Another not-so-good experience concerned a group of St Francis boys who were caught with a huge bag of grapes they stole raiding the grapevine of a nearby neighbour's back fence. In their haste to stuff themselves with the delicious fare, the boys must have dropped and crushed a few. Whatever evidence they left in their wake, Mr Sutton discovered the culprits. As punishment, the boys were summoned to the courtyard. There in front of them were tubs of grapes.

'George Kruger and the three others step forward. I know who you are, so step forward lads.'

'Now boys,' Mr Sutton declared, 'I want you to eat all of the grapes on display. No one is to leave the courtyard until they are all eaten – by you four boys.'

Never again did any one of those four boys steal another grape, at St Francis House or anywhere else.

One day when George was walking along Semaphore Beach he saw something shining in the sand. He lent down and picked up a large silver coin with a big hole in the middle of it.

Could this coin have been the famed holey dollar? When George showed the other boys his prize find, there wasn't too much interest. One of them said, 'Mate, there's a bloody hole in that coin. It's no good. Chuck it away.'

There have been a number of shipwrecks off the South Australian coast where a holey dollar could well have been washed overboard. South Australia was not one of the Australian cities to take convicts, but the odd escaping prisoner jumped ship at Port Adelaide or Glenelg in the hope of forging a new life in the colony of 'free settlers'.

In 1812 New South Wales's Governor Macquarie imported 40,000 Spanish silver dollars and commissioned convicted forger William Hershale to cut the centre out of each one to double the amount of available coins. Macquarie set the value of the holey dollar at five shillings, with 15 pence for the piece cut out which was called the dump.

The holey dollar and dump went into circulation in Sydney Town in 1814. In 1822 the holey dollar was discontinued when replaced by Sterling coinage.

Rising from the ashes

In 2013 a holey dollar sold for a world-record price of $495,000.

Ms Linda Downie, numismatics expert and managing director of Coinworks, said, 'This holey dollar was created from a Spanish silver dollar that had been minted at the Lima Mint in Peru in 1808. Only 20 of the 200 specimens held by private collectors have ties to the Lima Mint. And this is the absolute finest of them all. A world-class rarity, the coin was purchased by a private collector from Western Australia.'

That day over coffee in Katherine, Trevor Woodhead quipped mischievously: 'Have you still got the coin, George? We could go halves.'

George isn't too sure what happened to that old foreign coin, but he suspects he did throw it away. Today, with hindsight a-knocking, he ponders what might have been.

After he left school, George returned to country in Darwin. He worked as a ringer and a drover at various stations (among them a huge station at Newcastle Waters) in the Northern Territory and Queensland. In 1961 George travelled to Darwin, then worked for a council in Alice Springs, operating all manner of machinery: trucks, bulldozers and front-end loaders.

George spent more than seven years in the Alice, then went off diamond drilling with water resources, working in remote areas in the Northern Territory such as the massive gold mine at Pine Creek, situated off the main track from Darwin to Katherine.

'My job was to interview station managers when the mining company wanted to get a bore drilled. Then they sent me out to the Simpson Desert looking for likely places to drill and the rig broke down. I was stranded there for eight weeks. I needed to be able to find water in the desert and I was lucky to meet a Pitjantjatjara man, probably a medicine man, who told me the best way to find water. And I did, every time. He said the spirit will always protect you and guide you: "At night you will be protected by the owl; by day you will fly with the eagle."'

In 1981 George's career pathway took a new and exciting turn. He met and then worked under the famous eye specialist Fred Hollows.

'I met Fred round the time he met Gabby. They turned up in Katherine, his team treating people's eyes within the remote communities. Professor Hollows asked me if I'd like to help and I didn't hesitate. My first role with the team happened at Wurli Wurlinjang, a community across the river here.'

George travelled to Darwin where he talked to Ella Stack, a former lord mayor and medical doctor. After that meeting George became a regular member of the Hollows team.

He learnt to screen people's eyes for a variety of diseases, the most common being trachoma, a serious bacterial infection of the eye which can cause blindness.

'I'd use a matchstick to flip the eyelid inside out and if trachoma was present it was evident by the sight of little black dots.'

He even treated people with laser work.

George Kruger could do the work of an optometrist, but he never studied to become one, despite the encouragement of one of his mentors, Dr George Burke, a leading Sydney-based eye specialist.

'I should have done the study,' George said, a faraway look in his eye, 'But they wouldn't let us ...'

'Who wouldn't let you?' I asked.

'The government. If you got so far in the business that was it ... they didn't want you to get too high ...'

'They would bring you down?'

'Yes, you'd immediately lose seniority. This discrimination was real, not my imagination. So that was why I didn't get the necessary qualification.'

George worked with Fred Hollows throughout remote communities in the Northern Territory and the Islands for 18 years.

He was another of the fabulous St Francis House high achievers.

George's brother Fred lives in a caravan park in central Katherine. Fred doesn't articulate much about his life at St Francis House and after his school experience he worked in various manual jobs, mainly in the Top End. These days he teaches boxing every Saturday morning and says with pride maybe his greatest claim to fame is the fact that he sired a son at the age of 71.

Des Price remembers vividly Father Percy Smith reading the story of Dr Doolittle in the common room at St Francis House. Des was born on 11 March 1942 at Queen Victoria Hospital in Adelaide. He was among the hundreds evacuated to Adelaide from the Northern Territory over fear of the Japanese invasion in World War II. And he has no idea why Father Smith left St Francis House, virtually 'abandoning' his young charges.

Des recalls raiding the fruit trees in and about Semaphore and after he left school he worked in the railways and became a member of the Australian Federation of Locomotive Enginemen.

Des was married to a woman named Alma but the marriage didn't last long. In the time they had together they produced two daughters, Alison and Jacqueline. He had a son from 'another liaison'.

He often talks about 'jumping fences' and that son eventually brought a grandson, Eddie Sandsburg, who played Australian Rules football for North Adelaide.

These days Des lives in Whyalla. Everywhere he drives he takes his little dog.

Des Price is a soul man.

Noel Hayes liked his days at St Francis House.

He doesn't say much about the experience, but he knuckled down and worked hard at school. After leaving St Francis he worked on various stations and as a council worker driving graders and other huge machinery.

Noel didn't move mountains but he did shift a helluva lot of dirt and gravel in the outback. He got involved in the Centre for Appropriate Technology (CAT) in Alice Springs with a white man named Bruce Walker and another St Francis House old boy, Jim Bray.

Born at Harts Range, 30 km east of Alice Springs, on 30 June 1941, Jim Bray was the son of Mary Perkins and Bill Bray. His siblings numbered nine: Richard, Ronald, Lawrence, Norman, Harvey, Olnie, Elsie, Hilda and Jesse.

'As with many of the boys I started at St John's Hostel,' Jim says.

Later he was taken to St Francis House where among his best mates were Gordon Briscoe, Clifford Bray, Trevor Reid and Gerry Tilmouth.

'I found my time at St Francis House a marvellous experience. There were always new things to do and to try. And we – the boys – bonded.'

Rising from the ashes

*Reunion at St Francis House, c. 1973. Pictured left to right:
Vince Copley, Tim Campbell, John Moriarty, Wilfred 'Boofa' Huddleston,
Father Percy Smith, Malcolm Cooper and Ken Hampton.*

Jim Bray worked, as most of the boys did, in manual jobs. He was first a boilermaker/welder for F. Miller & Co. engineering in Rosewater. He hadn't completed his apprenticeship when St Francis House closed and he needed to find accommodation. Jim found 'refuge' with a family in Clifford Street, Ethelton. Richie Bray, 'Boofa' Huddleston, Gordon Briscoe and Tim Campbell were there with him.

Jim says they were cared for brilliantly by the woman they always called 'Mum'. A young man with a future in mind, Jim worked branding bags at the Colonial Sugar Mill in Port Adelaide, cleaning the church hall and helping old people go shopping at five shillings a turn.

'In less than a year I had stashed away in excess of £300. In those days you could buy a pretty decent house for that sort of money.'

Later Jim worked for water resources on drilling rigs in the Top End, and on the Nullarbor Plain. He got involved with CAT with Bruce Walker. Jim Bray was chairman of CAT from 1989 to 2010.

These days Jim lives in Alice Springs. He paints and has never-ending gratitude for having been brought up at St Francis House.

'It was marvellous. My pathway to a good education.'

Brian Butler was born in 1938 at the Bagot Reserve Detention Centre in Darwin.

His mother, helped by two aunties, Daisy Ruddick and Dolly Jamieson, cared for Brian there before Japanese Zeros began bombing Darwin and the government organised a mass evacuation, sending the people to relative safety in Alice Springs.

Sadly Brian witnessed extraordinary cruelty in his early growing years.

'My mother, along with other Aboriginal ladies married to white men, endured terrible physical and mental abuse,' he recalls. 'My father would go out having all manner of liaisons with other women about the town. He'd return, accuse my mother of being promiscuous, and bash her in front of the children. He used to drag her about the floor by her long, black hair and sink those big army boots into her ribs. That was the way things happened in Alice Springs.'

Brian says his father would flog him, his five brothers and three sisters if they did not wear a shirt or a hat on hot days.

'He'd bellow at us, "because you are black enough as it is . . .

you don't want to end up like the boongs out there in the bush, do you?"'

His grandmother on his father's side, Ollie, often took up a scrubbing brush, the one she used to scrub the floor, and tried to 'rub the black out' of them. Brian attended St John's Hostel, run by Father Percy Smith, and soon enough he joined the first six boys at Pembroke Street, Kensington, the stepping stone to St Francis House.

Brian's time at St Francis House was short-lived for, after a year or two, his father sent him to Sacred Heart College in Somerton Park. His strongest memories of those early days was returning to Alice Springs in the holidays.

'It gave me a chance to sit with the old people. My fondest memory is sitting down with Albert Namatjira in the sandy creek at Simpson's Gap and Honeymoon Gap watching him paint.

'I also witnessed the pain of the families. The cries of the mothers and grandmothers, all of whom yearned for information about the children who were taken away, some never to be seen again.'

Brian decided to devote his life to finding the children who were taken. So at the age of 14, the tall, strong teenager had no trouble in pretending he was the required 16, and he joined the merchant navy.

'That gave me a chance to travel throughout Australia. After a few months of doing this I finally got from Western Australia right up to Cairns and I was able to tell where those kids came from, which families they belonged to, because I knew their features, I learnt the features of the people from the various

The Boys from St Francis

towns. You can always know just by the way they look, pretty quickly you can tell the difference between a Northern Territory, Darwin, Alice Springs person as opposed to somebody from New South Wales and so on.

'When I went back to Alice Springs I would go out and speak to all the old people and say, "I saw this one, I saw that one". I would be able to tell them that they were still in the land of the living.'

Brian got involved in a string of organisations trying to help bring mothers and children back together while working toward better medical assistance for Indigenous people across Australia. Today Brian and his wife, Nicola, run Lateral Love Australia: 'lateral love and spirit of care for all humankind'.

The boys from St Francis have made a great impact on Australian society, individually and collectively. Their story is unique in that they came together in an institution where by circumstance and an extraordinary will to make something of their lives they bonded and they excelled. They are wonderful role models and their story should be told far and wide. A good start would be to have access to their story, this book, in every school in the land.

Like a phoenix rising from the ashes of a stolen past, the boys from St Francis rose to high achievement in Australian society. Their heritage is a mix of the white fathers of a long-established European people and the black mothers of the most ancient culture on earth.

Indeed, as Brenda Copley attests: the boys from St Francis 'came as boys and left as men'.

Author's note

Much of the material I gathered to write this book came from interviews with St Francis House old boys and/or their relatives. However, information and quotes came from other sources, most of it in the public domain: newspaper articles, documents, private papers and four books, in particular – *A Bastard Like Me* by Charles Perkins (URE Smith, 1975); *Racial Folly* by Gordon Briscoe (ANU E Press, 2010); *Charles Perkins: A biography* by Peter Read (Viking, 1990) and *The Flower in the Desert* by John McD. Smith (Seaview Press, 1999).

References by chapter

Stolen

1. The death of Horace Foster at Manangoora in 1941 as told by Bessie Marshall (nee a-Kithibula) in her native tongue, translated and transcribed. The document is now in the hands of Jim Foster and family.
2. 'Bush nurse braved outback perils: Territory women heroes' actions were taken for granted', *Northern Territory News*, 3 November 1983.
3. 'Wally McArthur: A tribute' by Tom Collins, 27 January 2014, abbreviated extract from *The Glory of Their Time: Crossing the colour line in Rugby League* (Skipton Vertical Edition, 2004).

The Boys from St Francis

The first six
1. *Racial Folly* by Gordon Briscoe (ANU E Press, 2010, pp 3–4).
2. *The Story of St Francis House* (a transcribed document) by the Reverend Canon Percy McD Smith MBE, March 1997.
3. *A Bastard Like Me* by Charles Perkins (URE Smith, 1975).

A 'better place'
1. *A Bastard Like Me* by Charles Perkins (URE Smith, 1975).
2. *The Story of St Francis House* (a transcribed document) by the Reverend Canon Percy McD Smith MBE, March 1997.
3. 'Abos. find fairy god-father' (front-page story), *Truth*, Adelaide, Saturday 27 September 1947.

The house that 'Jack' built
1. Painting of Glanville Hall by John Ford.
2. 'Bass Strait to ship of state: Daring whaler John Hart gave up sea trading to become a leader of his state' by Francis Murray, *People*, 3 January 1962.
3. *Glanville Hall Development* by W.B. Hagan, city engineer, Port Adelaide Council 15 May 1968 (document courtesy Port Adelaide Library archives).

The boys from St Francis
1. *Racial Folly* by Gordon Briscoe (ANU E Press, 2010).

Our own 'William Tell'
1. *A Bastard Like Me* by Charles Perkins (URE Smith, 1975).

By a hand so cruel
1. *Racial Folly* by Gordon Briscoe (ANU E Press, 2010).

Author's note

Sunshine and shadow
1. *Racial Folly* by Gordon Briscoe (ANU E Press, 2010).
2. 'Column 8' (on bodgies and widgies), *Sydney Morning Herald*, 1 February 1951.

The Colebrook girls
1. Obituary for Fred Raggatt, Port Elliot *Argus*, 5 September 1946.

Faith
1. 'Faith Coulthard scored 28 and took 9/15', *Eden News*, 1 February 1957.

The flag
1. 'True Colours', *Deadly Vibe,* March 2005.
2. 'Aboriginal flag has many roles, says designer by Debra Jopson', *Sydney Morning Herald*, 3 September 1994.

Their hero
1. 'Wally McArthur: A tribute' by Tom Collins, 27 January 2014, abbreviated extract from *The Glory of Their Time: Crossing the colour line in Rugby League* (Skipton Vertical Edition, 2004).
2. 'Betrayal of Wally McArthur' by Peter Hackett, *Sydney Morning Herald*, 1999.
3. 'A new Black Flash is on his way to England' by Jack Bentley, *Daily Express* (UK), 20 November 1953.

Charlie
1. *A Bastard like Me* by Charles Perkins (URE Smith, 1975).
2. Transcript of Charles Perkins interview conducted by Robin Hughes, 5 May 1998, *Australian Biography*.

Home
1. *Charles Perkins: A biography* by Peter Read (Viking, 1990).

A year to remember
1. *A Bastard Like Me* by Charles Perkins (URE Smith, 1975).
2. 'Jan 6, 1965: The colour bar' by Graham Williams, *Australian*, reprinted 12 July 2014.

Joy and sorrow
1. 'Bastion of culture and community' (a tribute to Bill Espie), *Sydney Morning Herald*, 15 October 2011.
2. 'Source of inspiration' (tribute to Les Nayda), *Advertiser*, 21 June 2014.
3. *Racial Folly* by Gordon Briscoe (ANU E Press, 2010).
4. Peter Goers tribute to Les Nayda, *Sunday Mail*, 12 July 2014.

Two brilliant careers
1. Biography of Ken Hampton, *The Australian Dictionary of Biography* (MUP, 2007).
2. 'Champion of his people' by Graham Cornes, *Advertiser*, December 2009.

Acknowledgements

My thanks to Vince and Brenda Copley for their friendship and help in this project. Vince Copley, AM, is a man of great strength and vision. He envisaged the power of this story and dearly wanted *The Boys from St Francis* written and the book available in all school libraries; indeed to all Australians. Thanks also Vince for writing the foreword. I have conducted many interviews with St Francis House 'old boys' and their families. Some of the old boys have passed, but I have acknowledged many of them here.

St Francis House (Glanville Hall) stands on Kaurna land. In 1836 the early colonists happened upon King Rodney (Ityamaiitpinna) in the Port Adelaide area. King Rodney ruled the area. In winter he ventured east and set up camp on land which is now the site of the Adelaide Botanic Gardens. All South Australians are indebted to the Kaurna people for they handed down the wisdom and traditions that are indelibly etched into the souls of the Indigenous people of the area.

Special thanks to Trevor Woodhead who kindly drove me about Darwin, Katherine and Humpty Doo in search of Harold Thomas, the artist who created the Aboriginal flag, and to interview the brothers Kruger, George and Fred.

Please forgive me if I have missed a name in the following people I wish to acknowledge. They helped me piece this story together in some shape or form. Those marked with an asterisk are deceased.

The Boys from St Francis

Thanks to Josie Agius,* Vince and Brenda Copley and their children Vincent (Junior) and Kara, Don Dunstan,* Jim Bray,* Lawrie Bray,* Gordon Briscoe, Brian Butler, Dr Charles Duguid,* Bill Espie,* Jim Foster, Judy Foster, Cyril Hampton,* Malcolm Cooper,* Aileen Cooper, Evonne Goolagong Cawley, Wally McArthur,* Charles Perkins,* Eileen Perkins, Ernie Perkins,* Hetti Perkins,* Millie Glen, John Moriarty, Ros Moriarty, Fred Kruger, George Kruger, Peter Tilmouth,* David Woodford, Judy Woodford,* Paul Keating, John Smith, Father Percy Smith,* Pastor Sir Douglas Nicholls,* Nick Nikoleaff, Fos Williams,* Von Williams,* Mark Williams, Margaret Thatcher,* Harold Thomas,* Fred Vickery,* Max Wilson, Faith Thomas, Lowitja O'Donoghue, King Cole (Bripumyarrimin),* Wilfred Huddleston,* Elliott Johnston,* Muhammad Ali,* Lionel Rose,* Margaret Mibus, Rudyard Kipling,* Nelson Mandela,* Professor Fred Hollows,* Gabi Hollows, Noel Hayes, Des Price, Les Nayda,* Peter Goers, Sonny Morey and Carmel Morey.

My thanks to Michael Bollen and his Wakefield Press team for taking on this important project. I also greatly appreciate the skill and professionalism of my editor, Margot Lloyd.

And my thanks to my wife Patsy who always provided wise counsel and sage advice after reading the chapters as they were created. A former television executive, Patsy has an image in mind when reading the text. Her concepts were enlightening to this wordsmith. Thank you also to journalist-author-PR man Trevor Gill for his ongoing encouragement and sound literary advice.

Ashley Mallett, Adelaide 2018

Index

A

A Bastard Like Me 162
Aborigines Advancement League 133, 175–176, 224–225
Aboriginal Employment Education Development 242
Aboriginal flag 115, 142, 146, 147, 149–152
Aboriginal Legal Service 227
Aboriginal Youth Orchestra 140
Aborigines' Friends Association 43
Aboriginal Progress Association (APA) 224–225, 227
Aborigines Protection Act 175–178, 223–224
Acorn Cricket Club 173
Adelaide Botanic Gardens 60
Adelaide Airport 250
Adelaide Oval 35, 138
Adelaide Swimming Pool 97
Adelaide University 140, 233
Advertiser xv, 64
Agius, Fred 102
Agius, Josie (nee Copley) 99, 102
Ali, Muhammad xiii–xvi, 235, 236
Alice Springs Airport 250
Alice Springs Hospital 139–140, 249
All Souls School 28, 39
Almond, Jim 53, 54, 55, 103

Almond, Judith 'Jingle' 54, 55, 103, 128
Almond, Judy 54, 55, 103–104
Almond, (Mrs, senior) 35, 38,
Amata 140
Ampol Cup 174
Angel, Roy 116
Anzac Hill 18, 73
Ardrossan 102, 103, 109
Arrernte Council of Central Australia 208
Ashford Hospital 125
Australian 188, 203, 233, 246
Australian Aboriginal Cricket team 47, 149
Australian Board of Missions 39, 40, 54
Australian Communist Party 227
Australian Constitution 177, 202
Australian Cricket Board 204
Australian Crime Commission 255
Australian Dictionary of Biography 246
Australian Federation of Locomotive Enginemen 263
Australian Labor Party 111, 176, 189, 200, 205, 227, 228, 233
Australian National Railways 161
Australian National University 218
Australian Soccer Federation 217

The Boys from St Francis

Australian Sporting Hall of Fame 247–248
Australian Wool Corporation 218

B
Bagot Reserve Detention Centre 266
Bailey, Macdonald 156
Baker, Henry 74
Balaklava Railway Station 13
Balarinji 218, 221
Bald, Malcolm 92–93, 127
Balfour's Cake and Coffee Shop 64
Bannon Labor Government 111
Barassi, Ron 254
Barnes, Jeff 175
Barossa and Light Football Association 255
Bay Sheffield 246–247
Bean, Charles 194
Bentley, Jack 156–157
Birmingham Symphony Orchestra 140
Bishop Auckland Football Club (UK) 168–169
Black Lords of Summer, The 151
Blight, Malcolm 254
Bodyline 136
Bolt, Usain 11
Borroloola 2, 3, 5, 6, 8–9, 155, 210, 213, 214, 221, 222
Boy's Own Annual 154
Bradman, Donald (Sir) 35, 136, 204
Bradman, Jessie (Lady) 35
Bray, Clifford 264
Bray, Elsie 264
Bray, Hilda 264
Bray, James 'Jim' 58, 147, 264–266
Bray, Jesse 264
Bray, John (Dr) 233
Bray, Lawrie ix, 57, 62, 63, 78
Bray, Norman 63, 264
Bray, Olnie 264
Bray, Richie 48, 58, 224, 226, 264, 265
Bray, Ronald 264
Bringing Them Home (report) 30, 122
Briscoe, Bill 241
Briscoe, Dennis 241
Briscoe, Gordon ix, x, 12, 21–23, 42, 51–55, 58, 60, 62–63, 70, 76, 81, 87, 82–93, 101, 115, 164, 172, 175, 176, 182, 202, 209, 224, 228, 229, 240–241, 244, 257, 264
British Tube Mills 165
Broken Hill Proprietary (BHP) 246
Brooks, Frederick 133
Brumby, Aileen 119
Brumby, Murial 119
Brumby, Nancy 119
Brumby, Rose 119
Buck's Flat 45, 48–49
Bugner, Joe xiv, 236
Bungalow, The (Old Telegraph Station) 13, 18, 19, 24, 26–27, 48, 51, 123, 213, 248–249
Burke, George (Dr) 262
Burke, Laurel 8
Burke, Marie 210
Burke, Wendy 8
Burnt Bridge Station 191
Busby, Matt 169
Butcher, Peter 250
Butler, Brian 42, 51–52, 57, 58, 71, 123, 226, 243, 266–268
Butler, Keith xv
Butler, Nicola 268

Index

C
Cahill, John 217
Campbell, Mabel 130
Campbell, Tim 8, 14, 77, 224, 265
Cardwell, Roger 229
Carroll, (Matron) 138
Carter, Linda 'Lilly Kruger' 257
Casserley, Tony 254
Ceduna 131, 229, 230
Central District Football Club 252–255
Central Hotel 143, 146
Centre for Aboriginal Studies in Music 140
Centre for Appropriate Technology 264, 266
Channel 7 198
Cheltenham Cemetery 34
Chifley, Ben 54–55
Christ, Joyce 137
City of Port Adelaide Enfield xi
Clements, F.T. (Mrs) 125
Closing the Gap program xi, 255
Cochrane, Bill 255
Colebrook-Blackwood Reconciliation Park 119
Colebrook Home 118–122, 129, 130, 131–132, 134, 136, 225
Colebrook, T.E. 119
Colonial Sugar Mill 265
Commonwealth Games 11, 152
Commonwealth Railways 245
Congress of Racial Equality (CORE) 182
Coniston Cattle Station 133
Connelly 18–19,
Cook, Cecil (Dr) 29
Cooper, Aileen 127, 224–225
Cooper, Dido 17
Cooper, Malcolm x, 17, 34, 36, 48, 52, 57–59, 61, 96, 106, 175, 224, 238
Copley, Alan 99
Copley, Brenda (nee Thomas) 75, 112–113, 198, 205, 239, 268
Copley, Colin 99
Copley, Maureen 99
Copley, Valda 99
Copley, Vince xiii, xv, xvi, 15, 44, 48, 58–59, 62–63, 66–70, 72, 75, 77–78, 82, 86, 94–96, 99–106, 108–110, 112–113, 119–120, 130–140, 143, 145, 154, 158, 175–176, 198, 203, 206–207, 224–226, 235–236, 239, 246, 256, 265
Copley, Winnie 99, 101–102
Croatia Soccer Club (SA) 169, 171, 174
Crocker, Walter (Sir) 113
Croft, Joe 28, 39
Crouch, Edna 130
Curramulka Football Club 108, 110, 112, 226
Curramulka Town Hall 111
Curtin, John 195

D
Daily Express 11, 156–157
Daley, Aileen 135
Daly, Dominick (Sir) 47
Darwin Airport 146
Darwin Hospital 72
David Unaipon Award 152
Deakin government 194
Department of Aboriginal Affairs (federal) 28, 113, 177, 205, 206, 207, 214, 218

Department of Aboriginal Affairs (SA) 121, 122, 139, 246
Department of Native Affairs (NT) 28, 33
Dial M for Murder 229
Dixon, Geoff 220
Dixon, Tom (Father) 231
Dove, (Sister) 15
Dow, Ruth 136, 138
Duggan, Mary 137
Duguid, Charles (Dr) 42–43, 54, 125–126, 133–134, 176
Duke, Neville 190
Dunstan, Don 114, 176, 203, 227, 228

E
Eden News 136
Edwards, Kathleen Winifred 99
Elizabeth Boys' Technical High School 252
Elphick, Gladys (Mrs) 113
English Channel 166
Ernabella Mission 133
Ernst, Anne 243
Espie, Bill 17, 34, 36, 44, 57–58, 83, 90, 161, 209
Espie, Edie 17
Estcourt House 87, 116
Ethelton Primary School x, 75–76, 95, 170, 212, 251, 252
Ethelton Primary School Football Team 78
Ethelton Primary School Soccer Team 147
Ethelton Railway Station 46
Eudunda Football Club 255
Eustice, Ken 254
Evans, (Mrs) 128–129

F
F. Miller & Co. 265
Family Planning Association 140
Family Wellbeing Program 242
Federal Council for the Advancement of Aborigines and Torres Strait Islanders (FCAATSI) 175–177, 202
Federal Court of Australia 152
Federation of the Advancement of Aborigines (FCAA) 175–176
Ferguson, Bill 55
Ferguson, James (Sir) 47
Ferguson, John 169, 171
Ferguson, Yvonne 171
FIFA 217
Filipi, Brenko 174
First Fleet 153
Firth of Clyde 149
Fitzroy Football Club 106–107, 114
Ford, John 46
Foster, Alice (nee Bajamalanya) 1–4
Foster, Horace Mole 2–7
Foster, Jim x, 1, 3–4, 7–8, 14, 21, 59, 62, 84, 86, 91, 119, 125, 155, 160–161, 211–212
Foster, Rose 1, 3, 7, 9, 14, 119, 125–126
Fraser, Dawn 97
Freedom Ride 180, 182–193, 199, 200
Freedom Riders 182–193
Freeman, Cathy 152

G
HMS *Galatea* 47
Gallagher, Phillis 72
Gardiner, Walter 250

Index

Gawler Centrals Football Club 252
Gillespie, Jason 145
Glanville Fort 87
Glanville Hall xi, 40–42, 45–46, 49, 54, 55, 243, 256, 258
Glanville, Mary 46
Glen Helen Station 13, 123–124
Glen, Millie 13, 118, 119, 122–129
Globe Timber Mills 116
Glynn, Topsy 210
Goers, Peter 244
Goodes, Adam 154
Goolagong Cawley, Evonne 30, 162–163
Gorey, John 252
Gorey, Thomas 248
Gosper, Kevin 10
Government House (Adelaide) 113–114
Graham, Bradley 105
Graham, Michael 105
Granite Downs 120
Grant, Kris 255
Grasby, Al 200
Great Western Mine (White Range) 21
Griffin, Merle 221–222
Groves, Bert 175
Guy's Hospital (London) 149

H

Hack, (Sister) 191
Hackett, Peter 154
Haerney, Bill 2, 3
Hale, Tilly 241
Hall, Carey 8
Hall, Fay 1, 8
Hall, Harry 184–185
Hall, Steele 227
Hall, Trevor 8
Hamilton, Arnold 9
Hamilton, Betty 8
Hamilton, Eileen 8
Hamilton, Hubert 8
Hamilton, Joan 8
Hamilton, Melva 8
Hamilton, Phyllis 1, 8
Hampton, Cyril 14, 91
Hampton, John 14
Hampton, Ken 14, 106, 219, 224, 245–248
Hampton, Robert 116
Hampton, Timothy 245
Hart, John 'Jack' (Captain) 45–49, 117
Hattam, Mary 229–230
Hawke, Bob 207
Heathcock, Ruth (Sister) 5–7
Heathcock, Ted (Constable) 5
Hecht, Ernest 151
Heffernan, Margaret 251
Helsinki Olympic Games 10, 11, 154, 156
Henbury Station 237
Herbert, Alfred 8
Herbert, Joyce 8
Hershale, William 260
High Court of Australia 30, 229
Highland Games 159
Hill, Gerry 14, 63, 76–77, 164, 219, 224
Hill, May 63
Hilton Hotel, Kuala Lumpur xiii
Hilton Hotel, Mile End 172
Hindmarsh, John (Governor) 148
Hodge, Andrew 228
Hollows, Fred (Professor) 143, 262–263
Hollows, Gabby 262
Huddleston, Cecily 8

The Boys from St Francis

Huddleston, Ida 9
Huddleston, Robert 1, 8
Huddleston, Wilfred 'Boofa' 8, 14, 48, 77, 214, 217, 224, 265
Huddleston, Wilton 2, 9
Hunter, John (Captain) 153
Hyde, Ruby (Matron) 119–120

I
Independence Day 153
Indigenous Team of the Century 224, 255
International Women's Cricket Council 137
Interstate Commerce Commission 182

J
Jackson, Syd 139
Jacobson, Peter 229
Jay Creek 25–27
Jefferson, Thomas 101, 153
Johnson, Sarah 245
Johnston, Elliott (QC) 227
Jones, Dennis 254
Juventus Soccer Club 215

K
Keating, Paul 28
Keighran, Jack 2
Kemp, Brian 254
Kempsey 183, 188–191
King Cole (Bripumyarrimin) 149–151
King Rodney (Ityamaiitpinna) 60
Kingston, George Strickland 45
Kipling, Rudyard 235, 239
Kloden, Leo 252
Knightley, Phillip 30

Konrads, Ilse 97
Konrads, John 97
Kruger, Freddy 143–144, 146, 263
Kruger, George 143–144, 146, 257–259
Ku Klux Klan 144
Kunoth, Charlie 57

L
Larwood, Harold 136
Law Society of South Australia 231
Le Fevre Boys Technical School x 75–76, 95–96, 212, 237, 245
Lendill, Jack 157
Lester, Grace 119
Ligertwood, Andrew 228
Light, William (Colonel) 47
Lima Mint 261
Listening to Country 219
Lloyd, William 188, 189
Lock, Annie 118
Lord's Cricket Ground 149
Lords Dreaming 151
Lorella Station 2
Lush Studios 132, 136

M
Macquarie, Lachlan (Governor) 14, 260
Magarey Medal 254
Maitland Hospital 103, 109
Manangoora Station 3
Manchester United Football Club 168–170
Mandela, Nelson 203–204
Mao Tse Tung 227
Marshall, Bessie (nee a-Kithibula) 6, 7
Mascot Airport 193, 195–198

Index

Matthews, Stanley (Sir) 97
Mattingly, Christobel 247
McArthur, Marlene (nee Newchurch) 158–159, 161, 168
McArthur, Wally x, 10–14, 21, 58–59, 87, 90–92, 125, 153–161, 168, 211–212, 219, 226, 245–246
McCaw, Frederick 9
McDonald, Normie 107
McEvoy, Alex 258
McEvoy, Joe 259
McGee, (Mrs) 240–241
McLean, Bob 106, 217
McMaster, Moree Hospital 190
Meath Gardens 150
Melville, (Alderman) R. 189
Merdeka Stadium xv
Metropolitan Business College 186
Mibus, Margaret 239
Mick Simmons Sports 181
Miller, Tilly 15, 17
Mirror 200
Moir, Alan 230
Moree 183, 187–190, 193
Morey, Carmel (nee McSkimming) 255–256
Morey, Sonny 146–147, 154, 248–256
Moriarty, John x, 2, 8, 12, 14, 58, 76–77, 115, 125, 154, 164, 174, 175, 176, 182, 209–212, 213–228, 245, 265
Moriarty, Ros (nee Langham) 212–216, 218–221
Morphettville Race Course 154
Morris, Graham 159
Motley, Geof 217
Mount Barker Creek 127

Mulgoa x, 8, 12, 13–16, 21, 53, 58, 59, 63, 65, 90, 91, 125, 127, 155, 209–212, 217, 221, 245
Murdoch, Rupert 232–233
Murphy, (Miss) 34, 40
Murphy, Thommy 86
Murray Bridge 92, 136
Myers Department Store 34

N

Nalanji Dreaming 221
Namatjira, Albert 35, 52, 123, 267
National Aborigines Day 151
National Indigenous Council 218
National Indigenous Cricket Advisory Committee 145
National Indigenous Cricket Strategy 145
National Museum of Australia 212, 222
Nayda, Ken 219
Nayda, Les 219, 241–244,
Nayda, Shane 243
Nayda, Sharon 243
Nepabunna Mission 131
Neville, A.O. 29
New South Wales Police Force 36
News 232
Nicholls, Doug (Pastor Sir) 107–108, 110, 113–114, 139, 175, 177, 228–229
Noffs, Ted (Reverend) 180, 190
Noonuccal, Oodgeroo 177
Norrie, William (Sir) 35
Northern Territory Cricket Board 145
Nunga Anglican Ministry 247
Nungas, The 226–227

O

Odeon Theatre, Semaphore 85–86, 171, 173, 201
O'Donoghue, Lowitja 119–122, 132
O'Donoghue, Lily 120
O'Donoghue, Tom 120
Old Gum Tree 243
O'Malley, Mick 215–216
Oodnadatta Children's Home 118
Opperman, Hubert 200
Orchard, Barbara 137
Orr, Bob 165–167
Osborne Power Station 92, 216
O'Shea, Pat 214
Overland Telegraph Line 48

P

Page, Bruce 233
Palmer, John x, 17, 34–35, 52, 53, 57, 58
Palmer, Melva 17
Pan Hellenic (Sydney Olympic) Soccer Club 179
Panunga, Nancy 248
Parramatta (sailing ship) 48
Paul, Mona 119
Pearce, Nettie 9
Penrith High School 91, 155
Perkins, Adam 201
Perkins, Charles 'Charlie' xiii, x, xv, 17–21, 23–24, 26, 34, 36, 44, 57–58, 61–62, 72, 76–79, 81, 87, 90, 91–92, 162–168, 170–173, 178–180–182, 183–187, 190–194, 196–204, 208–209, 211, 215, 219, 224, 226, 228, 235–236
Perkins, Eileen (nee Munchenberg) 178, 180, 182, 191–192, 198–199, 201, 205
Perkins, Ernie 57–58, 63, 69, 164, 236–237
Perkins, Hetti (senior) 17–21, 26, 181–182
Perkins, Hetti (junior) 201
Perkins, Mary 264
Perkins, Nellie Errerreke 21
Perkins, Rachel 201
Peterson, Norm 111
Phillip, Arthur (Captain) 153
Pienaar, Francois 204
Pine Creek Gold Mine 142, 261
Pitjantjatjara Land Rights Act 242
Playford Council 255
Playford, Tom 176–177, 232
Point McLeay 101, 139
Point Pearce 58, 101, 112, 140, 228
Port Adelaide Council 60
Port Adelaide Football Club 48, 91, 107, 217
Port Adelaide Soccer Club 215
Port Thistle Soccer Club 79, 91, 164–165, 209, 212, 215
Powditch, Roy 194
Powditch, Sandra 194
Prague Soccer Club 179, 215
Prasad, Nancy 193–200
Price, Des 74, 219, 226, 256, 263–264
Prince Alfred, Duke of Edinburgh 47–48
Prince Phillip, Duke of Edinburgh 113–114, 159
Privy Council 232
Protector of Aborigines 29, 133, 139, 223

Index

Q
Quartermaine, Harry 14
Queen Elizabeth II 113–114, 159
Queen Elizabeth Hospital 208
Queen Victoria Hospital 126, 136, 138, 263
Queen's Medal 36
Queensland University 28
Quinn, Bob 96
Quorn Primary School 120, 136

R
Racial Discrimination Act 195
Racial Folly 22, 51, 87
Raftery, Judith 246
Raggatt, Fred 13, 123–124
Raggatt, Hannah (Miss) 125
Rainbow Town 18, 123, 236, 241
HMS *Rapid* 47
Rayner, Keith Rayner (Archbishop) 247
Reed, Geoffrey (Sir) 231
Reid, Trevor 58, 264
Repatriation Hospital 122
Richardson, Victor 'Vic' 135, 136
Richmond Hospital 125
Rioli, Cyril 218
Rivett, Rohan 232–233
Roberts, Alice 210
Roberts, Glen 8
Robertson, Geoffrey (QC) 233–234
Robin, B.P. (Archbishop of Adelaide) 39, 43, 67–68
Rochdale Hornets 11, 156–159
Rochdale Observer 157, 159
Roper River 1–2, 8–10, 12–14, 209–10, 245
Rose, Lionel 236
Roseby Park Station 191

Rowe, Colin (Attorney-General) 177
Royal Adelaide Hospital (RAH) 121, 132, 134
Royal Air Force (RAF) 143, 257
Royal Flying Doctor Service 5–6
Royal North Shore Hospital 114
Rudd, Kevin (Prime Minister) 30
Ruddick, Daisy 266
Russell, Harry 14, 79, 90, 91, 155, 224
Rutter, Delia (Sister) 119

S
Sacred Heart College 267
Saltbush Riding School 259
Saltwater Fella 218
SANFL 104, 224, 252, 253, 255
Sarra, Grant 150–151
Scott, Harry 230
Semaphore Beach 45, 55, 59–60, 86–87, 98, 119
Semaphore Rugby League Club 155
Shaw-Lefevre, John George (Sir) 149
Sherwin, Goff (Reverend) 'General' 84–87
HMS *Sirius* 153
Smith, Isabel (Mrs) 17, 32–37, 42, 51–52, 66, 71, 80, 178
Smith, John 42, 66, 219, 226
Smith, Len 107
Smith, Norm 107
Smith, Percy McD (Father) 13, 16–17, 24–25, 27–28, 31–35, 37–43, 47, 51, 54, 56–58, 60, 62, 64–66, 68, 72–73, 79–81, 101, 162, 164–165, 174, 178, 210, 219, 245, 267

Smits, Margaret 246
Sonny Jim 230
Sorry Day 30
South Adelaide Football Club 111
South Australian Aborigines Act 175
South Australian Cricket Association 35
South Australian Education Department 40–41, 91, 121, 132, 252
South Australian Harvest Board 104
South Australian Railways 37, 241
South Australian Rugby League 156
South Australian School of Art 35, 148
South Australian Soccer team 223
South Australian Under-17 Soccer team 97, 115
South Australian Under-18 Soccer team 76–79, 163–164
South Coast District Hospital 121
Southern Argus 124
Southern Yorke Peninsula Football League 108
Spears, R. (Professor) 240
Springboks 202–204
SS *Orsova* 171
St Edward's Church (Kensington) 38
St Francis of Assisi 44
St Francis House xi, xvi, xv, 10–11, 15, 24, 41–42, 44–45, 48, 50–51, 54–55, 58–59, 62–63, 65–69, 71, 74, 76, 79–84, 86–91, 93–95, 99, 102, 110, 115–17, 119, 122, 125–128, 140, 142–143, 146–149, 153, 158, 160–164,

St Francis House *cont'd* 174–175, 182, 209, 211–213, 216–217, 226, 228, 235–237, 247, 252, 257–259, 263–264, 267–268
St John's Hostel 13, 32, 213, 257, 264, 267
St Mary's Convent 249, 250, 251
St Paul's Anglican Church 43, 44, 71
St Peter's Cathedral 68, 247
Stack, Ella 262
Standley, Ida 25
Stephen, Bill 107
Stirling, James 91
Strehlow, Ted (Professor) 26, 54, 231
Strong, James 220
Stuart Arms Hotel 25
Stuart, Robert Maxwell 229–234
Suchanek, Les 179
Sultan, Betty 241
Sultan, Daphne 246
Sunday Mail 244
Survival in Our Own Land 247
Sutton, (Mr) 259–260
Sydney Morning Herald 98, 232

T

Talking Heads 220
Tatten, John 150
Taylor, (Mr) 'Squizzy' 81–84, 87, 95
Taylor, (Mrs) 81, 84, 93
Tell, William 66, 70, 82, 237
Thatcher, Margaret 44
Thomas, Alfred 140
Thomas, Alice Esther (nee Clift) 109

Index

Thomas, Bernard 140
Thomas, Faith (nee Coulthard) 129–132, 134–140
Thomas, Harold 115, 142, 145–149, 151–152
Thomas Holt Ltd 157
Thomas, Khatija 243
Thomas, Nutter 68
Thomas, Watkins Holmes 109, 112
Thompson, Peter 220
Thomson, Elkin (Professor) 54
Thomson, Jeff 134
Tilmouth, Colin 239
Tilmouth, Gerald 116, 147, 239
Tilmouth, Margaret 238
Tilmouth, Peter ix, 17, 34, 37, 56–59, 62–63, 67, 70, 78–79, 82, 87, 237–239, 264
Tilmouth, Richard 239
Tilmouth, Tilly 63
Tilmouth, Trish 238
Tilmouth, William 243
Tomkins Medal 104
Tongene, Maud 113
Tonkin, David 241
Top Gear 142
Truth 42–43, 99
Tucket, (Mr) 102
Turner, Fred 258–259
Turner, Jim 19
Turner, J.M.W. 148
Turner, Paul 232

U
Uchida, Shoji 236
United Aborigines' Mission (UAM)188–120
United Nations 122, 175
University of Sydney 54, 182
University of Western Sydney 36
Unley (Girls' Technical) High School 121, 126, 136

V
Vickery, Fred x, 95–96
Victor Harbor 53, 54, 121, 132
Victoria Station 166
Vorster National Party 203

W
Walgett 183–187, 193
Walkabout 222
Walker, Brian 211
Walker, Bruce 264, 266
Walker, Faye, 238
Walker, Kath 177
Walker, Ken 211
Walker, Murray 90
Walker, Robert 58
Wallace, Donald (Reverend) 147
Wallace (Mrs) 147
Wallaroo Government Hospital 99, 103
Wanganeen, Bob 228
Watkins, David 159
Watters, Rex 110
Weetra, Spencer 105
Wesley, Billy 8
Wesley, Heather 8
Wesley, Helen 9
Wesley, Kenneth 8
West Adelaide Football Club 102
West Australian 29
West Broken Hill Football Club 106
Whelan, Ted 217
White Australia Policy 11, 154, 194–195, 200
Whitlam, Gough 205, 233

The Boys from St Francis

Wigan Rugby League Football Club 11, 160, 167–169
Willard Hall, 54
Williams, Fos 105, 111, 139, 217, 224
Williams, Graham 188
Williams, Mark 111
Williams, Mary 225
Williams, Von 111
Willunga High School 148
Wilson, Max 58, 72–76, 79–80, 89, 93, 96–99, 115–117
Wilson, Morris 'Whickey' 89–92, 250
Wilson, Richard 77
Wilson, Ronald (Sir) 30
Wilson, Steve 72
Wilson, Susan 77
Wilson, 'Turtle' (Mrs) 89–91

Wingard, Chad 48, 218
Winnie the Pooh 38
Woodford, David ix, 17, 34, 44, 51, 56–59, 63, 70–72, 78, 85, 104, 219, 224
Woodford, Millie 17, 63
Woodhead, Trevor 143–145, 261
Woomera Rocket Range 238
World War II 68, 73, 129, 142, 159, 164, 183, 195
Workington Town Rugby League Football Club 159–160
Wright, Freddy 87
Wright, Jimmy 87
Wunala Dreaming 220–221

Y

Yamba Station 248

Wakefield Press is an independent publishing and
distribution company based in Adelaide, South Australia.
We love good stories and publish beautiful books.
To see our full range of books, please visit our website at
www.wakefieldpress.com.au
where all titles are available for purchase.
To keep up with our latest releases, news and events,
subscribe to our monthly newsletter.

Find us!

Facebook: www.facebook.com/wakefield.press
Twitter: www.twitter.com/wakefieldpress
Instagram: www.instagram.com/wakefieldpress

www.ingramcontent.com/pod-product-compliance
Lightning Source LLC
Chambersburg PA
CBHW020745160426
43192CB00006B/247